LIVING IN TWO WORLDS

LIVING IN TWO WORLDS

A LIFE OF LOVE

JOSEPH BARRY MARTIN

First Published in Canada 2013 by Influence Publishing

Book Cover Design: Adam Mountstevens
Typsetting: Greg Salisbury
Portrait Photographer: Jon Fitzpatrick

This book is lovingly and respectfully dedicated to the Spiritual Masters who work with and support us through all times and places, and also to our Ancestors and Descendants who share this beautiful planet. And to you, dear reader, infinite blessings as you open your heart centre daily on the life path—you are the reason I wrote this book. May we be worthy participants in this co-creation with Source.

TESTIMONIALS

"The life of Joseph Barry Martin is not only a story of mind-body-spirit integration, but a showcase of the alchemy between humanity and divinity. Two of the most profound questions we can ask ourselves are "who am I" and "why am I here." Joseph's hero's journey will help you revisit these questions and answers based on the makings of your own life story."
Brian Luke Seaward, Ph.D. Author, Stand Like Mountain, Flow Like Water

"I cannot remember a time when Near-Death Experiences (NDEs) have been so widely discussed, and readers of this book will discover why they are important. Joseph Martin has lived a very dramatic life, claiming to have spoken with Jesus as a child and to have had his first NDE at the age of eight. Readers may agree or disagree with Dr. Martin's view of reality, but they will certainly not be bored with his stories and some of them may even begin to question their own beliefs."
Stanley Krippner, Ph.D. Co-author, Personal Mythology

"Dr. Joseph Martin's life story is the epitome of the struggles and successes of a person born into extremely challenging family dynamics who learns to honour his soul's spiritual truth. This book will inspire readers to reflect on their own remarkable lives."
Michael Gurian, Ph.D. Author, An American Mystic; The Miracle

"Very early in my life, I learned that it isn't what a person does that matters. It's who that person is. The same holds true of authors. What Joseph writes in Living in Two Worlds is interesting. It's insightful and entertaining. This is an easy read that makes the reader a better person. And yet...it's about him. It's about Joseph Martin. Joseph is kind. He is loving, giving and extremely sensitive. Joseph was aptly named by his Mohawk elders "He Lives in Two Worlds." I, for one, am happy that he lives in mine. This is a good book."
David Bouchard, Metis author of more than 50 books including Seven Sacred Teachings with Joseph Martin, storyteller, public speaker, Order of Canada recipient

ACKNOWLEDGEMENTS

An immense open-hearted thank you or nyaweh ko:wen to all my spiritual mentors, along with my friends, peers, counselors, fellow academics, clients and students who have taught me so much throughout my life. Gratitude flows to Miriam Sanua, best friend and ongoing editor, and Julie and Greg Salisbury along with all those at Influence Publishing for their suggestions and endeavours. Thanks to my friend Jon Fitzpatrick for my photographic portrait on the back cover.

CONTENTS

PREFACE

Sharing my true story with you was something I never intended until my successful third heart operation three months ago, which gave me another chance to inspire others through my love. Many of the integral experiences you will read may surprise and even astonish you. As they say, "truth is stranger than fiction."

May you be encouraged, heartened, emboldened, and strengthened to live your own passionate life. My friend Joseph Campbell says, "follow your bliss." This is the reason I am writing this book.

This life story is for everyone who wishes to learn new subjective ways of understanding and living love, light, truth, freedom, beauty, and the good. You can choose in your heart, mind, and will to have a perfectly joyful life while you are briefly here during your adventuresome Earth-walk.

Life's truest goal is to seek happiness for all others through your love and showering them with your inner soul light. Only then will you be happiest. This book is for the openhearted of every historical time, generation, age, race, religion, creed, sexual orientation, and background.

I sincerely trust there will soon be born some new "scientists of the spirit and soul" opening to their own true natures. This book is meant to be a deeper, higher revelation of cosmology, ontology, epistemology, and eschatology. As I already have, you can make research and clinical advances in biochemistry, genetics, electrophysiology, neuroendocrinology, organ cleansing, and physical longevity, as well as in socio-cultural community-based, compassionate compatibilities. No matter how long it takes, much or most of what I share will be the common experience of every soul on earth.

Always seek your highest, best vision. Find out the deepest, most core reasons why you have chosen this particular earth-walk. Knowing the intuition of your heart, take action with every breath and each step of your day and night. May you be always blessed on your journey. Go forth into your positive, highest possible future in love, peace, fortitude, and joy!

MY MOST RECENT HEART OPERATION

"Namaste," I proffered to the two Hindu nurses as I was being wheeled into the operating room for my second heart surgery.

"Namaste!" they returned in quick, surprised voices. "Are you Hindu?" they queried.

"Yes, I am Hindu!" They tittered and looked at each other and then giggled some more.

"We'll take good care of you!" they promised.

Namaste is the traditional greeting in India since ancient times and it means, "I bow to the god-goddess in you." Within a few minutes, I had them scurrying around like two little squirrels.

My heart surgeon, Dr. Jovan (John) Bozinovski came late to the waiting room at the Jubilee Hospital in Victoria, B.C. Canada on the early morning of my surgery, October 10th, 2012. My operation was previously scheduled for October 4th; however, Dr. Bozinovski was attending to a patient whose operation was not going well, and he operated from the day before well into the night and early hours of the following morning, which was the day scheduled for my operation. I had been waiting for my operation since dawn. My pre-operation procedures were completed by 2pm and I waited all day for twelve hours in the hospital, only to be told at 8pm that evening that the operation was postponed.

After this, my open-heart surgery was rescheduled for six days later. That morning, I arose at 3am, showered with special antibacterial soap I was given, and my best friend and business partner Miriam Sanua drove me to the hospital. In a private room, I was shaved from chest to ankles, had a gown put on me, and was given a paper bag that contained just my toothbrush, toothpaste (or truthpaste as I like to call it), my new slippers, and one book.

At 6:30am, a chatty nurse wheeled me to the large waiting room where the people to be operated on for the morning were lined up in a row. I was the first to arrive. Eleven other beds followed. I used the washroom three times, nervously making my way back and forth from the washroom at the other end of the large room, intently watched by the nurses and staff. My operation was scheduled to start at 8am. By 9am, my surgeon had not yet arrived.

I was sure that I would survive this second heart surgery. The first one was done in 1958 at The Hospital for Sick Children in Toronto, which was when the heart-lung machine had just been invented in Chicago. Doctors in Toronto tested the machine by doing heart surgery for the first time on a few dogs. Then they tried it on a young girl my age, eight years old. She died on the table.

I was the next to have open-heart surgery. I survived, and was touted on CBC National News, local newspapers, radio, and the media. Much later, a photo was taken outside the front of the hospital with the 258 staff required for my surgery.

However, I "died" for 32 minutes during this first 18½-hour operation. I'll tell you that story in a wee bit, because this is the substance and purpose for this life and the story you are reading. It's about whom we really are, where we come from, where we will be going when we "die" and what the major purposes for a life can be.

Back to my beginning story: Dr. Bozinovski came in about 9:15am that morning. He was not in his scrubs yet, and jolted up to my bedside in the waiting area. I could see the concern in his eyes on his pallid, stiff face. I looked at him and asked how he was doing. He just nodded.

"Are you ready for the operation?" he asked.

"Yes," I said, "I know it will go well, and all will be fine." For months, my intuition and discussions with my Spiritual Masters who live inside me told me that all would go well and I would survive.

The reason for the operation was a structural one. I was born with a hole in my heart the size of a silver dollar, and the mitral and atrial valves did not quite properly close. My first operation at eight years of age dealt with the first issue—well, sort of—more on that later. For at least the last two years, I suffered from severe heart failure, lack of breath, and an inability to do all my treasured exercise, swimming and weight training.

In early 2010, after a serious bout of pneumonia, which brought on cardiac failure, I put on about 100 pounds of water, which my body could not release. This situation lasted over a year into June 2011. My weight went from 190 pounds to 290 pounds.

Water pills and other heart pills saved my life several times in the Emergency Department at two local hospitals.

By 2012 I was somewhat on the mend, but still not strong enough for surgery. So I waited, exercised, hoped, and prayed that all would be well. Finally in August, Dr. Bozinovski called me to meet for the first time, and he assessed me for a possible operation. We soon realized that I knew his father's and uncle's Macedonian restaurant back in Toronto, very near my psychotherapy clinic at King Street East and Parliament Street, in the lower east side of the downtown. It was very likely that I saw him playing in the churchyard and park nearby at Little Trinity Anglican Church, and also possibly saw him running in and out of the restaurant where I sometimes had my lunch if I did not bring my own.

During my assessment in the office with Dr. Bozinovski, I told him I would like to have pig skin valves put in since I did not want to be on rat poison (warfarin) the rest of my life, which would be the case had I chosen the metal valves. He demurred, and also mentioned angiogram and Cat-scan tests showed that I needed a 7-inch Dacron repair to my aorta.

"Okay, let's do this—pig valves it is!" I beamed. "When can we do this?"

"Well, I'm going away in the middle of October for conferences, so…"

"Can you do it in early October?" I interrupted. This was late August, and I had a feeling that my physical body could not hold on until November. My intuition told me it would be too late for me by then.

"Sure," he chimed in. "Let's do it in early October. Sign here."

I merrily signed my life away because I knew he was the right doctor for me.

"Two kids growing up in Regent's Park and meeting up again here in Victoria! Who would have thought?" Said Dr. Bozinovski.

There I was on the table in the waiting room with Dr. Bozinovski by my side. I sent him positive energy to calm his trepidation that I could plainly feel and see.

"It'll all be just fine, I know it will," I assured him.

"I'll see you in there in five minutes," he said, and then he ran off to change.

I was wheeled down the corridor to the last room on the right, which was the reoperation room for those with previous experience. The doors opened, I was rolled in and then I saw the two Hindu nurses, "Namaste," and so the story continues.

I saw the heart-lung machine on the right side of my metal trolley.

"Wow, it's much smaller and totally computerized!" I marveled to the two doctors who managed this high technology. "The first heart-lung machine was the size of this hospital!" I informed them.

"I'm sure it was," one rejoined.

Then the chief anesthesiologist on my left put a huge intravenous tube into my left wrist and another on my right.

"We're going to have to cut you up and down through your sternum to get at it," he advised. My last operation was a lateral one from left armpit to right armpit. So after this I would have a huge cross cut into my chest for the rest of my life. As you'll see, this acts as perfect symbolism for me and my journey.

Dr. Bozinovski suddenly popped up to my right side as he looked down at me with a great concern for the complexity and materials for the surgery. I thought I should say something to him because there was something I needed to know.

"If you were me," I popped the question, "what would you do? Pig skin or metal valves?"

"Metal," he quickly answered, "metal, otherwise, I'll be re-operating again in 7 to 10 years from now."

I had visions of yet another operation at age 70 and wondered if I would make it through yet another heart surgery. "Okay! Metal it is!" I spontaneously decided. Dr. Bozinovski looked around at his staff.

"Everyone heard him say it—he's changing his mind, right?" Dr. Bozinovski confirmed. I guess I was supposed to sign something, but I was five seconds away from going under. I could see the anesthetist about to open the valve to put me into my unconscious journey. Dr. Bozinovski turned to the two Hindu nurses and ordered, "go get the two metal valves, and hurry!" One nurse rushed by and grinned at me. Then I was out.

Did I tell you the doctors said I would need a cut on my upper right chest to feed a long tube into the back of my skull to oxygenate and keep the blood flow while my body was taken down to 16 degrees Celsius? Well, that's what they did, along with seven various external shunts that they applied to my left chest as well as three holes for drainage just under my ribcage.

The operation was supposed to last 6-8 hours. When Miriam didn't get a phone call by then, she phoned the hospital.

"Still operating… scar tissue… they have to go very, very slowly… not sure how long it will take…" Finally, after 10 hours, she received a call at 7:34pm. "He's done, and it's looking good," confirmed Dr. Bozinovski in a tired voice. "You can see him tomorrow."

Sounds good. Well, actually, I was under anesthetic all night. Along with copious amounts of liquids draining from my lungs, there was too much blood, which caused great concern. So the intensive care staff called Dr. Bozinovski back in for a re-operation the next morning at 7am. He opened me up again. Were my valves leaking? From where was I bleeding so profusely?

"It looks good, the valves are functioning." I imagine later they just got the Hoover out and sucked me dry.

By 10:30am the next morning, after 25 hours of anesthetic and yes, someone else's blood in my arteries and veins—yuck, a transfusion, something I did not want, for reasons that you'll discover later—I was slowly being drawn back to waking consciousness. Here I was, coming out of the massive, blazing, comforting, glorious Light of the Great Central Sun – the centre of the multiverse—and I knew I was back on Earth in my physical form.

I was overjoyed and strongly satisfied that I got another chance at finishing my unusual life. I saw Miriam on my left and the anesthetist at my right. Prior to the operation, he told me that I would have a ventilator tube in my mouth for half a day or so when coming out—well, coming out of the anesthetic, I mean.

I had some questions for him, like where, how much, what, when, why… He had told me I wouldn't be able to talk. I tried anyway, babbling and gurgling inanities. I finally resorted to sign language, writing letters in the air.

"Give it up; you won't be able to remember anything anyway," he sighed.

I nodded my head up and down with as much strength as I could muster, meaning, "Oh yes I will, so let's carry on."

As it turns out, this story is really about what I remember of my pre-birth existence, what happened before I came back to Earth, while I was in the womb, at birth, and afterwards… up until this moment about which you are reading.

Miriam looked somewhat anxious about all the tubes and my fat, swollen face. However, she was relieved that I had survived. I knew I would. How did I know? Why and how I know these things is the substance of this stirring story, probably unlike any other story you have ever heard or read. This adventure is even more heavenly, and hopefully more inspiring, than the usual stories about NDEs (Near Death Experiences) you might have heard.

THE GREAT CLEAR LIGHT
AND MY SPIRIT AND EARTH LIFE EXPERIENCES

Soon I'll get to my first all-out, full-spectrum NDE at age eight and then the one at 32; and then this one here. Fascinatingly enough, though, my whole life has always been lived in both worlds simultaneously—the rich, full, marvelous Spirit world, and this fleeting, illusory dream of an Earth-world.

The Great Central Sun of the multiverse in Spirit is our true home, where The Creator made us, so we could go and play in his lila. We are great goddess-god children of Her-His grand astronomical playground of swirling galaxies, star-beings, flaming suns, and feminine moons. Most of us have spent a lot of time on Earth, even millions of lifetimes as Buddha states. We come down from the fourth dimensional astral plane into this third dimension of beauty, truth, good, righteousness, and pure perfect love. We are meant to be fully trusting in Spirit while here, and learn the deepest and highest "Whys" of our existence and our individual Earth-walk.

When I was 24 years old, and living with the spiritual Longhouse chief's family of the Kanienkehaka (Mohawk) of Kanehsatake (Oka), Quebec, I was given the name Dehanakerehkwen—"He who lives in Two Worlds at the same time" —Spirit and Earth, The Void and Creation, Native and non-Native, masculine and feminine, past and future…

"For most of us most of the time, the world of everyday experience seems rather dim and drab. But for a few people often, and for a fair number occasionally, some of the brightness of visionary experience spills over, as it were, into common seeing, and the everyday universe is transfigured."
Aldous Huxley, Heaven and Hell

For most of my life, my true deep inner experiences have remained untold. When I realized I had successfully pulled through this last operation three months ago, the mortality of this earthly mineral frame hit me hard. Upon getting home, after six long sleepless nights and days in hospital, I thought, "This is it! Time to step out boldly! I must do this now or never!" So that's how this personal mythological tale came to be in your hands.

Most importantly, I want you to realize that everything I am sharing with you is true, no matter how far-fetched it might seem to your present perceptions. What's the main reason I am sharing this story with you? So that you can know that you have real, untapped, latent possibilities hidden within your heart, unconscious mind, and soul that will lead you to your own best Self, your spiritual centre, your psychological wholeness. By taking my search to heart, you can also find and live your Immortal, Illuminated Love-Light Self.

Near Death Experiences are not the key and not really necessary. Here is what is core and essential: constant, intuitive, moment-to-moment listening (not talking) to the innate, deeply interior Divine guidance of Source and the Great Spiritual Masters of all traditions and Spirit realms is the true and everlasting, ever-fresh, fundamental passive and active process of finding your Self.

You are an angel and god-goddess in ape's clothing. Each one of us is a tiger of the heart, not a lamb to be slaughtered or led by the nose to our spiritual, psychological and physical destruction and death by others.

PART ONE
BEFORE BIRTH TO MID-LIFE

CHAPTER 1
DESCENT FROM SOURCE AND HEAVEN BACK TO EARTH

For some reason that I don't yet fully comprehend—though I deeply feel and experience this as an ongoing knowing, I am an eternal, infinite being of Great Clear Light from the One Source. And so are we all—all our sisters and brothers and All Our Relations, including the star-beings.

As I continue writing this story, I see a beautiful redheaded hummingbird outside my window. He is sitting on a wintry branch beside his hummingbird feeder. He turns his head, this way and that, looking up and around, watching and wary of attack by intruders. Isn't this how most of us live our lives? When he is certain he is alone and free, he comes to the feeder for another sip of joy – for joy is what Hummingbird Medicine means in our Native way.

"From joy I came, in joy I live here with you, and to joy I return."

For millennia, scientists, the religious, and mystics have been in a quandary about the nature of the soul, the afterlife, and the origin of the universe. Humbly and truly speaking, I am 99.99 percent sure that there each of us is a soul, the afterlife is one and the same as what you feel and perceive at this moment, and the origin of the universe-multiverse is one point of Clear Light that is Pure Perfect Love.

I recall my descent from the central Source Clear Light when I decided to take rebirth on planet Earth. There are cycles within cycles, and there is some choice. I decided to choose parents with whom I had had no previous lives. These parents were typical simple folk of their time – ones who had both been in WWII during the 20th century, which was such a momentous time of hatred, murder, and bloodshed.

When one leaves Source, there is often a council who helps to plan the process of descent and taking rebirth. It is said that there is a clamor among one million souls for each Earth rebirth. Such is the need; such is the treasure of the life of each person who makes it here.

THE GREAT METAGALACTIC CENTRAL SUN COUNCIL AND SPIRITUAL MASTERS

For me, members of my High Spirit Council are members of the Sananda Christ holographic energy field of the Great Metagalactic Central Sun Source. These include Babaji Nagaraj, Metatron, Melchizedek, Jesus Christ, Shekinah, Dendreah, Krishna, Shiva, Yogananda, Vivekananda, Ramakrishna, Buddha, Zoroaster, Mother Mary, Mary Magdalene, Kwan Yin, Rabi'a, Avalokiteshvara, Mohammed, and many other important Spiritual Masters who walked the earth.

Others with whom I am connected are somewhat less known on Earth: Milarepa, Gandhi, William Blake, Saint Francis, Nostradamus, Rudolf Steiner, Emanuel Swedenborg, Paracelsus, Newton, Kuthumi, Isis, Shams-i-Tabriz, Rumi, and many Tibetan Tulkus.

All along my path of descent down through the dimensions, my great Spiritual Masters and friends accompanied me. Primarily, the ones I choose to share are Babaji Nagaraj, Jesus Christ, Mother Mary, Archangel Mikael, Metatron, Paramahansa Yogananda, and Dendreah the Earth Mother. They are my very best friends. We continuously have discussions about any and all major or minor concerns. They directed my meetings with the various souls on my downward path and still do now throughout my life here. At all times, they each give me comfort, insight, wisdom, and mostly pure love. For me, this is key for living a joyful life. We have loving friendships with deep Divine-human affection for one another. They are my sisters and brothers.

Leaving Source can only be explained in metaphor, as language has its limitations. My personal experience is this: the descent is a lessening of the light, a deepening of the darkness of the ether, the dark energy of akasha or space. One feels it in terms of a lowering of vibrations of the soul consciousness, a moving into matter. Along the way, which does seem like a downward vertical descent, within this dense darkness, one sees the small orb lights of great souls with whom one chooses to meet.

Some are upward bound after an earth life; others are downward bound, preparing for their upcoming Earth-walk.

Coming from heaven to the Earth world feels like a cascade, a cataract plummet of the soul into greater and greater density of energy while becoming more material—from the ninth to the seventh dimension, from the seventh to the fifth dimension, and from the fifth to the third dimension of the Earth's physical body. One can think of these as a chain or ladder if one likes – that would be a good visual—something like descending Jacob's ladder. For me, I experienced this as a calibrated ladder-like descent, a free-fall sensation within consciousness and inner vision.

When one leaves the higher reaches of Divine-human nature in Source, there is a freedom to fly. One wants to make a real swan dive of it. The extreme radiant golden-silver-diamond mist or cloud of knowing feels infinite, eternal, and gloriously joyful. This is how one subjectively experiences the flow. One carries this golden halo of light and pure love with one through the full descent into the womb. Along the way, one meets other great soul lights and merges with them. This connection is a full or partial conscious mind-heart-soul melding. Even more spiritual and emotional than the Vulcan mind-melding of Spock in Star Trek.

From a detached observer perspective watching this from the outside, it is somewhat like one would see on a clear night in the sky. It seems to be mostly darkness with great brilliant lights dotting the expanse of akasha. Some lights are fainter, perhaps more distant to your awareness and interest. From a personal experience, one is love-light, and feels love and sees light. If one is to look outside of oneself, one is aware of the great expanse of darkness through which one is moving and notices other lights one passes.

In the descent, one goes through innumerable changes of lessening vibrations. Between each level, there are energetic frequency fences. In spiritual terms, one can call these "spiritual energy veils."

One chooses whom one wishes to connect with. There are meaningful purposes to each meeting. The interaction creates knowledge, focus, direction, and guidance for the up-coming life. This is my experience.

MEETINGS WITH REMARKABLE SOULS

AN AUTHOR, POLITICIAN, TWO PSYCHOLOGISTS, A SCIENTIST AND A DOCTOR

In this particular descent into my life, whom did I meet? Apart from those mentioned above, who travelled with me, I will describe just a few of my conscious connections on the way down and why these were important for my life to come.

TOLSTOY

The Russian writer, Leo Tolstoy, was a significant connection for me. His heartfelt knowledge and extraordinarily detailed psychological understanding of human nature had a powerful effect on my life choice to be a psychotherapist and psychologist. Tolstoy was able to *"lay bare man's intimate gestures, acts and thoughts: murder and sacrifice…greed and devotion…lust and affection…vanity and love…-one by one."*
Back cover, Leo Tolstoy, The Death of Ivan Ilych.

Tolstoy's powerful consciousness-raising for peoples' liberation through non-violent confrontation was key to Gandhi and to myself. The Tolstoy–Gandhi letters are remarkable for their insight and cultural, historical significance that created major change within the 20th century.

The bright light that is Tolstoy's soul emboldened my own, thus courageously heartening my Earthbound journey into the "illusion" of another Earth life.

ABRAHAM LINCOLN

Abraham Lincoln was another seminal social, political and mind-heart changing catalytic soul. Although somewhat depressed in his inner mind and demeanor, he nonetheless created massive civil rights and social change through the abolition of slavery by bringing the southern and northern peoples together in the American Civil War, 1861-1865. He strongly encouraged my choice to focus on my life's ongoing social issues of justice, civil liberties, equality of rights and privileges for those of differing gender, race, sexual orientation, religion, and skin colour.

CARL GUSTAV JUNG

Carl Gustav Jung was most definitely a great light for me in my dive into my Earth body. He is one who magnetizes my interest in the farther reaches of human nature, Jungian Depth Psychology, the unconscious, alchemy, anthropology, sanity, mysticism, and personal individuation as a life goal. As a teenager, I read all of Jung's work, and during my late thirties, Jung and I had ongoing discussions, visitations and dreams, which helped me to chart the changing course of my life from a university professor to a full-time dreams and past-lives Depth psychotherapist.

SIGMUND FREUD

I spent some time with Sigmund Freud. As a forebear and early compatriot of Jung's, Freud was foremost in helping me understand the nature of human instincts, in particular the life, death, and sexual wishes and issues of humanity—individually and collectively. Freud also interested me in mythologies, particularly those surrounding the father-son Oedipus complex, which is the unconscious basis for much war and corruption.

ALBERT EINSTEIN

Albert Einstein was another soul whom I met along the way. Although I was to study physics, calculus, and chemistry at university, it was Einstein's notions of relativity and inter-dimensional time-space-motion interweaving that continued to interest me the most. They are apt descriptions of the soul's conscious journey. Dimensions are interwoven within one another, just as string theory predicts. The part is contained holographically within the whole. The whole is constantly evolving through the conscious change of all the parts simultaneously—yet paradoxically beyond time, space, and motion at zero point.

Presently on planet Earth, there is a coming-together in consciousness of quantum mechanics, holograms, morphogenetic fields, and black holes on the one hand, and ancient traditions such as Buddhism and mystical knowledge on the other.

ALBERT SCHWEITZER

Albert Schweitzer, the great humanitarian medical doctor and winner of the 1952 Nobel Peace prize for his philosophy of "Reverence for Life," inspired me to enter the medical profession from the vantage points of spirituality, compassion, social justice, and kindness for All Our Relations.

Albert was a scholar of Johann Bach's music and influenced the Organ reform movement. His proficiency as an organist motivated me to take organ lessons early in life, along with piano lessons starting at 4 years of age. Whenever I play church organs, I feel the presence of Albert. These have been some of my most mystical and glorious moments in this life.

Powerful and meaningful texts of his are *"The Mystery of the Kingdom of God: The Secret of Jesus' Messiahship and Passion," "The Decay and Restoration of Civilization,"* and *"Civilization and Ethics."* Schweitzer's autobiography is a memorable read entitled, *"Out of My Life and Thought."*

SIX CLASSICAL MUSIC COMPOSERS AND MUSICIANS

Six classical music composers exceedingly transformed my understanding of the musical and mathematical melodies, harmonies and rhythms of the higher and lower universal spheres. For me, music was, is, and will always be the greatest energetic vitalism and healing harmonizer of and for souls in the universe. And it is so much more than angels singing while playing harps. These composers are, in no particular order, Johann Sebastian Bach, Johannes Brahms, Ralph Vaughan-Williams, Sergei Rachmaninoff, Pyotr Ilyich Tchaikovsky, and Ignacy Jan Paderewski. Gifts of musical and compositional ability and understanding were given to me by each of these great men.

I have been a musical composer in many past lives. During the progression of these on Earth, I endeavoured to memorize every piece of classical music I could find. And I have accomplished this during my life. Whenever I choose, at will, I can turn on and listen to any composition in my mind. This is a true joy for me!

JOHANN SEBASTIAN BACH

Bach is undoubtedly one of, if not the greatest spiritually enlightening composers of all time. His dancelike, joyous melodies, and mathematical precision and timing of his harmonies and rhythms are exquisite. Bach gifted me with these capabilities and musical awareness.

JOHANNES BRAHMS

Johannes Brahms empowered me with a deep sense of the full musical ranges of human emotionality, courageous striving, massive will, and spiritual longing. The paradoxical oppositions of surging warrior nature, juxtaposed with tender, caring sweetness are found in Brahms's music, and these were given to me for my compositions and my piano playing.

RALPH VAUGHAN-WILLIAMS

English composer Ralph Vaughan-Williams is a highly unique individual of intense inner piety, nature-orientation, spiritual interiority, emotional passions, and broad engaging musical feelings of human fulfillment and earthly evolution. His *"Lark Ascending"* for viola and orchestra is among the most popular pieces of all time.

Ralph and I have a great friendship, with a very high affinity between our two soul matrices. Vaughan-Williams's earthy, lyrical, and soaring melodies are akin to my own inner music that I constantly play on the inside. I rarely have thoughts going on inside—just the music I choose to play or listen to at any given moment. I find this experience very calming, inspirational, and transformational. From Vaughan-Williams I received the gifts of heart-rending melodies and harmonies that shatter the ego and shake open the sacred heart. I love spending time with him.

SERGEI RACHMANINOFF

Sergei Rachmaninoff is a deeply introverted, nervous, and massive talent. One of his gifts to me is the ongoing flow of melody over 32 or 64 bars, rather than the usual four-bar or eight-bar sequences used by other composers. His harmonies and massive orchestration abilities in his symphonies and piano concerti were gifts to me. Among my most favourite compositions that I regularly listen to are *Piano Concertos #2 and #3, Symphony No. 2* (especially the second movement Adagio), *Rhapsody on a Theme of Paganini with 24 Variations, and his Vespers.* I thoroughly enjoy playing his *Preludes* and *Etudes-Tableaux* on my piano.

PYOTR ILYICH TCHAIKOVSKY

Pyotr is a deeply emotional, sensitive, gay human being, who is a stellar and massive musical talent, unrivalled in the realms of pure emotional expressiveness. Unlike most of my past lives, I chose to be gay in this life in order to challenge myself emotionally and be able to better understand human prejudice and suffering. I needed some inspirational guidance from a soul like Tchaikovksy. He supported my decision and we did a heart-meld so that I could first-handedly experience every step of his emotional torment and musical outpourings of his deep longings for male companionship. Later in my life, I read all his autobiographical notes, and all the biographies of his life. I determined that I would enjoy being gay and celebrate joyously until the end, unlike Pyotr's grievous, sad and depressing self-suicidal denouement.

IGNACY JAN PADEREWSKI

Ignacy Jan Paderewski is a somewhat unknown Polish composer and pianist of the early 20th century. He was the first pianist to travel the world concertizing. His romantic melodies, often based on cultural motifs, are very stirring. Jan's gift to me is his unique style of playing the piano with *tempo rubato* or expressive use of subjectively timed phrasing. Besides this, the use of intermittent extreme *fortissimo* or loudness, and exquisite *pianissimo* or softness is his signature. The perpetual flow from soft to loud to soft provides great emotional effect on the listener. Jan's supreme vibration of heart-moving melodies and intense feeling values reside in me every time I play the piano. I have a photo of him on my piano at all times.

HISTORIC ANCESTOR SPIRITS

For millions of years, our Mother Earth planet has enjoyed many previous civilizations that may be unfamiliar for you. In particular, during my descent, I connected with the Pangeans, Hyperboreans, Polarians, Lemurians, Atlanteans, Druids, Tibetans, and First Nations from every continent and culture. There exist various interlinking ancestral energetic collective soul fields surrounding the Earth in the fourth dimension of astral awareness. These are holographic meme memories of each and every known historical event and culture. We call this *The Akashic Record*. As I was descending, I entered these mind-heart energy fields, and read these ancestral historical records. This was important background knowledge for my life as a social-cultural-historical anthropologist.

Foremost among those Spiritual Masters who supported me in this process were Dendreah or The White Buffalo Calf Woman who is the Earth Mother, Rudolf Steiner, Nostradamus, Swedenborg, and Paracelsus.

Paramount to my life has been the direct communication and influence of great Native Spiritual Masters from Turtle Island (North America). These well known historical persons with whom I parlayed in my pre-life consciousness are Tashunke Witko (Crazy Horse), Tatanka Yotanka (Sitting Bull), Goyathlay (Geronimo), Tecumthe (Tecumseh), Hinmaton Yalatkit (Chief Joseph, Nez Perce), Pontiac, and Hehaka Sapa (Black Elk).

You might notice that some of these individuals were still in their Earth bodies when I descended in the fall of 1949, such as Paramahansa Yogananda, Vaughan-Williams, Hehaka Sapa, and Albert Schweitzer. It is essential to note that each of us always exists in two worlds at the same time—the real Spirit world and this passing, changeable Earth dream world. Hence, it is easy to connect with anyone at anytime at the speed of thought, which is much faster than the speed of light.

In my descent, I knew that a core mythological element to our times is the true story and related spiritual-psychological theme of Avalon, so I connected with King Arthur, Merlin, and the 12 knights of Camelot. Our discussions centered on this reigning powerful Holy Grail mythology of our 21st century, which will prevail for many centuries to come. This is a key topic about which I am presently writing. The focus is the true nature of the Holy Grail in its multi-faceted, archetypal, spiritual, psychological, and evolutionary aspects—for individuals and the collective of all cultures.

ARCHANGELS

The majority of our world population—whether Christian, Jewish, Muslim, Buddhist, First Nations, or animist, believe in the presence of angels. They are said to protect, guide, and heal us. Some believe that each of us has a guardian angel, perhaps several. Renaissance art, cave drawings and art from almost all cultures show the high spiritual and psychological relevance of angels.

Archangels are on a higher spiritual vibrational level than angels, and thereby hold more power and position of authority in the ongoing history of the earth for which they are responsible. It is known that each of the four major Archangels rule in various times.

ARCHANGEL GABRIEL

For instance, Archangel Gabriel was the one who announced the birth of Jesus to Mary and ruled in the age of Pisces from the time of Jesus to 1873. Gabriel foretold the births of Jesus and John The Baptist. In Islam, Gabriel revealed the *Qur'an* to the Prophet Muhammed over a period of 23 years. In Jewish angelic hierarchy, Gabriel is sent as a messenger of YHWH to the prophet Daniel during the Babylonian Captivity of the Jews. Gabriel interprets Daniel's visions written up in the *Book of Daniel*. In the *Book of Ezekiel*, Gabriel is understood to be the angel that was sent to destroy Jerusalem.

ARCHANGEL RAPHAEL

Archangel Raphael is well known in the Old Testament and in the Apocryphal stories before the time of Jesus. Raphael is mentioned by name in the *Book of Tobit*, when he was seen walking in the flesh. Raphael routinely binds demons and devils, casting them into the darkness. He is the prime Archangel of Healing, Health, Real Estate, Joy, and compassion. Raphael has been a dear friend of mine for many millions of years.

ARCHANGEL MIKAEL OR MICHAEL

In 1873, Archangel Mikael or Michael took over the reins of spiritual rule from Gabriel for the coming few centuries in this Age of Aquarius, until approximately 2250. The date of 1873 is a watershed for world societies in several ways. Many great changes have happened since 1873—the birth of cultural changes in art, music, architecture, sciences, consciousness, and psychology—including the lives and theories of Freud, Jung, Adler, and scores of others. On the side of evil, the world has seen massive, catastrophic conflagration—World Wars I and II 1914-1918 and 1939-1945, respectively, the Korean War 1950-1953, the Vietnam War 1945-1973, and the Iraq War 2003-2011, to mention a few.

We have many Western images of Archangel Mikael showing him with blazing blue light, an upheld sword, and sometimes slaying dragons. He is a foremost spiritual warrior for the Christ energies and the "turning of the ages" in which we find ourselves. During the great wars of the 20th century, Archangel Mikael gave much courageous spiritual power to those in the trenches and the populace. Mikael will preside over the coming century of terror, destruction and our final peaceful resolution.

What is the Michaelic Impulse? It is the Sun power at work upon the Earth and us humans. The Sun is the source of all intellectual life operating in the service of the Spirit. That is how we are able to cooperate in the service of Michael at the turn of the 21st century and beyond. Utterance of this truth may evoke a certain inner resistance today, in this age of emphasis on intellect and rationality. Those who have a real understanding of the spiritual life will not set much store by the cognitive concepts of materialism and reductionism prevailing in this post-modern age. Abstract and formal thoughts invade the human mind with ideas utterly remote from living reality; these thoughts and theories are cold, dry, and barren as compared with the warm, radiant life pulsing through the world and through humanity's heart.

LANGUAGE OF THE ARCHANGEL
AND SPIRIT BEINGS OF THE HIGHER REALMS

What is the language of the Archangels and angels? There is a non-auditory awareness through each heart's intuitive telepathic connection amongst the Archangels, and between Archangels, angels and human-kind. Even though humans have devised a plethora of languages over millennia, the true communication is the language of the heart. Besides this, there is a language spoken throughout the galaxies, and this is called Intergalactic. There is nothing on Earth like this, not even glossolalia. Intergalactic communication, which is a spoken language, is the Christ power of pure love and infinite joy.

Without the supreme protection, guidance and knowledge of Archangels Mikael, Raphael, and Gabriel, I could not have lived this life. The rekindled friendship we manifested in my descent to Earth has lasted in a felt kinesthetic sense every day of my life.

TWIN SOULS

Prior to each incarnate life, we can make an agreement and meet up with those we deeply love. Over hundreds and thousands of lifetimes on Earth, on other planets and galaxies, and in the Spirit world, we can build and co-create with another soul a unity of tender, affectionate loving friendship. For me, there are many such "twin souls" on Earth and in the heavens. In fact, I truly feel that each Divine-human is my sister and brother, regardless of skin colour, eye or hair colour, race, religion, age, gender, sexual orientation, or infirmity.

Although I love everyone's heart, there are several souls who have ac-companied me, and I them, in my Earth world journey this time around. In particular, there are two, and together we live pure joy and co-create what will hopefully be of lasting importance to the future of Earth, All Our Relations, and humanity.

CHAPTER 2
IN THE WOMB AND CONSCIOUS BIRTH

I consciously chose my parents for the role they could play in teaching me the lessons I needed in order to grow and take on my responsibilities in life. It is said in Ayurvedic medicine that some aspects of the personality of the child are given by the feelings and emotional-mental states of each of the parents at conception. As I will explain later, this is partly true in my case.

While a portion of the soul vibration clearly embeds in the zygote and the growing multi-cellular fetus, most of the soul does not incarnate until the last few days or hours before the actual birth. Even so, some or most of the soul will only come into the physical form after birth. One can see this by the quickly changing lines on the palms of a newborn, which like the colour of the eyes and hair, can change very quickly for a baby. These changes are representative of the soul's past lives in previous physical incarnations. Indeed, higher aspects of the soul may take years and decades to incarnate, which has been my case. A seven-year cycle is the baseline for a stage of human growth–biologically, endocrinologically, neurologically, and psychologically.

My mother smoked and drank during my pregnancy. For these and other reasons, I stayed out of the womb until near the end of her term. I feel deep gratitude towards my mother for carrying me and giving birth to me. I was born with a hole in my heart—a Ventricular Septal Defect or VSD. I always knew that, as a gift to my mother, I took on all her considerable past lives' karma. This was verified when I was 32 years of age, and was studying with Dr. Vasant Lad at The Ayurvedic Institute in Albuquerque, New Mexico. He told me, in front of a group of students, that I had done this out of gratitude for my mother giving me birth.

I cried when I came into this world. Typically, at birth babies cry and parents rejoice. At our death, we rejoice and our families and friends cry. Such is the nature of the very mixed Earth world of fear, sadness, grief, anger, and mostly selfishness—for now.

PARENTAL AND ANCESTRAL KARMAS

Karma is a very specific universal law. It's like the Second Law of Thermodynamics in physics—for every action, there is an equal and opposite reaction. In human terms, it means that every thought, feeling, word, and action you send to anybody will be repaid—whether good, bad, or mixed—down to the last vestige of emotion and intention. You will need to love and forgive yourself now in this life or come back and meet up with the same souls in a future life. This karmic law is ineluctable. Just as everyone who is born will eventually die, every iota of karma will be revisited, and you have the choice and chance to transmute and transform it whenever you wish.

MY MOTHER'S FAMILY KARMA

My mother was born in Holland. Her relatives were hard working horse people. Her father was an architect. She planned to be a nurse. At the age of 22, World War II started and Hitler invaded Holland. War has a way of tearing apart dreams and somehow it can give us the opportunity to develop courage. My mother became a member of the Dutch Underground Resistance to wartime occupation; she travelled between villages with written messages rolled up and stuffed inside her bicycle handlebars. German soldiers raped her several times. The psychological, emotional and physical tolls during 6 years of war were incapacitating and gruesome; eventually she and her family were reduced to eating tulip bulbs.

Her ancestor's lives were mostly short, brutish, and nasty. Europe in the last five or six centuries has been a maelstrom of war, colonization, and plagues, thus requiring courage and deliberate hard work. These conditions create human realities of alienation, loneliness, depression, and many kinds of fears and dreads.

MY FATHER'S FAMILY KARMA

My father is from many generations in Canada from England, Scotland and Ireland. On his paternal side, there are many generations of British and Canadian military, as well as pirates who were so much part of the British Empire. My father grew up as a young man in the Depression and rode the rails out West looking for nonexistent employment. At the age of 27, he enlisted in The Queen's Own Rifles in Toronto and became a Sergeant. During his 6 years overseas—from North Africa, through Italy, France and Belgium—the Canadian troops eventually liberated Holland in 1945.

Back then, we knew little about Post-Traumatic Stress Syndrome or PTSS; they called it "shell shock." My father lived with his untransformed, buried emotions, memories, and tragedies for all his life. He suffered from yellow fever, malaria, and weak kidneys and he had seven heart attacks before he finally succumbed.

Karmically and emotionally speaking, I would like to emphasize the enormous spiritual, psychological, emotional, and physical side effects of daily battle stress in wartimes, as well as in so-called postwar peacetimes. This heavy, deep, degradation of psyche, mind, emotion and will becomes part of the collective unconscious and collective conscious energy fields. From both sides of my parent's lineages, heavy karma has been passed down to me—psychically, energetically, and physiologically.

Familial, ethnic, and ancestral karma became one of the key foci for my life. It is why I became a scientist, psychologist, marriage and family therapist, and social-cultural anthropologist.

CHAPTER 3
BIRTH TO 3 YEARS

I feel it's important for you, the reader, to view my early life as a significant marker of what the vast majority of souls have to deal and cope with when they incarnate on Earth during this century. My life stands in for an everywoman, an everyman—in fact, for you!

Because both my mother and father were seriously psychically, psychologically, and physically damaged by the war, these energies were transmitted to me in various ways—psychically, genetically, and by being in my mother's womb. Of course, one is always closer with the mother, given that one is inside her for nine months.

ABUSE BY MY MOTHER

My mother was the second youngest of a family of thirteen children. So psychologically she was a baby, and very early on I fulfilled the parenting role for both my parents. As a result of the terrors, dread, and physical-mental-emotional torture and raping by the Nazi soldiers, my mother's hold on her psyche was minimal, even though at times she was a mentally strong woman. Like most people on the planet today, including the collective itself, my mother was bipolar. At my birth, she suffered from post-partum psychotic depression. Later in life, she often went into a manic phase, and had to be hospitalized and severely sedated—the usual banal treatment given by psychiatrists in this century showing severe lack of knowledge of human nature and mental health care.

She was also very beautiful; people thought she was the twin of the Swedish actress Ingrid Bergman. Being physically gorgeous was definitely a liability for my mother—she was singled out and became a sex toy for the Nazis.

Although my mother and father did truly love each other on one level, there was always lack of authentic communication. There were also unconscious negative projections from both sides throughout their life together.

I am not sure my mother wanted a second child; my older brother was her first child. She had issues with men and boys as a result of her experiences and perceptions. When I was being carried in the womb, there were definite feelings of self-loathing and hatred for children that I picked up from her. For she felt that her young adult years had been destroyed by the war, and she was unconsciously raging against her loss. During my decades of therapy, including hypnotherapy, I discovered she did not want me to have what she didn't have and could never retrieve— a good life. All this was palpable to my soul in the womb and at birth.

At my birth, there were many strains on my mother, the marriage, and our family. She smoked and drank throughout her pregnancy with me. Shortly after my birth, she fell into post-partum psychosis and deep depression. This was never really treated, although much later during my thirties, as mentioned, she was in and out of mental institutions for psychotic breaks.

What I am about to share with you has been recovered by me through life-long dreams, body sensation memories, working with four therapists from the ages of 26 to 49, Ericksonian Hypnotherapy, Neuro-Linguistic Programming (NLP), and in my clinical therapy groups with other people who are also survivors of abuse. These hundreds of my mind-body kinesthetic recollections of actual experiences attest to the veracity of my experience. It is wise to remember that, minimally, over 70 percent of girls and women in the world have been abused, and over 55 percent of boys and men. Hopefully in future, individuals will uncover their hidden truth and become whole authentic divine-human beings.

Firstly, there are seven kinds of abuse: spiritual, mental, emotional, physical, sexual, verbal, and non-verbal. And what exactly is abuse? Why does it happen so frequently in relationships, families, and all ethnic groups of humanity throughout time? Abuse is about taking away someone's power and soul and belittling them, making them feel a complete lack of self-worth.

Why do humans do this? It is because they themselves do not feel and are not self-empowered. Most individuals have little or no self-confidence or self-worth. They must compensate for this lack by torturing others and stealing energies from them. This is aligned with humans' long interest in vampires, werewolves, ghouls, zombies, and such.

What did my mother do to me? From early months, she would pick me up from the crib, and throw me against the wall or floor. She would burn my skin with lit cigarettes. I am omitting the majority of hundreds of memories; my point is to let you know that I have gone through what the majority of children worldwide have suffered. The healing of this global issue is paramount if our species is ever to survive and evolve. On an overall scale, I felt unloved, unwanted, lonely, and totally alienated from my mother and others around me.

ABUSE BY MY FATHER

Again, from decades of body memory recall, I now know and have also healed and forgiven my father for the massive abuse I suffered at his hands. This part of the story will interest you, because as you will read in a later section, my father is physically reincarnated and became one of my students.

My father was the youngest of over a dozen children as well—and no, we weren't Catholic—nominally Presbyterian. Both my parents were babies and very psychologically immature. As a child, his older brothers and others sexually, physically, and emotionally abused him. His mother and father were tough-minded, closed-hearted military people who went by the rod. Just as he was physically beaten, he beat me.

I will cut this part of the story short, for there is too much to tell. I was physically beaten and punched by my Father when he went into his alcoholic rages, and even when he was sober. Dinner times were a misery; I never ate much, knowing I would be slapped hard on the side of my face by his strong hand. When I didn't eat, he sent me to bed without food. He was a rage-aholic. This was caused by his past karmas, his abusive childhood, and six years of wartime trauma, while he had also lost his youth and dreams.

After every time that he beat me, he would feel guilty and cry, and then he would ask me to sit on his lap. That's when the sexual abuse would happen, and also in his bed when my mother was not there. From a very early age, until the age of 13 years, I was anally raped, and made to per-form fellatio on him. When my father had his wartime compatriot drink-ing parties at our house—for he was a good-times kind of fellow—one

19

of my uncles would often come into my bedroom late at night and rape me. Two of my cousins also abused me over time.

POOR HEALTH

Early on, within a few months of my birth, it became clear that there was something seriously wrong with my physical health. The pediatrician told my parents that I had a very large hole in my heart between the left and right ventricles—the size of a Canadian silver dollar. It's called a Ventricular Septal Defect (VSD) and is quite common in babies.

In the early 1950s, there was nothing medicine could do for me. Nowadays, children with this condition are operated on within days or weeks of birth. My mother and father must have unconsciously felt guilty, but there was nothing they could do to save me.

CONTINUOUS SPIRIT-INFILLING *KUNDALINI* ENERGIES

Throughout my babyhood and my life, I have felt at all times of day and night the infilling of the Universal Spirit of Oneness, Wholeness, Pure Love, Clear Light, and energizing Kundalini energies. With it comes a feeling of being perfectly loved and a warmth and friendship with all the Spiritual Masters and Source. The immediate peace filters through my nerves, bones, muscles, mind, and heart and instantly calms me. It happens even when I don't ask for it; it comes when I need it. It is infinite healing. This unified holographic field energy of the Akasha brings knowledge, wisdom, and empowerment from the Akashic Records, which exist for anyone to tune into. It's easy—one just asks to be there for information on a particular topic. I jokingly say these records are easier to access now because they are on CD and online!

JESUS AND THE GREAT PURE PERFECT LOVE

I used to cry day and night. Wail in fact. I recall crying myself to sleep every night of my childhood. Not only was I in physical pain with poor heart functioning and physical abuse, I was in spiritual pain from the lack of love. As well, at this time, my mother sexually abused me by sticking fingers and objects up my anus until I screamed. I was not a happy camper in the least. Nor did I feel safe. Nor did I want to stay on the planet in this body.

I recall through those long, sad years from age two to four that my soul would call out into the night for comfort, protection, and solace. Starting just before the age of two, Jesus came to my succor every night. I immediately felt comforted. I already knew Jesus, based on our many past lives together and time with Him in the spirit world in preparation for this journey. He has been my lifeline for many millennia, and always will be.

Here's how the dialogues went:

> Me: "Why are my parents and relatives treating me this way?"
> Jesus: "Because they do not know themselves, nor care for themselves."
> Me: "I thought all people were like me…"
> Jesus: "You must always remember that others are not like you or have your personal experiences—yet…"
> Me: "Do I need to stay here? Why am I here?"
> Jesus: "Because you have a great life ahead of you that you will enjoy immensely, and also a role for the planet with others at this time."
> Me: "I see others around me full of hatred, greed, selfishness and fear. Are they mostly like this?
> Jesus: "For now, sadly, yes…"

And here is my most often asked question of Jesus.

> Me: "What is the most important reason for people to come to Earth? Is it money, fame, fortune…"—those being what I was observing in people.
> Jesus: "No, Joseph, it's Love!"
> Me: "Love? What's that? I don't know the word and I don't think I've ever experienced it with my family."
> Jesus: "Love is the relationship you and I have together. We are friends who deeply care for one another and have great affection, sweet emotions, and respect for one another."
> Me: "Love, you say. Well, I do know and remember the true nature

of our relationship, Jesus! If this is love, then I understand truly what love is, and why I am here."

Jesus: "Remember to always Be the Love you Are! For pure love is the key to all life, here, and everywhere in the universe."

Me: "I will love my parents and brother, and all my relatives then."

Jesus: "Though your life is a great challenge to you on all levels, you will succeed when you fill your heart with love, and learn to give and receive it in every circumstance, with every person you meet."

This is the main heart of my ongoing discussions with Jesus Christ, night and day.

LUCIFER OR SATAN AND OTHER DARK FORCES

You may or may not believe in Lucifer and all his Dark Forces and minions. He is described in detail in the Old Testament and New Testament of the Jewish and Christian Bible. He is also present in the Holy Qur'an. In Hinduism, we have many millions of demons of various sorts. In Buddhism, likewise, there are traps and attacks laid by all kinds of named and known Dark Forces and demons. Likewise, in First Nations and worldwide Aboriginal traditions, we have many Dark Beings and entities.

Every culture expresses belief in and shares experiences about all manner of Dark Beings. These include the Lemurians and Atlanteans; the aboriginal shamans' battles between the good and the evil; the African tribes; Mayan, Incan, and Toltec civilizations; the Tibetans; the Druids and Celts; the Asian and Middle-Eastern traditions. All these cultures know about the Dark Forces. It is just a question of whether or not you have actually experienced them firsthand.

For me, Lucifer or Satan, as he is called, is another complex and important part of my life's story. Lucifer or the Antichrist is the antipode to Jesus and the Christ Consciousness or Kutastha Chaitanya as we say in Hinduism. Whereas Jesus brings love, light, hope and joy to the Earth, Lucifer brings hatred, darkness, fear, desolation, despair, and loneliness.

Lucifer's main role in each of our lives, and indeed on the Earth with our collective humanity is clear. Satan chooses to destroy each of us—spiritually, mentally, psychologically, emotionally, and physically. He is always on the march and watches us, choosing auspicious times when we are weakest, in order to render us helpless and hopeless. Lucifer is said to be the twin of Archangel Mikael. Mikael's sword of light and life is opposed by Lucifer's force of hatred and death.

According to the Bible and other mythologies, Lucifer was at the right hand of God, one of Her-His chosen. When Lucifer refused God's wish to bow and serve God's new creatures—humankind—then Satan's pride and ego got the better of him. He refused. God-Goddess then sent him down to the depths of Hell, into utter darkness and loneliness, nevermore to see the bright shining face of God, the one being Lucifer had previously loved so much.

Other than my joyous inner celebratory loving friendship with Jesus, my early life and teenage years were definitely one long, continuous Dark Night of the Soul. I lived the via negativa, the left-hand or the faster and more challenging dark path to higher consciousness.

MY ONGOING BATTLES WITH LUCIFER-SATAN AND OTHER DARK FORCES

From when I was two years of age, Lucifer savagely and viciously attacked me many times. These mostly happened at night, while lying in my crib. Sometimes, it was during the daytime when I was assailed. If the Big Evil One and the Dark Side have never forcefully threatened you, then pray this never happens to you. One feels as if one is losing one's mind, having all soul, hope, and emotions crushed into non-existence, and the physical body about to be killed and obliterated. The fear and terror is of the most extreme intensity imaginable. The one saving resolution that I intuitively knew to use, at the age of two years and upwards, was to call upon the name and blood of Jesus Christ. This always works like a charm, so to speak. There are other techniques to use; however, this is the main one that stops the attacks.

Good trumps evil every time. Righteousness is infinitely more powerful than hatred. One small light can fill a stadium of darkness. Love always heals and frees, while enmity always closes, hurts, destroys, and imprisons.

Why did this happen to me? Where there is Christ and Light, there is Lucifer and Dark to oppose it. In fact, these two energies rule the

Earth world and the Milky Way Galaxy. This third dimension is a world of duality and always will be. For every power, there is an equal and opposite force. And humans get to choose where to align our hearts and consciousness—and each of us needs to choose. With good and evil, there is no fence sitting, though most of us already carry mixed karma regarding this issue. One of our great purposes in our Earth walk is to forgive ourselves of past evil deeds, love ourselves, and choose the path towards our innate goodness, truth, beauty, and love. Only then can and will we eternally be free.

Even though we are a century and a half past the abolition of slavery in America, humans on earth are still slaves to Lucifer and their own egos. Satan continues to entice each one of us into using our own possibilities for inner hatred, ego judgments of self and others, and wanting to use force over others to feel important.

I was alone in all this. I never spoke of this to anyone, certainly not my family members. I knew they would never understand. It wasn't until my early teens, when I started reading pertinent books by C.S. Lewis, George MacDonald, and Charles Williams that I found some solace in the truth of what I suffered. Most helpful was C.S. Lewis's The Screwtape Letters, which are glib yet direct letters of advice from a senior demon, Screwtape, to his nephew Wormwood, on the best ways to tempt a particular human and secure his damnation.

In C.S. Lewis's other books, such as The Great Divorce, the Space Trilogy novels, and The Chronicles of Narnia series, the central theme is always the eternal fight between light and dark, good and evil. It is up to each person to be a heroine-hero in their own lives, conquer their dreary, fearful, disempowering ego, and open their heart to the infinite love in their own soul.

CHAPTER 4
THE EARLY YEARS, 3–12 YEARS

SPIRITUAL REMEMBRANCES

A major reason for sharing my story is to let you all know that ordinary people like myself can make a difference. When you share your love, you can bring happiness and friendship to everyone you meet.

My early life challenges impulse me to find the best ways to allow people to heal themselves, which is why I studied so much about ancient and modern healing techniques. I know that our soul and spirit are the keys to all healing. It is my pleasure and honour to sit with so many people and witness their own healings when they open to pure love.

At ages three to seven, there were many mornings when I sat on the living room carpet and watched the sunlight streaming through our floor-to-ceiling southern windows. I easily and naturally went into trance watching the sunbeams. It seemed to me that I could see the atoms and energetic lifetrons of the smallest particles of the universe and all matter. I found glory in this deep, quietude, and solace of the heart for hours at a time. It was always the movement of the sunbeams that led me to these spiritual epiphanies. During this time, I heard the voices of Jesus, Vivekananda, and Yogananda—the latter two being the first and second pre-eminent Hindu guru monk teachers to come from India to Turtle Island, North America--Vivekananda in 1893 and Yogananda in 1925. You might recall they were with me on my descent from Source to Earth.

It was during my listening to their heart words that I understood anew the unity of the cosmos—the Spirit and Earth worlds being one, interplaying and dancing one with the other in synchronous non-time and time, spirit and matter. Here I received my remembrance of my special vocation from God and Jesus again—to be pure love and thereby, even without words, to open others' hearts. It is my great joy, which I am being to the best of my abilities, though I am human and have faults and weaknesses like everyone else. As Gautama Buddha relates, "Learning is only remembering."

MUSIC AND THE PIANO

Music is one of the best ways to open your heart and soul to love. At age four, one of the first pieces I learned was "Heart and Soul." Music is cross-cultural and universal; it goes far beyond language of the mind. Music is the eternal infinite communication of the heart.

My cousin Sally was my first teacher. When I was five, I went to see her teacher in the Beaches in Toronto. There was a young man at the end of our street, Steve, who drove me weekly from Don Mills to and from my piano lessons. I am forever grateful for his sacrifice. I learned so much from Barbara Gilroy. She enchanted me with the feelings, power, and precision of classical music. During this year, I started to compose my own little tunes, such as "The Little Tin Soldier," a Mozartian styled tune, and "The Happy Little Toymaker."

At age six, Barbara sent me to her teacher, Mona Bates, a seasoned, world-travelling pianist of the highest caliber. During the 1910s and 1920s, Mona played the Liszt Fantasy and Beethoven's "Waldstein" Sonata, among others, at Massey Hall in Toronto and in New York. She studied and concertized throughout Europe and the Far East under the exotic name, Anom Setab (her name spelled backwards). She gave up concerts in 1925 to open a studio at the northeast corner of Jarvis Street and Wellesley Street East. (The mansion is now a Keg restaurant.) During World War II she set up the Musical Manifesto Group and the Ten-Piano Ensemble with her best students and gave numerous performances, raising thousands of dollars for charity.

I vividly recall my first session with Mona Bates. There was a large, curved, drive-through red granite portico. Trembling, I got out of the car, walked to the large double doors, and pressed the buzzer. A manservant came and told me to wait in the hall on the pew-like bench. I could hear a lesson going on in the large European-style drawing to the left of the grand hall where I was seated. I had a major inferiority complex, and my nervousness created a stultifying near-catatonia within. Was I good enough? Would she take me on as a pupil?

MONA BATES AND THE MAGIC OF SPIRIT COMMUNICATION WITH GREAT CLASSICAL COMPOSERS

Finally, after an exhausting fifteen minutes, the other pupil rushed out, and Ms. Bates swished out into the hall. At the time, she was 67 years old, and still a very spry energetic person. Her two small fluffy white dogs with pearl necklaces happily rushed to greet me. With a quick, bristling walk, Mona strode up to me. She was 4'11" and exuded a Victorian pomp and circumstance. Her long whitish hair was parted in the middle from front to back, and wrapped and coiled at her ears in the biggest buns I had ever seen. She looked positively otherworldly. Now, I see her as a female Yoda. She had rings on every finger of both hands.

"So, you're young Mr. Martin, are you? Well, let's hear you play something."

"Ooookay," I stammered shyly.

I was even more terrified when I was ushered through the double stained-glass doors into her lavishly decorated grand studio. Standing starkly in the centre of the space were two monumental, lustrous black Concert Grand Steinways of 8' 11 3/4", side by side. They were like two sentinels, guarding the mystical realms of higher pianistic magic. Did I deserve to be in this hallowed sanctum? Did I merit this once-in-a-lifetime chance? Would she take me on as a student?

Treasures of unimaginable beauty bedecked the high-ceiling, light-filled room. I noticed large teak chests from Asia, and booty from all over Europe and the world. The skylights and large windows made this conservatory feel like a jungle with its large palm trees and other large-leaved foliage. There were budgies in cages hanging in the large 30-foot tall indoor trees. Eccentric is not enough of a descriptive moniker for this unique, intense powerhouse of a woman. She could have matched Queen Victoria with her searing hawk-like gaze and direct powerful demeanor.

"Well then, have a seat at the piano on the right!"

She flicked open a massive, glittering gem on the ring finger of her left hand and glanced at the watch inside the ring!

"We have exactly 30 minutes, even though your parents could only afford 15 minutes… I am giving you extra time," she smiled demurely with a stern look.

As I recall, 15 minutes of her time was $25; that was a lot of money for our poor family of four with $6,000 annual income back in the mid-1950s!

"We'll see how you do," she chirped.

I played a little ditty by Haydn that she had open on the piano. She tightly smiled and said, "go on…" So I played Brahms's Waltz in A-Flat," a most memorable, world-beloved melody.

"Hmm…," she opined.

She stood up from her seat at the other Steinway Grand to my left. A photo of Johannes Brahms in his prime was placed in front of me, covering the music I was playing. What she said next forever changed my life experience.

"Do you know how Brahms felt when he was composing this piece of music?"

"No," I quietly said.

"Well, please stare into his eyes while I tell you the story. Brahms was very much in love with Clara Schumann, the wife of his good friend, Robert Schumann, the composer. Yet this was to be an unrequited love for the whole of Brahms's life…"

I fixedly looked into Brahms's eyes, and was drawn ever more deeply into his personality and soul while she continued in a more pensive, almost tearful manner.

"The deep passionate love in Brahms's heart and the pure melodies that can only come from this kind of love were what he was feeling when he wrote The Waltz in A-Flat."

Suddenly, I felt Brahms's own soul speaking to my heart! I recognized these feeling sensations and the inner verbal conversations that were similar to those in the deeply emotional-spiritual relationships I have with Jesus, Babaji, and my many other Spirit world friends. I could feel Brahms, know what his heart was experiencing, and sense him breathing and thinking inside me now. I was floored, and immensely and excitedly thrilled.

"You must get to know each composer, their innermost heart feelings, and what they experienced when they composed each of their compositions. This is the only way to play their music. Play it the way it was created and meant to be played by the composer."

I had never been told this before. One simply memorized a song and played it in a technically proficient manner—analytically. Heaven opened my musical heart! I was given permission to do what I do best—listen to others' hearts and respond. I could feel Brahms's love and passion in my own heart. At Mona's behest, I played the song once more—only this time with authentic feeling!

"Excellent!" she joyously exclaimed. "Excellent."

Then she gave me a lesson on how to let all four lines of melody in the harmony of Brahms's Waltz sing on their own.

"Most people are trained to let just the top soprano melody line take prominence," she demurred. "This is not the proper way. You must let each line have its own voice in its uniquely beautiful flow—the soprano, alto, tenor, and bass lines of the harmony each alternatively emphasized."

Then she played it for me. Heaven on Earth! What a glorious transformation from the normal way of hearing this piece. I tried, and it was a marvelous revelation to my heart and ears.

During my next few weekly lessons, she brought out photographs of the following composers: Bach, Haydn, Handel, Mozart, Beethoven, Rachmaninoff, Chopin, Liszt, and others. I stared transfixed at each one's eyes and face. Then I played a piece of theirs. I could hear the composer speaking to me in my heart-mind—"a little less fortissimo, more flow of the notes, not so harshly rigid! Don't use the sustain pedal so much." This was pure magic!

Mona told me to take all the inner liberties I wished with the melody lines, tempi, and rhythms of each piece.

"Play tempo rubato and use your emotions to connect with the composer's feelings to express the infinite and ultimate beauty of the music. This is what musical performance really is!"

Ms. Bates, as she like to be called, invited me to play in one of her annual recitals when I was seven years old. All her famous student pianists, much older than me, would be tickling the ivories as well. When it came to my turn, I sat at the piano in a wretched, uncontrollable inner fear. I was playing the famous Brahms Waltz in A-Flat. My terror was so intense that I lacked control over my right leg and foot, which pushed down on the sustain pedal and I couldn't get it off. One is supposed to alternatively press and lift their right foot off the sustain pedal according to the musical phrasing. What horror when the first half of the piece had all the notes mushing together. During the second half, my self-controlled, nervous foot would alternately go up and down on the pedal—at the worst times for the phrasing. I felt it was a disaster. Ms. Bates grimaced and we had a long talk about how to get over nerves at my next lesson.

More so than ever, my inner world started to revolve around music and these particular composers. I practiced six to eight hours a day. Alone in the basement, I was in ecstasy and entranced by what I heard and felt coming through my fingers. From the local Don Mills Public Library, I took out all the biographies I could on all the composers mentioned. I recall being especially excited by Johann Sebastian Bach, Georg Frideric Handel, and "Papa" Franz Joseph Haydn. Seated at my upright grand piano, I spoke with each composer for hours while I learned their songs. I heard their voices, felt their emotions, and I lived my life with them as I let them inside my heart and body—just as I always have done with Jesus and the others Spiritual Masters.

There is an important proof of heaven in these experiences. Souls are eternal, and you can communicate, listen, and ask questions with them at any time. You could call what I experience heart and mind telepathy. It's the "telepaphone" that I constantly and consistently utilize every moment of my life to connect with anyone I choose in Spirit. I laughingly joke that many people would think I am out of my mind in "hearing voices." My rejoinder to this would be, "perhaps, but most likely not! You may misperceive that I am 'out of my mind,'" I joke, "however, I am also more in my heart."

I continued my lessons with Mona Bates and Barbara Gilroy simultaneously until I was 15 years old. I did my RCM Royal Conservatory of Music Toronto Grade 10 Piano, along with the requisite Music Theory, History, and Harmony. I had long-standing, serious thoughts of going on to the Associate of The Royal Conservatory (ARCT) diploma for Performers and Teachers. However, in the end, I decided that the highest use of my time was further explorations in academics and sports. In studies, I was interested in math, physics, chemistry, biology, psychology, philosophy, and anthropology. In terms of sports, I was not allowed to participate until I was 12 twelve years old, and felt very inferior in team sports where I had not been able to develop skills. Therefore, my choice for my late-coming to my physical competitive skill sets were individual sports—swimming, diving, 100-yard dash, high jump, downhill skiing, canoeing, wilderness solo hiking trips, and bicycling.

PLAYING IN THE WOODS

Having this heart condition meant I was constantly out of breath. I sometimes fainted while walking about due to lack of oxygen. I was never really allowed to play rough, though I did hike in the forest near our house a lot. We had an underground fort and a tree fort. Back then, Don Mills was the first suburb in North America, and we were on the outer limits of Toronto. We had the forest behind our small street of 12 houses; we lived at 4 Waxwing Place. As a result of the street name, I always loved cedar waxwing songbirds.

I spent time botanizing for berries and roots; I liked to identify and draw the flowers and leaves of all kinds of plants and trees. When we played "Cowboys and Indians," I was always the Indian—sometimes the only one, which speaks volumes for the lack of acceptance of and respect for our Aboriginal Ancestors in Canada.

During my years of five to twelve, I played with the kids on the streets, most of whom were just a few years younger. I became the leader. I made paper kites for them and we played with them in the spring winds. In summer, I would teach them to ride a bicycle, or hitch up a wagon, cover it with a structure and cloth and make stagecoaches. We often sold lemonade and other homemade articles to raise funds for the Toronto Star newspaper Relief Fund for inner city children. I even had my photo taken with an article about this in the local Don Mills "Mirror."

PUBLIC SCHOOL

My life at home with my parents and older brother was hell. My first day in kindergarten turned out to be likewise. Having what Alfred Adler calls a psychological condition of organ deficiency as an aspect of my personality, I felt a massive inferiority complex in regards to others— adults and children—even though I knew my real Soul Self was the real me, and very different from my ego personality. This was key for me, knowing there are two worlds in which each of us live and participate, whether knowingly or unknowingly—the innermost spiritual, invisible Soul Source of pure love in the heart, and the outer, visible, six-senses, familial, socially acculturated perception of the material world perceived by the ego mind.

My brother escorted me to school that initial day of kindergarten. Some other boy in Grade One made fun of my skinny frame, my awkwardness, and my physicality. He could tell that I felt inferior, and he acted upon it. I suppose that's how bullies are made. He swung at me. I hit him back. It was the only time in my life that I struck out at someone. The school principal and a teacher saw us; it was just before the bell at 9 am. I was sent home with a bloody nose. I felt badly that I created suffering and I vowed to never do it again. However, a part of me was elated that I stood up for myself—and that was my ego and false pride.

Recently, since my third heart surgery, I have recalled smells and tastes from our regular daily naps in kindergarten. I now remember the smell of the room, the taste of the simple water cookies and the apple or orange juice in the paper cup, the sight of the coats hanging on hooks and boots all lined up. I became sociable during that year. While education is really just planned amnesia for the soul, it can be good for learning to share and play kindly with others, or not.

However, Grade One at Greenland Road Public School was a misery. My teacher did not like me; neither did the Principal, who was a strict, duty-oriented middle-aged man. They thought I was too big for my britches. I could read and write easily, and spelling was something at which I excelled; I seemed to be gifted, as we all are, with an eidetic memory for words, sounds, and kinesthetic experiences. We just have to work at improving these innate skills, that's all.

The school adults had it in for me. I asked them if during the thrice-weekly gym class I could go to the library or play the piano.

"Absolutely not, under no circumstances," commanded the Principal in a brazenly militaristic manner, "you, young man, will sit on the bench on the sidelines in the gymnasium and watch the other children play and learn skills."

That man stole my creativity and childhood sense of personal adventure in learning. There and then, I planned to prove to myself that school was a waste of time except for socializing, and that learning must be self-directed. This became a great life goal that I have accomplished.

The other children knew something was wrong with me physically— they just didn't know what. I was made to sit there for 50 minutes each time and endure the gloating looks of the other kids and the gym teacher. They made me feel shame, guilt, and embarrassment; I was treated like a non-entity.

I liked my male Grade Two teacher, Mr. Slack; he was kind, gentle, and had beautiful dark hair and blue eyes. He recognized something in me and encouraged me in many ways. Isn't that what most teachers are meant to be and do?

MY FIRST HEART SURGERY, OCTOBER 26, 1958, HOSPITAL FOR SICK CHILDREN, TORONTO

My health was deteriorating quite rapidly during the summer of 1958. I was more frequently short of breath and lost energy even though my spirits were and are always high. My family doctor, Dr. Gordon Stewart, was very solicitous and concerned about me. He was soft, intuitive, and likely knew about the abuse in my family. Dr. Stewart sensed my precarious future. He and I had a deep feeling and intuitive relationship. He gave me his stamp collection to keep me busy during my days in bed. This is how I learned about the many cultures of the world, and intrigued my interest in anthropology. Early on, I knew I wanted to be an Egyptologist! His soothing presence is one of the main factors in my choice of being a health practitioner over 38 years. He was a very kind, compassionate, and smart man. Whereas my family relationships were horrendously emotionally and physically painful, Dr. Stewart was someone with whom I could relate.

Being concerned about my future health, he had sent me to a pediatrician at the Hospital for Sick Children on University Avenue in Toronto. This man knew about the new heart surgeries being done on dogs at the local Banting Institute. The pediatrician set up an appointment for me with Canada's first cardiac surgeon.

Canadian physician and cardiac surgeon Dr. William (Bill) Thornton

Mustard (1914-1987) was one of the first to perform open-heart surgery using a mechanical heart pump and biological lung on a dog in 1949. He developed the "Mustard cardiovascular procedure" used to help correct heart problems in "blue babies." Now, I was not a "blue baby," just a "Clue" baby; someone who knew that Colonel-Doctor Mustard in the operating room with the wrench, knife, and sewing kit, would do a marvelous job for me—at least I truly hoped so.

In 1957, Dr. Mustard trained with Dr. Alfred Blalock in Baltimore, Maryland, to learn pediatric cardiology and surgery techniques for Tetralogy of Fallot, the "blue baby" syndrome. My issue was a little different; it was a Ventrical Septal Defect (VSD). In 1957, Dr. Mustard was appointed Chief of Cardiovascular Surgery at the Hospital for Sick Children.

According to my recollections, Dr. Mustard had done one surgery before mine was to take place. It was on a young girl my age, and she had died on the operating table. Very sadly, there was also a fellow student my age in my Public School class with a VSD, and in the spring of 1958, he died before having surgery.

My first meeting with Dr. Mustard was in the spring of 1958. In his office at the Hospital, he was describing to me what he intended to do in the surgery. He told me that the previous first operation on the girl was unsuccessful. It didn't sound too promising. He wanted time to experiment on other dogs before doing me. Also, in Chicago, they were developing a new heart-lung machine that he would use. I was instructed to rest and take it easy over the summer to get ready for my operation in the fall.

"What chance do I have of living through the operation?" I inquisitively stammered.

"You have a 20 percent chance of living through the operation. Without it, you will certainly die."

Only staring death in the face—knowing you have only a few months before it actually happens—can give you the terror I felt in that moment, and the fear continued to increase exponentially up until the operation.

Two weeks before the operation, I ran away from home. I hid in the forest in one of our forts. My brother knew where I was, hidden underground, though he did not come to drag me home. Eventually I came to grips with the greatest fear any human can have—the fear of death. Thus early on, I dealt with the thought that my life might soon be over.

While in the woods, I quieted, and listened to my heart, and a deep calm and peace came over my whole mind, emotions, and body. I knew that I had to be courageous and go through with the operation. Along with my attacks by the Dark Side, this was another seminal turning-point moment, when I realized that my entire life's goal was to transform all my fears—one at a time—into courage, love, strength, decision, devotion, and action! I decided I would go through with the operation, even though Dr. Mustard had said there was only a 20 percent chance I would make it through alive.

Because I trusted Jesus, I would go through this operation, even though it was likely that I would die. Such is the trust of an innocent child, and this is what eventually pulled me through—then, and in all my various illnesses and operations throughout my life!

No words can describe my feelings the days before the operation. Prior to it, I was given all kinds of barium and blood tests. Tubes were inserted from my right inguinal or groin artery to my heart, and another from my left arm artery. This was painful enough.

When the day of the operation came, I was easily out-of-my-body since I had learned to do this so consciously during my many times of abuse. I was somewhat aware of being wheeled down to the operating rooms, all built below ground in the basement of the Hospital. Had they done this for wartime purposes?

THE OPERATION ITSELF AND NEAR-DEATH EXPERIENCE

The heart surgery was 18½ hours long. Here's the story of my Near Death Experience (NDE). To this day, it is one of my most vivid, easily repeatable, inner full-spectrum memory replays. About midway through the operation, I had the NDE, which apparently lasted at least 32 minutes. During this time, I felt, saw and heard myself leave my body. I soared out through the roof of the Hospital; it seemed to be early evening. I recall flying straight up and off the planet. I saw the moon on my left, and then the sun on my right. As I passed through the centre of the Milky Way Galaxy, I saw distant swirling galaxies going by.

When I reached the Source, the Great Metagalactic Central Sun, I landed in a paradise landscape where everything was vibrantly alive. The blades of grass, with their glistening dewdrops, sang their harmonies; the celestial grass seemed like a field of dazzling diamonds. To my right, falling gently from distant mountains and hills was a joyously burbling living creek, resplendent with celestial light shining on its rippled surface. To my left was an orchard of apple trees, with gorgeous, colourful spirit birds singing with pure hearts of love—just for the majesty of it all!

Directly in front of me, about 7 feet away, in a dazzlingly magnificent brilliant white energy body, was Jesus Christ. His beatific smile and generously compassionate and kind heart showed in His outstretched arms and sparkling glow of goodness, truth, and beauty. Yet most of all, it was His scintillating, infinitely eternal, gloriously pure love that entranced and drew me in. I moved closer, while Jesus leant forward, reaching out with His hands of light to touch my shoulders.

Astonished and more than pleased, I was glad I came Home once again. My being was overflowing with joyous sensations of the greatest love and gratitude. Peripherally, I watched the deer and sheep grazing behind Jesus; they looked up and meandered over to us. There were rabbits, grasshoppers, and a multitude of rainbow-coloured butterflies, such as golden Monarchs, yellow Swallowtails, and iridescent Blue Morphos. It seems like I was there for an eternity, for the reason that in Source there is no concept of time.

I can still vividly hear the glorious angelic choruses of perfect, peaceful, joyous melodies within harmonies of greatest wonderment. This is probably why I still love and listen to Bach, Handel, Vaughan-Williams and Respighi's music every day.

"I'm so glad to be Home, Jesus!" I exclaimed in absolute joy. I had supreme relief as I left behind my family, and the emotional-psychological traumas of my Earth life.

"Well, Joseph, actually, you're not staying here; you're going back to Earth."

I was stunned! Why was I here, if not to stay? Why would I need to go back? How was this possible? I had come all this way on my intergalactic journey; now I was Home.

"You have a great and important life ahead of you. You will learn many things, and most importantly, you will enjoy sharing your love with everyone and everything. I want you to go back to your Earth life. I will be with you in your heart every step of the way."

In the love of our two hearts as one, much more passed between us, an understanding that comes only from being one inside a deep friendship of the heart in full love.

I gulped. I gasped at the thought of returning to Earth. I looked Him squarely in His loving eyes. My heart pondered this possibility, this opportunity.

"You know I would do anything for you, Jesus. I always have. If you wish me to go back, I will." We stood there, completely mesmerized with each other's love, eye-gazing soul to soul. The light of His love was blazing into the core of my soul, pulsing me with infinite courage, strength, and faith—and above all, hope.

Everything in life is a trust walk. This was one more chance to experience the glorious challenges of an Earth walk. I sensed there was a higher divine purpose for me; I knew it would only be accomplished if I went back immediately. There was a yearning to stay, and opposed to this, a dire sensation that if I didn't return to my body soon, this door of possibility would close forever.

Jesus and I hugged deeply, and we smiled. Then I turned away and immediately went into a clockwise spinning tunnel of burning, swirling diamond-white and turquoise-blue lights. Though it is timeless, it was instantaneous, at the speed of intentional thought. I had my compass set for Earth. I began to slow down and came out of the tunnel after I went through the Milky Way Galactic Centre.

From there, I made my way back to our solar system. This next part is still so visually and kinesthetically powerful for me. I recall traversing through the middle of the sun, then transiting by our moon, ending up flying towards Earth from a distance of over 384,000 kilometers away. It was dark; it was nighttime on earth on Turtle Island, North America. I could see multitudinous lights of electrified cities and towns. Earth resembled a glowing spherical Christmas tree or bell.

I had to focus on my coordinates. I voiced to myself, "Ah, there is Lake Ontario. There is Buffalo on the south shore of Lake Ontario, and Toronto on the north shore." I aimed for the centre of the downtown, as I knew all the major hospitals were on University Avenue. As I flew in over the lake, Sick Kids was on the right side of the street. I saw a Hospital sign and flew through the building, searching for the operating rooms. "Here we go, I found it!" I chuckled with relief. Flying through the walls from room to room, I realized that all the bodies on the tables were adults. I was in the wrong hospital, Toronto General. Which way to go?

Time was ticking. I could feel a sense of urgency from the doctors and nurses. If I didn't hurry up, I would be too late, and I would die. One's sensations and intuitions always tell when one will live and when one will die. I knew it was down to a few seconds now. Apparently, I had been clinically dead for quite some time, and the staff members were more than worried; they were panicking.

This was epic. Could I find my body in time? I was terrified—this time for the opposite reason. Before I had not wanted to start the operation—now I had to find my mortal frame and finish the operation before my time was up.

I roared through the halls of the Toronto General Hospital and flew out through the south wall, heading for the neighbouring Sick Kids Hospital. I knew all the operation rooms were below ground, so I dove down and went through so many walls, room after room, looking for myself. Finally!

"There's a young lad. That must be me." I zoomed in and screeched to a halt. "Whew, I made it!"

Then I heard, "Hey, what are you doing in here? This is my body; get out!"

"Sorry, you look like me! I'm off! Okay, where am I?"

Still on the hunt for my body, I went to the next room. "There, that must be mine!" Out of sheer panic, I crash-jumped into myself with such force, that I assertively woke up, opened my eyes, and lifted my head. "Yeah, I'm home!" I shouted inwardly to myself as I quickly viewed my open chest, clamps, gloved hands, and beating heart. Omitting the expletives used by my surgeon and anesthesiologist, I heard, "Quick! Give him more anesthetic!" I wasn't at all surprised; I had seen my open heart from above when descending into my body. I never asked them, yet I bet the doctors were totally shocked! I saw them scurrying; they must have opened the line of anesthetic because I soon went under.

Chapter Four

POOR RECOVERY

A day later, I woke up in the Recovery Unit. I had an oxygen tent around me, which covered the entire bed—yes, that's what they used in the middle of the twentieth century. I was very weak, I could hardly focus, much less talk. I was aware that I was on the painkiller heroin. Often, through my tears, I had to ask and even plead for more.

During the first two weeks inside this heavy opaque plastic, grey tent, I felt very lonely and isolated. Only my mother came to visit, usually for five minutes every other day. Into the third week, I raised the left side of the oxygen tent with my hand so that I could see her better. I was so desperately disconnected from human affection that I asked her for a kiss. She did give me one. It turned out to almost be the kiss of death. Within a few hours, I got serious pneumonia; my lungs filled up, and I could scarcely breathe.

Dr. Mustard was furious. He angrily phoned my mother, and asked her "What do you think you're doing? I had forbidden you to touch your son. Do you want to kill him? He may not recover now."

Apparently, she cried and cried. However, in my heart, I knew that—on deep unconscious and partly conscious levels—my mother did want to kill me. She actually wished I had never been born. This I found out later through my hypnotherapy yet had always known through reading her mind while in I was in the womb. Here is a great lesson for mothers and fathers—be careful what you think and say to your unborn and birthed children!

It was another two months until I was well enough to get out of that tent. I was happy enough to be sitting up in my hospital bed all day, eating only hot dogs with ketchup and strawberry milkshakes. That was it. I hated eggs—probably as a result of the massive Negative Mother complex I had inherited, with eggs as a symbol of the Mother. Sometimes I would nibble on a peanut butter and strawberry jam sandwich of white Wonder bread. I could handle macaroni and cheese with lots of ketchup.

The next biggest shock came about three months after my surgery. Dr. Mustard came to my hospital bed, which he rarely did, and wanted to talk.

"The hole in your heart was as big as a Canadian silver dollar. The hole was so large; I could only put a Teflon patch on half of the hole. I had to leave the other half open, as doing any more surgery would have put too much strain on your heart muscle. I am very sorry, but you will need another operation in a year from now," he said.

While my mind sank at this tragic news, my inner intuitive heart spoke up loudly to myself, saying, "You will not need another operation. All you need to do is pray, and visualize the rest of the hole closing up and the heart mending itself."

I was shocked by what I heard from my soul, and of course, I never mentioned it to my doctor or anyone.

During the intervening months after my surgery, I spent hours daily visualizing the hole in my heart muscle closing naturally on its own. I prayed with Jesus to make sure this was done completely, perfectly and successfully. All along, I felt an inner spiritual and emotional assurance that all would be well. So I persevered in my positive ways, and it worked wonders. I was healed. I knew I was going to go home and finally find my life and path.

I went home for a few months in the middle of the summer of 1959. I was called back to the hospital in September, 11 months after my first operation. Dr. Mustard did all the scopes, tests, tubes, and analysis in preparation for my second operation. Then I went home to wait. Two weeks later, he ordered all the very same tests done over again. What was up? I went home again and then my mother got a call. We went to see Dr. Mustard at Sick Kids.

He called me into his office alone, and said, "Please… sit down there in that chair," gesticulating with his right hand to a chair in front of his desk. He stood up, pulled his glasses down to the tip of his nose, and stalked around to the front of his desk. He leaned back, breathed, and folded his arms across his chest. I clearly remember every one of his following words. In a rather perplexed and serious manner, he very slowly pronounced, "I don't know what has happened, but the hole in your heart is gone. I don't know how or why. I have no scientific explanation for it. You won't need another heart operation."

Immediately, I thought to myself, "Should I tell him what I have done?" Very quickly from inside came my stirring loud inner voice, "No! Don't tell him what you did! He will never understand! Don't tell anyone! Not even your mother and father!"

Doctor Mustard thought this was a big success. I was invited to a research clinical teaching session at the hospital with doctors from all over the world. I was the specimen on the gurney table all over again. They were describing the cardiac surgical procedures to fellow clinicians. It was a tiring three hours for me. Afterwards, the 256 staff that attended and had something to do with my operation took a photo with me out front of Sick Kids Hospital. I was on the National CBC TV news. I was the headline in the Toronto Star and the Toronto Globe newspapers.

FINDING THE KEY TO LIFE - A LOVING IMAGINATIVE HEART

One thing prompted my awareness more than anything else. I said to myself, "If, with the help and grace of God, I could cure myself of this complaint and condition, then I now know the keys to self-healing! I know that all healing comes from inside my soul, mind, and body. The body always knows how to heal itself. Doctors only set tissues on the right path. Spirit does the rest. I will explore this in every way I can, until I have all the answers."

My friends, this is what has been the driving power that has gifted me with profound wisdom throughout my life. I turned over every book and looked inside every spiritual healing technique, until I had learned them all—Western, Eastern, and Tribal Medicines; ancient and modern; energetic and materially physical; metaphysical and biochemical; esoteric and exoteric; mental and emotional; unconscious, conscious and super-conscious; shamanic and surgical; extraterrestrial and terrestrial. This is my gift to you and future generations—the gift of miraculous eternal life through the divine-human healing power of the Great Christ Love and Light. All you need to do is open your heart, believe, admit to Grace, feel infinitely grateful, take action, and do it for your higher Self.

Thomas Edison claimed that, "The doctor of the future will prescribe no medicine, but will interest his patient in the care of the human frame, in diet and in the cause and prevention of dis-ease."

I will take this a few steps further. The lack of unity with the Source Love and Light is the major cause of all illness for humans. When an individual releases karmic-emotional blocks within his or her unconscious astral and physical bodies, accepts his or her true nature as a spiritual being with a soul, and then opens his or her heart, mind, and body to the highest celestial Light and Pure Love, then she or he will heal themselves perfectly.

We are meant to SOARR—Surrender, Open, Allow, Release (old energetic emotional-psychological blockages,) and Receive the Great Pure Love We Are.

GOING HOME

I spent most of Grade Three in the hospital, but I passed anyway, having done a few reports from my hospital bed.

I was exceedingly happy to be alive. There was great joy in botanizing alone in the woods, listening to the plant and tree spirits, and communing with Mother Earth. I found rocks that talk, sharing ancient memories of this place, Delundu (Toronto), the Mohawk name for "the place where the logs come down the river to the lake." There in the woods is where I most felt at peace and at home and I felt my Native roots. I rode my bicycle around the surrounding streets thereby exercising my legs, which rejoiced to be strengthening after all that lying in bed.

Archery became one of my favourite pastimes. I took my longbow and arrows with my target to practice in the backfield at Don Mills Collegiate Institute Junior and Senior High Schools. Early on, I missed and shot a few arrows into a neighbour's roof; I had to climb the outdoor TV antenna to retrieve them. Mostly, I improved with long hours of diligent application.

During these summers, I lived in a tent in the backyard alone. I preferred to be out with the plant, tree, rock, and animal spirits. I transplanted May Apple, white and rose-coloured trilliums (even though it was illegal to move our provincial flower) and wild ginseng and ginger, along with double-flowering bloodroot. Some nights, at 3am, I sneaked alone over to the Don Mills Shopping Centre to the 24-hour donut shop, and bought a whole dozen of the apple-cinnamon donuts. These were my all-time favourites.

Since I was five, between the window wells at the back of the house,

I planted potatoes, lima beans, squashes, and corn. Looking back, I suppose this was my unconscious memory of my Kanienkehaka and Haudenosaunee or Mohawk and Six Nations past lives. Our Three Goddesses or Sisters, in common with the Hopi, Maya and other First Nations, are Corn, Beans, and Squash.

In the summer of my ninth year, my family took a holiday to Manitoulin Island. The ancient energies of this land of Kitchi Manitou captured my soul as nothing had before. The power of Ancestors' voices brightened and informed my spirit. Playing with the young Aboriginal children on the beach gave me an exhilarating sense of community and pride. I have always felt myself to be Native, as well as a Universalist—someone who feels connected to all ancient and modern spiritual and cultural traditions.

FAMILY ILLNESSES

During this time, my father's health deteriorated. He had more and more heart attacks. His kidneys and liver were shot. My mother, too, went into her own deep depression, and became hospitalized. Her diagnosis was phlebitis or swelling inflammation of the legs caused by a blood clot in a vein, although the reasons I intuited were much more psychological and emotional, in particular the depressive side of bipolar manic-depression. The painful clot was in her right leg, which symbolically means the fear and pain of consciously moving forward in your life.

When I was ten, and my brother eleven, my father was in one hospital downtown and my mother in another uptown. I walked to the Don Mills Shopping Centre Dominion store to buy food, cooked, cleaned, and organized the house, while my brother did the other chores. I remember cooking chicken and macaroni as our favourite dishes. The neighbours next door at 2 Waxwing Place looked in on us every night and sometimes took us to the two hospitals for visits.

FAMILY EMOTIONAL CHALLENGES

As a child, one knows what roles one plays within the family and ex-tended family system. Mine were given to me by my parents, brother, pa-ternal grandmother, uncles, aunts, and cousins. I never knew my paternal grandfather who died after the Boer War, or my Dutch grandparents who stayed in Holland.

I was the "sick one," "the unwanted one," "the runt," "the baby," and "the one who never should have lived." These unconsciously projected roles stuck and blossomed into "the sick one," "the guilty one," "the bad one," and "the evil one." I felt deeply burdened by all these negative roles projected onto me at the time and throughout my growing up and teenage years. The shame, guilt, and embarrassment were heavily toxic and made me sometimes think of suicide. Shame feels like heavy wet blankets on one's heart, mind, and body all the time—a self-hating burdensome load.

Typically, the childhood family victim of abuse wrongly believes and perceives that they are to blame. The blame always lies with the victimizers, the perpetrators. For all the vast majority of billions of humans on Earth now who take on this victimized blame, I wish they find the truth and set themselves free. For me, growing up and now, only the love of God, Jesus, and my other dear Spiritual Master friends heartened me.

My mother, father, and brother were incapable of dealing with their own unfathomable feelings, so they unconsciously and consciously dumped these onto me. Even though I knew that these heavy wet blankets of shame were not mine, I knew that my family members were doing the best they could for what they knew at the time. So I carried on. As you will see, it took many decades of therapy for me to completely heal myself. So yes, it is possible to heal oneself with grace, gratitude, guts, and supreme love and forgiveness. When one person in the extended family system heals, then all the individuals in the system can have the opportunity to heal too—if they take it.

Please always remember the depths of despair one can drive one's children into, when they are dealing with family systems issues of shame and rejection. You can prevent the bullies of the future, and create beautiful, loving children.

Growing up, my parents were still abusive and swirling further into their own despair, boredom, and loneliness. My brother's anger at having a sick younger brother turned to pretend comedy when he tried to smother me with a pillow, which often ended with me fainting. Then and now, I honestly feel that he was trying to kill me. And yes, at other times, he was solicitous and somewhat trying to befriend and protect me. For the most part, however, there was no emotional or psychological support in my family of origin. Nonetheless, I am eternally grateful for a roof over my head, a piano, food, and the clothes on my back from a poor, lower-middle-class family.

I stayed out of the way of all my family members. Luckily, I had the middle back bedroom—between my parent's room at the end of the hall, and my brother's room on the other side of mine. When I wasn't practicing piano in the basement, or hiding in the downstairs cold cellar closet under the stairs to stay away from being beaten in a drunken rage by my father, I was in my room with the door closed. The downstairs closet was both physical and psychological, for I knew I was a spiritually gay man as a child. Many men and women down through the centuries have been of this inclination. This closet, which was stocked with tins, macaroni boxes, water, and a flashlight, was to be our home when the nuclear bombs were dropped. At school, we practiced hiding under our wooden desks.

I trust that the coming-out of the gay men and women of the world will synchronistically mean the coming-out of closet peacemakers who will "Get Up, Stand Up" for the human rights of all people everywhere, including those who want to put an end to war—inside and outside.

Dinners at home were constant panic, as any adult child of an alcoholic comes to know. My mother stopped smoking and drinking, but not my father. I never knew if I would be backhanded or merely tolerated as non-existent at the kitchen table. "Speak only when you're spoken to!" my father thundered before or during a rough backhanded slap to the face. I was hit for eating too slow because I was afraid, or too fast because I wanted to leave and go to the seeming safety of my bedroom. I was often sent to bed with no food because my father was in a rage fueled by his massive inferiority complex and his hidden gay orientation. He evidently intuitively knew I was gay because he would say, "No son of mine will be a homoscxual! I will send you to a psychiatrist and put you in jail!"

The hilarious truth is that later, in my early and mid-thirties, I went to several psychiatrists in order to feel extremely good about coming-out, and was able to transmute my own internalized homophobia, which I had inherited from my family and society at large. My life proves you need to fight openly for your own liberation and do all your own inner healing work as soon as you feel the need.

There are many things you can say about the British Empire and a Victorian upbringing. Physical corporal punishment of children at home and school is one of the most destructive and shameful things of this lost devolving civilization. And yes, I did get the strap at Public School, just for being rebellious and being myself, which most children need to be if they are ever to grow up and live their soul life.

When I came home from school and on the weekends, I preferred the safety of my bedroom with the door completely shut.

"Open your door, or I'll smash it in!" my out-of-control, rage-aholic father demanded. He swung it wide open and inquired as to what I was doing.

"Nothing of interest," I stammered.

"Well, okay," he muttered, and turned to walk away. I simply closed the door tight again.

SPEAKING WITH THE SPIRITUAL MASTERS AND SAINTS

What was I doing in my room all that time? I was listening to and conversing with the Spiritual Masters and Saints, and writing it all down in my notebooks, along with noting my dreams since the age of seven. Eventually I acquired a blackboard, with boxes of white chalk, and a big eraser—just like at school. These I used to write down all that I heard from the Spirit world.

Typically, Nostradamus and I spent time together every day for most of my pre-teen and teen years. I wrote down the prophecies he shared with me about the future. In particular concerning the Apocalypse from John the Divine's book Revelation, which he wrote in solitude in a dark, hidden cave on the island of Patmos, Greece. By this time I read the whole Bible, the Old Testament and New Testament, cover to cover, and made underlines and notes in the columns. Over the years, I had seven or eight different translations with wonderful commentaries.

I intuitively knew as a young child that we were living in the time of the Apocalypse—the Four Horsemen, the breaking of the Seven Seals, and the Whore of Babylon. I knew this was why I had come back to planet Earth—to participate as an elder and leader to guide people and the world to the next stage of our evolution. Nostradamus told me of three Antichrists: Napoleon, Hitler and the one alive now. Who this last one is, I am not sure, although I have my surmises. All this must come to pass before there can be peace on earth. Jesus reminds his followers that "I come not to bring peace, but to bring a sword," Matthew 10:34. The 20th century and early 21st century has borne out this truth. Acknowledging this means we can take positive action and do something worthwhile about it.

As a budding spiritual historian, soulful psychologist, and metaphysical anthropologist, all this knowledge, wisdom and awareness became my central focus. I sought insights daily and nightly in dreams, visions, and visitations from the Spiritual Masters, Archangels, and Saints of all spiritual traditions. And I faithfully recorded all these conversations and revelations on the chalkboard and paper.

Somewhere around the age of nine, post-operation, I came across fascinating reading from the Don Mills Public Library, where I often spent afternoons and weekends.

There I found out about the lives of the great Saints, most of whom were Catholic, although we were nominally Presbyterian—a good Calvinist Scots and English religion. Thoroughly amazed and inspired, I read about St. Francis of Assisi and his love for animals; Teresa of Avila and her contemplative life of mental prayer; St. John and his Dark Night of the Soul, and Meister Eckhart's mythic imagery in his spiritual psychology.

Foremost for me at the time was a book that was to be central to my life, Jakob Boehme's The Way to Christ. He was a German shoemaker, who had his first mystical vision observing a sunbeam at age 25, then another at 35. His Neoplatonist and alchemical writings were several, although The Way to Christ, published in 1623, is a full summation of his spiritual cosmology.

Here's something from Jakob Boehme:

"Everything has its mouth to manifestation; and this is the language of nature, whence everything speaks out of its property, and continually manifests, declares, and sets forth itself for what is good or profitable; for each thing manifests its mother, which thus gives the essence and the will to the form. When you are art gone forth wholly from the creature [human], and have become nothing to all that is nature and creature, then you are in that eternal one, which is God himself, and then you will perceive and feel the highest virtue of love. Also, that I said whoever finds it finds nothing and all things; that is also true, for he finds a supernatural, super-sensual Abyss, having no ground, where there is no place to live in; and he finds also nothing that is like it, and therefore it may be compared to nothing, for it is deeper than anything, and is as nothing to all things, for it is not comprehensible; and because it is nothing, it is free from all things, and it is that only Good, which a man cannot express or utter what it is. But that I lastly said, he that finds it, finds all things, is also true; it has been the beginning of all things, and it rules all things. If you find it, you come into that ground from whence all things proceed, and wherein they subsist, and you are in it a king over all the works of God."
The Way to Christ, 1623

This is what I mystically experienced before birth, at birth, and since birth. I know and live in the Void of non-creation or prior-creation. Here the truth is Self-evident, Love is all-supreme, and the Light is epically stellar in the extreme! When you know this reality, then one sees and lives perfectly with compassion and wisdom in this maya world of illusion and Self-making and Self-manifesting.

Boehme saw the incarnation of Christ not as a sacrificial offering to cancel out human sins, but as an offering of love for humanity, showing God's willingness to bear the suffering that had been a necessary aspect of creation. He also believed the incarnation of Jesus Christ conveyed the message that a new state of harmony is possible. He also suggested that God is somehow incomplete without the Creation. Boehme experienced the non-duality between human beings and God. Carl Jung knew this—that our psychological-spiritual states and actions have a direct effect on God and Creation. Likewise, Rupert Sheldrake, in his awareness of morphogenetic resonant fields, shows how increased mental-psychological focus on certain thoughts become more prevalent and manifest positive habits of thinking and feeling, when so intended and willed.

In the Old Testament of the Bible, my favourite prophets to read were Jeremiah, Ezekiel, Daniel, Hosea, Joel, Obadiah, Jonah, and Habbakuk. I also thrilled to read all the stories I could find on King David and his good soul-mate friend Jonathan, as well as tales about Abraham, Moses and Noah. In many ways, these archetypal story memes are the foundational psychological underpinnings of our Western civilization. I was magnetically drawn to these reigning primordial personages and events, which still inhabit my heart and imagination, and inspire my life and writings.

In all ways, Jesus' passionate life of love, joy, compassion, and laughter warms my heart, and continues to do so throughout my life. Over and over again, I was magnetized by the emotions I felt when reading His story in the New Testament. When He was born, I rejoiced greatly in my heart, as did Mary and Joseph. When he died, I cried disconsolate tears for hours. Every Christmas, I wept for joy at the life I have with Jesus, and what He brings to all humanity—for all people, and for all time and space. Every Easter, I wept for His sacrifice with deep mental and psychological anguish, bereavement, and grateful joy. Nowadays, I am simply and humbly grateful for my deep personal brotherly friendship with Jesus, and I am filled with joy and thankfulness.

Jesus' mother Mary always felt close by my side and in my heart since I was young even though I was not Catholic. While my human mother was the unfeeling, emotionally shut-down Ice Queen—all for sad, believable reasons that she much later in her life fully transformed—Mary was and is the good spiritual, all-loving Mother I experience who keeps me feeling loved, thereby creating self-worth, and she holds compassionate space for me. She is truly a most remarkable Divine-human soul, and many millions worldwide know this.

ST. MARK'S PRESBYTERIAN CHURCH AND PLAYING THE CHURCH ORGAN

My parents were nominal Christians with no real personal relationship with the Divine or Jesus. Given my paternal grandmother's background, we attended St. Mark's Presbyterian Church at 1 Greenland Road, just beside my Public School. The Church was built in 1952, and we started attending after my successful surgery in 1958.

Who was St. Mark? He was born in Cyrene, Libya, and is the author of the second Gospel, a record of the life of Jesus as seen through the eyes of the Prince of the Apostles. He founded the Church in Alexandria, and the Coptic Orthodox Church in Egypt and Africa.

The pastor was Don Collier, a tall, thin, quiet, humble, and kind man. He became a good friend of mine, one of the only ones I had at the time. I really liked him because I felt he compassionately understood my needs and condition.

Knowing I loved music, Don offered to let me play the church organ anytime I wanted.

Starting when I was nine years old, I left school at 3:30pm and headed over to the church. I did this until I was 15, when I started attending Little Trinity Anglican Church on King Street East, where Harry Robinson presided. For St. Marks, I had my own key for the front door and the organ itself. All alone with my Divine friends, I let it rip. I loved hymns and played hundreds of my favourite tunes, too many to mention. I put all my heart and soul into my playing, and always felt ecstasy during my playing and deep peace afterwards. Soft like butterflies, or loud enough to rattle the windows, this organ became a portal, a gateway to God, for which I am always grateful. I give all my thanks to Don Collier as well.

CHAPTER 5
TEENAGE YEARS, 13-18 YEARS

Every Sunday, we had a roast beef dinner either at my family's home, or my Aunt Jean's. We ate dinner and then watched the hockey game on TV, always rooting for the Toronto Maple Leafs, following every excited comment by Foster Hewitt.

I would like you to get a balanced feeling for my family life. These were good people; they meant well. At the time, they were most likely incapable of changing their bad habits and stopping the abuse. When I confronted my mother in my thirties, she denied that there was any abuse. She maintained this until I was 38; that story comes later.

We did have some fun. We went camping in the summers at Algonquin Park or Manitoulin Island. Sometimes we had a picnic outdoors in a Toronto park. For me, these were few and far between. I had to create my own happiness inside my inner world—just like we all have to do.

When I was 13, Dr. Mustard did surgery on me for an undescended left testicle. I asked for him as my surgeon. It was far more painful than the heart operation. I was in Grade Seven of Don Mills Junior High School, which was my first year there. I was not yet in puberty. Life at home was extremely rough. I recall a blustery, cloudy twilight walking for hours on my own around Don Mills. I was extremely angry, despondent, desolate, and depressed. I was seriously thinking of suicide, just as each of us always does at least once or twice in our lives.

At one point, raging and crying vehemently, I looked up to the sky. Between the dark, thunderous clouds there was one tiny patch of blue. Just one. That was enough. I started writing a poem in my mind, and raced home. There, I wrote down a 12-page poem called A Patch of Blue. I poured all my pain onto the paper. It was transformative and marked a change in my mental attitude.

"I will survive and learn and grow through all this hell," I promised myself. I didn't know how, just that I would.

Not to find my own internal psychological support, and not to work my way through all this hell, misery, and despair would be tantamount to unintentional suicide—at least unconsciously and partly consciously. I could only do the best I could, one step at a time, reaching for the inner light inside to guide me. My Orphan archetype merged with my Warrior and Hero archetypes, and the way forward was set.

Things got worse. My father lost his job. He lost it because of his sixth heart attack and he was unable to work. He had no life insurance. My mother started Amway, and did some sewing to make ends meet. My father drank more and smoked more—Phillip Morris. At age 13, he forced my brother and I to take shots of whisky. I suspect this was to alleviate his guilt about drinking more.

"It tastes like gasoline! I don't want it!" I complained. After half a dozen tries, he stopped. I started smoking some of his cigarettes. At first he didn't mind, and then he tried to stop me. Eventually, after trying menthols now and then, a Sherlock Holmes pipe, and cigarillos until Grade 13, I stopped for good. My lungs are very happy.

My father had more and more War buddies over for Saturday night drinking parties. These were times when I was in fear. Sexual abuse often happened with my father and one uncle in particular. I dreaded these parties. Perhaps this is one of the reasons I do not like loud, reactive people in party situations.

PERTINENT TEENAGE REBELLION

I suppose I was rebellious, just because I was being my independent self. I never did drugs or drank much; I didn't need to. My friends said, "You're already out there! You don't need anything else!" My father did not know how to handle me, so one day he took me to the Don Mills Jail. He knew one of the police officers there, and he put me in jail for part of an evening—just to intimidate and scare me into being a dutiful, obedient son. It did scare me; however, I still went on my own journey.

The Beatles and the Rolling Stones have been part of our popular culture since 1963. By age 14, I grew my hair long, past my shoulders and down my back. I had golden brown, wavy locks; I enjoyed it. Now I feel it was a premonition of why Hindu men wear long hair—to hold in their spiritual power. My Junior High School Vice-Principal who was an ex-military man called me "Beatle Martin" and regularly threw me out of school until I got my hair cut. For Grades Eight and Nine, I cut off a little and then went back to school. By the end of Grade Nine, he simply gave up; by then half the guys in the school wore their hair long.

The American Empire revolution of blue jeans quickly caught on. We all had to have these blue jeans and later bell-bottoms. The school authorities would not let the young women wear jeans, though. A friend and I arranged on a Monday morning to have all the guys wear skirts or kilts—along with rouge for some of them who thoroughly enjoyed it—and all the young women wore jeans. The Don Mills Mirror did a story with flashy photos. We won the fight for girls to wear jeans. Fun, freedom, finesse, and intentional community can change the world—as long as the timing is fortunate and people are forbearing.

FAMILY CHALLENGES

My aunt Bessie was a blessing for me. I felt she was the only relative of scores of my extended family who understood me. At large gatherings, she and I would sit off in the corner of the back yard under a tree and talk. She felt like an outsider too, having married into the family with my Baptist minister uncle. When I was really young, she used to sit me on her knee and sing to me. Feeling her love helped me deal with being the "black sheep" and "sick one."

My grandmother never liked me, although she probably did love me. Of all her scores of grandchildren, my brother was her favourite and she spoiled him with many material gifts that I never received. I always felt her anger, criticism, and dismissiveness with me. I will always bless her for her gift of donating to me her piano for our house.

At her 106th birthday party, there were so many family members in a relative's backyard. Nana was sitting alone in a wheelchair. She had always been a large woman, and had not been able to move about much for quite a few years. When I noticed her alone while others chatted around her, I went over to tell her I loved her. When I said this, I could see tears well up in her eyes. I gave her a great big hug, and told her that everything would be all right, that Jesus would look after her every need. She looked up with some light in her eyes, and for the first time in a long while, she smiled thankfully.

This experience taught me the lesson of the great power of forgiveness. One or two kind words can heal and get the love flowing again. My Aunt Bessie had been kind and loving to me. I choose to be this way with everyone I meet. With my grandmother, I was happy, for at the end of her life I told her that I loved her. She died peacefully not long afterwards.

SPORTS

I was allowed by my doctors to buy my first pair of running shoes when I was 14 years old. Obsessively and determinedly I tried every sport I could. Soccer and baseball interested me, but they were not my sports. I swam as often as I could and the waters and physical movements soothed my body and soul. I took lessons. Then I became a Lifeguard and eventually received my Red Cross, Bronze Cross, Bronze Medallion, Intermediate Instructor, and then National Instructor (now the NCCP or National Coaching Certification Program.)

I did well enough at diving, archery, high jump, 100-yard dash and also downhill skiing at Blue Mountain and Georgian Peaks near Collingwood.

By the time I was 16, I could run a mile barefoot on a red cinder track in good time. I tried to impress my father. It didn't work; he didn't really care. He was too obsessed with his own numerous issues. I don't blame him.

MUSIC AND OTHER ACTIVITIES

In the school band, French Horn was my chosen instrument from Grades 7 to 13. I loved the mellow sound and holding this instrument. Now I cannot play because my embouchure is not adequate. Beside piano, I also played the 6-string acoustic guitar and 12-metal-string acoustic guitar. First Nations and African drums greatly appealed to me.

From Grades 9 to 13, there was a Christian youth group in our High School called Young Life. It is a worldwide non-denominational group, started in Colorado in 1941. The goal is to make a difference in the lives of teenagers through trained staff using time-tested methods, offering hope with spiritual values. I knew the leaders in Toronto and eventually became involved in the weekly meetings. 60 or 70 kids would meet weekly on Wednesday evenings in our home basement. There was spontaneous singing and joyous clapping to the over one hundred songs from our Young Life songbook. I was the pianist and choir director. Many of the songs were from Joan Baez, Peter Paul and Mary, Pete Seeger, Bob Dylan, and others in the cultural and folk music revolution of the 1960s.

After the singing, there was a short discussion on relevant spiritual issues concerning the soul. I immensely enjoyed all of it. It was a lot of fun. I made great friends then. On weekends, we held charity car washes, or went downhill skiing together near Georgian Bay.

These were spiritually revolutionary times in Toronto and around the world. I attended churches of all denominations—High and Low Anglican, African Methodist Episcopalian, Baptist, United, Catholic Pentecostal, and Pentecostal. I loved singing in the Black choirs—the gospel freedom songs moved me more deeply than the other hymns. These songs portrayed real soulful yearning for a deeper and more spiritual union with the Divine. Eventually I took confirmation at Little Trinity Anglican Church when I was 18.

I love languages, although I only speak a few besides English and French—basically some Spanish, German, Mohawk, and Deaf Sign Language or ASL. I spent two summers teaching swimming and canoeing at The Ontario Camp for the Deaf under footballer Bob Rumball in 1967 and 1968. Bob was a Toronto Argonaut halfback, is a Minister, and Founder of the Bob Rumball Organizations for the Deaf in Ontario. I was there because Jean Vanier of L'Arche and Mother Teresa of Calcutta had inspired me to give back to the less fortunate. I taught young deaf people to sing by placing their hands on the piano while I played so that they could feel the pitch. Teaching them swimming and canoeing were fun too, especially as I could not give directions by voice, only by banging the side of the canoe to get their attention; there were many hilarious spills as a result.

One of the most memorable moments of my life was working there with young mentally challenged people. In this case, the two-week program was over. All the kids were getting back on the bus to take them home to Toronto from Parry Sound. A young girl with Down Syndrome did not get on; she was holding something behind her back. Another counselor brought her over to me. She shyly offered me a gift. It was a portrait of me made of glued and painted macaroni on Bristol board. I was so happily surprised, stunned, and gratified that I burst into tears and hugged her for a long time. Love often comes more easily from those with less mental smarts, and much bigger and more open, caring hearts. As Kahlil Gibran notes, "Keep me away from the wisdom which does not cry, the philosophy which does not laugh, and the greatness which does not bow before children."

SUMMER HOLIDAYS AND JOBS

From 1965 to 1968, our family spent summer holiday time on Wistowe Island with family friends of ours. They owned the 10-acre island in Lake Joseph, Muskoka. The first July, we rented the boathouse cottage on the water. As we became good friends, we got invited back for the following two years. We were a group of young folks; we learned to water ski, surf, and we swam around the island. To make money, we painted cottages.

When I wasn't on Lake Joseph, I cut grass from May to October for Ontario Housing Corporation in South and North Regent Park downtown. I started a playgroup for young kids, aged 4 to 7, and sports like basketball for those 8 to 12. I had the Corporation rent buses and took the teenagers 13 to 16 up to Algonquin Park. My friends were the volunteers. Once we arrived at the Park, the teenagers were too frightened to get out of the bus at the campground. They had never seen a forest before and they were terrified. Eventually they learned to swim, canoe, and fish.

RELATIONSHIPS

Although I had kissed a girl in Grade 7, and had dated five young women by age 16, including Mary, my childhood sweetheart at age six, I was definitely 100 percent gay, and had known this since I was four. My being gay has more to do with my spiritual soul nature. I know that everyone's soul is psychologically and energetically androgynous—100 percent masculine and 100 percent feminine. And the way to one's true masculinity

is through one's feminine feelings, emotions, vulnerabilities, and recep-
tivities. Always. My male bonding power is spiritual energy I share with
the Creator, with my friend Jesus, other mystics, and my earthly male
friends. As well, I am a Warrior through and through, and loving male
friendships and bonding are key for me. It's not really about the sex; it's
the male heart bonding—to always have someone to count on, who has
your back, and who is truthful, honest, full of integrity, and trustworthy.
Besides this, it is the male creative power that drives my mental search,
my thrust for emotional heart openness, and my artistic, musical, and
poetic expressive originality of my soul.

My father was perplexed and he was visibly and verbally upset about
who I was. He kept saying, "I'll not have a homo in my house! I am going to take you to a shrink, and he will knock it out of you!" —all this,
even without me saying a word to him. The truth is that I saw that my
father was not able to deal with his own homoerotic nature. After all, he
had been in the War for six years with his buddies, and most had even
casual sex, let alone deep emotional connections, even though perhaps
unspoken, unconscious ones. As with most men his age, he had internalized his homophobia to the point where it was killing him. All because
he just could not open his heart, be vulnerable, be a real man, talk about
his feelings, and open to the male-male attraction that is so important for
men who want friendships and a way out of their deep alienation and
loneliness.

MY FATHER'S "DEATH"

I remember what led up to the final days of my father's life. He had a
great voice; in fact, he was a basso profundo, a low register singer of fairly
good quality. Sometimes he sang with The Toronto Mendelssohn Choir
in Handel's Messiah. Once in a while, he sang solos in our Presbyterian
Church choir. One Sunday, I accompanied him on the piano when he
sang Stuart K. Hine's version of the great Swedish Christian hymn, How
Great Thou Art. After the service, he felt queasy, nauseous, and was very
pale. His left arm pained him. He was rushed to Sunnybrook Hospital
with his seventh heart attack. He asked for a heart transplant. The doctors said he was not well enough. Two weeks later, on September 26,
1968, he died.

My father's death sent me into a heavy, neurotic, inner mental-emotional conflict and instability. On one hand, he was my father, and like all abused children of alcoholics, I had put him on a pedestal of what it means to be a man. On the other hand, I knew he was wrong to have stolen my power, diminished and belittled my true nature, intimidate, beat, and thrash me. How could I find forgiveness, resolution, and love someone when I could no longer communicate with him?

I found a way. I followed my father's soul into the lower astral worlds and travelled with him and Jesus up into the middle level astral worlds. Buddha was there to help him as well. I did this out of love for my father, and wanting to help him into his next life. In the Tibetan Buddhist tradition, recently departed souls spend forty-nine days in the lower bardo of purgatory or hell. And then one takes rebirth, if they are lucky enough to find a good family. So it is that one commences their next earthly life. I knew this is what my father was doing; I helped him all I could.

This was a highly mystical, visionary time for me. I was in the heights of the upper astral celestial realms and simultaneously in the depths of astral hell. Sometimes to lose balance in love and life is paradoxically to find balance in life. I wanted my father to know that I gave him my heart unconditionally, and in the spirit world, his soul ghost did come to know this—although he never asked for forgiveness even from the spirit world. That came much later on a blustery, snowy day in front of Maple Leaf Gardens in Toronto, when he was reincarnated.

It took many years for me to forgive my father after decades of energetic and Jungian Depth Psychology healing. Gandhi's words empowered me, "The weak can never forgive. Forgiveness is the attribute of the strong." There is a proverb that claims, "When you learn to love Hell, then you will be in Heaven." I followed this road to hell all the way to the very bottom and end of it, and then made my way back with the Light.

At the beginning of Grade 13, I was a basket case. I could not function much in the outer world. Our Senior High School Principal was an elder in our Presbyterian Church. Understandingly, in order to let me grieve properly, he let me stay away and skip school from late September 1968 until the end of April 1969. In May, I only came to write my exams, and passed well enough, although I had previously been an A+ student.

During this tme, I incessantly communicated with all the Spiritual

Masters and Saints. I had many visions, not just of my father's death, but my own deaths in past lives, and what death itself means for we humans. I was clearly descending into the depths of death, despair, desperation, disconsolateness, dejection, depression, downheartedness, dreariness, distress, dolefulness, and the worst doldrums.

During this most painful period, listening to classical music supported me on my great journey; in particular Bach's B Minor Mass and Handel's Messiah.

CHAPTER 6
UNIVERSITY YEARS 18-25

I always wanted to go to University since I was very young. I felt it was a way out of my poverty of family and finances. My family could not afford to put me through higher education. I started a house painting company to make money for my annual tuition fees, books, and my lodgings.

My inner psychological struggle with my father's death and loss was somewhat abating. My first year was at Scarborough College of The University of Toronto. I enjoyed meeting new friends of many different ethnic backgrounds. Joining Inter-Varsity Christian Fellowship (IVCF) was a blessing; I found some close friends there.

I studied calculus, physics, chemistry, philosophy, and psychology. I had thoughts of getting into medical school based on my great friend-ship with our family doctor, Dr. Gordon Stewart, and from knowing Dr. Bill Mustard. I wanted to give back to others.

I didn't do very well in calculus. I failed it and had to retake it in the summer; it was the only course I ever failed, and I had to prove some-thing to myself—that I could always succeed at whatever I put my mind's focus upon. I did well enough in the other courses, although I was not really psychically ready for more education. I socialized quite a bit, which is what first year is really meant to be anyways.

Some of the most memorable experiences of my first year included listening to W.H. Auden and Stephen Spender, who are both great British poets. Afterwards, I was able to speak with them. Auden spoke first. His emotional, pithy exclamations were like cannons; his voice was pugna-cious and strong. He must have been in his sixties then, and his face re-minded me of an old, dried-out potato because it had so many wrinkles. I have never seen a more heavily lined and creased face. I appreciated the depth of spirit in the glint of his eyes. He was like a big Yoda.

Stephen Spender, Auden's good friend, was tall, thin, elegant, debo-nair, and diplomatic. His shock of white hair made him look very regal. He spoke softly and slowly. The words were as singingly powerful as Auden's—just with a different emotional inflection in his voice.

While I have always loved their poetry, what inspired me most was meeting two openly gay men who had done amazing things with their lives. This gave me permission to be myself in the world. I experienced firsthand that the more I struggled with my challenges, the more I won my freedom and a greater sense of self-worth.

Staying out in the boonies of Scarborough in a low ceilinged, dingy, dark, one-room basement was very depressing. The landlady was not so pleasant either; she stole my leather making materials, which I never replaced. I made some money from selling handmade belts and pouches.

During my second year of university, I went to the downtown campus of The University of Toronto and bunked at Wycliffe Anglican College Residence. There were many "divine" students here training for the ministry. I had many great conversations with William from the east coast. Margaret, the joyous old laughing Scottish cook often put extra cookies in my lunch bag. The ham hash sandwiches always made me barf though. In the early mornings, or during an evening vigil, solitary in the Wycliffe chapel at the end of the hall from the refectory, I played hymns and blissed out. At Wycliffe College, I made lots of good friends and had more fun sharing spiritual experiences with friends in IVCF.

My first real boyfriend and I spent much time at his parent's farm on the Bruce Peninsula walking the trails and swimming in Georgian Bay. David and I were best friends. We later split up and he lived with another Anglican minister friend; he died of AIDS in 1989.

ASTRAL FAR JOURNEYS AND COSMIC CONSCIOUSNESS

It was during this time that I continued to extensively astrally travel day and night. More than ever, my father's death inspired me to understand what consciousness does and where it goes in the higher and lower astral worlds. I read Dr. Richard Maurice Bucke's Cosmic Consciousness. Dr. Bucke was Canada's first psychiatrist, graduating from McGill University in Medicine in 1862. He set up Canada's first Psychiatric Institution in London, Ontario, in 1877.

While travelling in the United States, he met poet Walt Whitman and they became fast friends, and often traveled together. Bucke eventually testified that he was "lifted to and set upon a higher plane of existence" thanks to Whitman. He published a biography of the poet in 1883 and was one of Whitman's literary executors.

While pursing further medical training in London, England, Bucke had the pivotal experience of his life, a fleeting mystical experience of "Cosmic Consciousness." In part, the passing of one of his relatives motivated this. During my second year, I read his book and it verified my own experiences. I searched far and wide for others' spiritual experiences that matched my own. In Dr. Maurice Bucke, I found another touchstone for my own expressions and memories since before I came into the womb.

The books of Carlos Casteneda about his nagual training with Toltec Master don Juan were all the rage for students at campuses. I read every one of them. Slowly, over time, I learned to dream and have visionary travels with don Juan and his group. My training in these astral realms became life-enhancing eye-openers for me and elevated my spiritual heart. From the high astral realities, I could see the history of the Earth, and what people were doing with their minds and energy fields. I mostly trained myself to clear and expand my mental consciousness. Most fantastically and crucially, this enabled me to look at my fears as simply projections of my own unconscious. My life goal has always been to realize that all my fears are just "false evidence appearing real." I've had to deal with over 500 fears in my life. I have accomplished this through Dreamwork, Meditation, Time Line Therapy, Past Lives Therapy, Rebirthing, and Ericksonian Hypnotherapy.

During the day I studied physical chemistry, organic chemistry, more physics, genetics, microbiology, psychology, and philosophy. My left-brain was getting an overload to memorize. At night, balancing this in counterpoise, my right-brain enjoyed the dreams, visions, and discussions with all sorts of spiritual beings in the higher worlds.

CONNECTIONS AND EXPLORATIONS WITH WILLIAM BLAKE

William Blake, (1757-1827) the engraver, artist, poet, painter, print-maker, and visionary, was one I spent perhaps the most time with in my inner world during this period. His life and experiences seemed so familiar to me. In reading about the death of Blake's brother Robert from tuberculosis at the age of 24, my mind catapulted into another reality. I was back there with Blake. Once I passed into the astral world, I saw and felt myself as Robert floating off the ground in my brother William's studio and conversed with him from Spirit. Beyond personal experiences, we spoke of how to create metal-plate engravings and the use of powerful, relevant archetypal images that became the core of his remarkable books and art.

William Blake had a profound effect on me in this life. His spirit and imagery of the Creator, Heaven and Hell, and the New Jerusalem became archetypal icons and grounding images for my own inner mental pictures and the paintings I have created.

Later, in 1974, when the Tate Gallery in London, England had a Blake Retrospective, I flew over there to be with the energies of his works. Blake's Ancient of Days and Glad Day are among my favourites. Glad Day is an icon of gay liberation.

So my time at University included much inner spiritual and psychological processing, deep scientific study, and fun socializing with my good friends. My professional academic liberation excited my hope for a good life beyond the devastation that was my childhood experience. I still had to make money to pay my way through University.

PART-TIME WORK IN NORTH AND SOUTH REGENT PARK

During summers and weekends in the spring and fall, I worked for Ontario Housing Corporation cutting grass in their many rental apartment complexes in mid-town Toronto and at other OHC holdings. This area encompassed North and South Regent Park bounded by Gerrard Street East to the north, River Street to the east, Shuter Street to the south, and Parliament Street to the west. Dundas Street East runs through the middle of the complex; there are high-rises on the south side, and townhouses on the north.

I started there when I was 18 years old, and after a few years of cutting grass, I got a job starting a playschool there for the young kids under five years. I took the older children camping, hiking, and swimming in Algonquin Park. When I saw the depth of poverty, loneliness, and gang fighting, my heart was touched. I have always felt close to street children.

SOCIAL JUSTICE AND CHARITIES

Friends of mine were interested in the local and global issues of social justice and charities. My friend David gifted me with a book on Mother Teresa called Something Beautiful for God by Malcolm Muggeridge. I felt awestruck by the courage, determination, and faith of this woman who helped the poor of Calcutta and around the world.

When I read Jean Vanier's In Weakness, Strength, I was deeply moved by the story of this ex-military man, brother of the Governor General of Canada, who started L'Arche communities for mentally, emotionally, and physically challenged people worldwide. The fact that he openly spoke of his journey with Jesus inspired me to walk my own path. Both Mother Teresa and Jean Vanier have been great mentors of mine.

CONSTANT COMMUNICATIONS WITH MOTHER MARY AND OTHER SPIRITUAL MASTERS

For all my life, I felt close to Mother Mary, the mother of Jesus. I am not, nor have I ever been Catholic. Nor was Mother Mary mentioned much in my church or home experience. Protestantism does not venerate saints or Mother Mary.

Nonetheless, I have always felt spiritually and emotionally close with Mother Mary. When I speak of or think of Jesus, I often spontaneously start to cry—enough to actually burst into uncontrollable tears. I have done this since I was a young child, and still cry easily when I feel the presence of the Spiritual Masters. More than anything else in my life, when I am communicating directly with Jesus and Mother Mary, I experience such overwhelmingly powerful emotions and memories. My life revolves around their lives, stories, and what they mean for the ongoing history of humanity and planet Earth.

I do remember coming into the womb in this life with Mother Mary at my side. Like Jesus, she has been with me every day of my life. Day and night, I have continuous contact with both Jesus and Mary about everything going on, in particular regarding what and where I should be, with whom to speak and connect, and the meaning and purpose of my relationships and actions.

I have an open line of communication with Jesus, Mary, Babaji Nagaraj, Metatron, Melchizedek, Archangel Mikael, Dendreah (who is the Earth mother Gaia and the White Buffalo Calf Woman,) and scores of others. These include, though are not limited to, Saint John the Divine, Saint Francis of Assisi, Bernard of Clairvaux, Saint John of the Cross, Saint Teresa of Avila, Saint Catherine of Siena, Hildegard of Bingen, Meister Eckhart, Jakob Boehme, Saint Anselm, Saint Sebastian, the Old Testament prophets Jeremiah, Daniel, Hezekiah, Hosea, and leaders like Noah, Abraham, Moses, and King David.

When I was a teenager, I phoned up The Catholic Diocese of Chicago and they sent me by mail Saint Francis of Assisi Omnibus of Sources, a red hardcover, 1900-page tome of worthy value on a most kind and gentle soul. Because of his love for nature and animals, Saint Francis has always been one of my very favourite individuals.

More modern spiritual humans that I have an open line with at any time are Rudolf Steiner, Emanuel Swedenborg, Isaac Newton, Gandhi, Martin Luther King Jr., and Bob Marley.

What do I talk about with them? I always listen to their hearts and ask questions regarding personal advice; they give valuable comments ever so lovingly and willingly. I want to know from them, "Whom should I call for the day?" "Who needs my love and support?" "What kind of work should I do?" "How can I get rid of the fears and upset I am feeling at this moment?"

These lifelong experiences have given me health, strength, courage, spiritual energetic support, and hope for the moment and our future. I would not be who or where I am without their constant, vigilant love. They often just appear immediately in my room and enter my body. I am immediately caressed with the sweetest, deepest waves of peace, pure joy, and true love—and above all, hope. I know that I will succeed and have the life I choose. They do not always tell me how this will happen; I just trust and know that it will.

Babaji often jokes with me, "Joseph, if I told you everything that would happen, there would be no surprises, and no fun and adventure! That would not be good. Life is for adventure, so that you can create Self mastery through all your many challenges."

THE SEARCH FOR THE HOLY GRAIL: WHAT AND WHO IS IT?

During my early years, I scoured ancient and modern documents and had many long discussions with theologians, historians, and archeologists regarding The Holy Grail. Although one may find partial answers here, my experience is that The Holy Grail is a subjective, innermost experience that requires a great journey over one's lifetime. For me, it is the most important task I engage upon—every day.

So what really is The Holy Grail? Where is it? Who is it? Why is it important? How can one find The Holy Grail?

The Holy Grail is the most pervasive, all-encompassing, spiritual-Earthly symbol of the last 2,000 years. Today, among all cultures of the world, people seek The Holy Grail. It is deemed to be the source of all eternal happiness, love, joy, deep peace, harmony, balance, great relationships, and prosperity.

For millennia since Jesus' resurrection, peoples of all nations have searched for the Holy Grail. Originally, The Holy Grail was the cup that Joseph of Arimathea, who was one of the few there at the Cross with Mother Mary and Mary Magdalene, used to catch the blood from the spear wound in Jesus' right side. Longinus the Roman soldier used The Holy Lance to pierce Jesus' side to make sure he was dead. Joseph of Arimathea held the cup that collected Jesus' blood, sweat, and tears.

Charlemagne King of France, Popes throughout the ages, King Richard the Lionheart, the Knights Templar, the Illuminati, and thousands of others have journeyed to Jerusalem and every continent in search of the actual physical Holy Grail. They seek it just as they have been looking for The Holy Lance of Longinus, Jesus' Shroud of Turin and other sacred relics. Although several recent books and internationally popular movies have focused on the ongoing search for The Holy Grail, no legitimate physical Holy Grail has yet been found. Over the 20 centuries, there have been many fakes, all discredited by archeologists.

What is The Holy Grail? I have spent my lifetime researching this spiritually, historically, and psychologically. In another manuscript I will present more material on this most essential topic for the existence of humanity.

Suffice it to say that there are many links we can follow. The Holy Grail may be several or all of the following: the Divine-human Feminine Spirit of Pure Love, Mother Mary, Mary Magadalene (whom some say is Jesus' wife,) Source, the Creator, the Self, King Arthur, Merlin, the Round Table, the Crystal Cave, the Lady of the Lake, the White Buffalo Calf Woman, Gaia, one's spiritual and psychological wholeness accomplished through the path of individuation, a pure heart, egolessness, the final liberation of the soul, the end of the need for reincarnation, an enlightened consciousness and mind, the Clear Light, childlike joy, regained innocence, Paradise, Heaven, beauty, truth, and the good. I have found that it may be these and more.

MY FIRST TRIP TO MEXICO, 1971

In the spring of 1971, twelve of my friends and I refitted a small yellow school bus to drive to Mexico from Toronto. We took out some of the seats, put in a propane fridge and stove, stocked up on some food and water, and headed southwest across the United States. It took us more than two weeks; we had many adventures and mishaps. For some reason, we had only one audiotape—Tea for the Tillerman CD by Cat Stevens! Even though we heard the album over 700 times on the trip, we still loved it so much. We memorized all the words and heartily sang every time we played it on the quest for our own Holy Grail. We were going to research some Toltec and Mayan sites, learn Spanish, and study with Ivan Illich at CIDOC in Cuernavaca.

At Teotihuacan, the massive Toltec site, I climbed the Pyramid of the Sun at sunset. It was a gorgeous, haunting, and memorable moment. I was forbidden to be up there after sundown, so I was chased down the rough backside of the pyramid. In the growing darkness, I tumbled over rocks and barely made it down. The police were after me with their dogs and whistles, but they never caught me.

I spent some time with a local Toltec family, plowing the fields of spring. Many small treasures like obsidian arrowheads, signet seal rings, and chert pottery pieces appeared in my hands as we worked the soil. I brought these back home with me.

As a group, another intention of ours was to learn some Spanish and attend CIDOC—Centro Intercultural de Documentation or Intercultural Documentation Centre—in Cuernavaca, Mexico. Ivan Illich, the great social justice writer and activist who supported the grass roots movement of liberation of the lower classes worldwide, founded this Institute. We had all read his books: Tools for Conviviality, Deschooling Society, and Medical Nemesis. The latter concerns iatrogenic or medically caused diseases.

I recall sitting in the front row, listening to this lanky, voluble man speak for four or five hours at a time. I took copious notes. Many of his ideas have influenced my thinking over my lifetime about personal and collective healing, liberation, self-responsibility, and social justice.

INTER-VARSITY CHRISTIAN FELLOWSHIP MUSICAL GROUP, 1971-1972

In the spring of 1971, five Canadian University students were selected to create a travelling musical group. With our sheltie dog and all our musical instruments and gear, we drove a remodeled Bell telephone window van from coast to coast. Starting in the east coast at Memorial University in St. John's, Newfoundland, we trekked to 54 universities over eight months from September 1971 to April 1972, ending up at the University of Victoria.

The songs we sang were hymns, carols, and lots of popular folk and pop music that were spreading "The Good Word." Playing piano is the joy of my life; and I do get a kick out of the 6- and 12-string guitars. Singing is another thing; I can carry a basic melody, and am not great at harmonies.

FINISHING MY DOUBLE UNDERGRADUATE DEGREES, 1972-1974

I went back to the St. George campus of The University of Toronto in the fall of 1972 to finish my Undergraduate degrees. Back then students did not pay per course. I paid my fee for the year and could take as many courses as I wanted and get credit for them. A typical four-year degree entailed 20 courses. I was so intent on learning as much as I could that I got credit for 40 courses within the four years. So I got a Double Honours Bachelor of Science, Microbiology, Chemistry, and physical sciences, and another in Psychology and Philosophy.

During this time, some of my favourite courses were the ones in ethnomusicology at the Music Faculty. Earlier, I thought of becoming a concert pianist and attending the Music Faculty full-time. However, I knew that if I had to make a living from playing piano, it would ruin the joy and inspiration I derived from it. I was also on the path of higher medicine, inspired by my early life experiences of healing after my heart operation and birth condition.

GRADUATE SCHOOL, 1974-1976

When I did not get in to Medical School, I changed plans and enrolled in the Institute for the History and Philosophy of Science and Technology, or IHPST, at The University of Toronto. I wrote extensive papers on the "History of the Discovery of the DNA Molecule," "The Mystical Writings of Isaac Newton," "The Discovery of the Heart by William Harvey" based on his De Motu Cordis: On the Motion of the Heart and Blood, in 1628, and De Humani Corporis Fabrica: "On the Fabric of the Human Body" by Andreas Vesalius, 1543. I enjoyed reading this in Latin—with white gloves on and all—in the Thomas Fisher Rare Book Library at the Robarts Library at The University of Toronto.

My most important researches were on the worldwide history and theories of the human body and condition, and health and illness from all cultures—First Nations, African, Arab, Greek, Roman, Hindu, Chinese, Japanese, Mayan, Incan, and others.

Based on my earlier interests in psychology, in particular Carl Jung, and philosophy, I decided in my second graduate year to study the history and philosophy of psychology and psychiatry, particularly in Canada. A friend had given me an early-signed copy of Dr. William Osler's Materia Medica Medical Textbook and material on Osler's The Evolution of Modern Medicine.

McGill University in Montreal has the archives of The Osler Library of the History of Medicine. I stayed with some friends in a student rooming house on Lorne Avenue just east of the campus on the side of

Mont Royal, the ancient volcano. I swam laps daily with a doctor friend who taught me to do flip turns at the ends of the pool, for which I am eternally grateful. I still love doing them.

Four or five hours at a stretch, I would pore through all I could find. There was not much on Jung, a lot on Freud, and of course, much on the history of western medicine from the Arabs, Greeks, Romans, and British. I read Hippocrates, Avicenna, Galen, and Moses Maimonides, filling my mind with the theories of the four humours—sanguine, choleric, melancholic, and phlegmatic.

I re-read the psychiatric notes of Dr. Robert Maurice Bucke, who studied medicine at McGill and whom I have already mentioned with respect to his Cosmic Consciousness: A Study in the Evolution of the Human Mind tome. I was curious to see how he had treated inmates in Canada's first psychiatric hospital, The London Ontario Asylum, 1877-1902, which housed over 900 patients. In alignment with other Victorian doctors, he declared, "insanity is essentially an incurable disease." Treatment consisted of sound diet, useful daytime employment, constructive amusement, and regular religious observances. He abandoned the medicinal use of alcohol, discontinued most forms of physical restraint, and initiated an open-door policy allowing the majority of patients' free access to the hospital grounds. A few years later, this had a profound effect on me when I worked in an Ontario Government Psychiatric Hospital. Most psychiatrists in Dr. Bucke's time had yet to grant patients the same degree of freedom that he did; I found this to be the case in the mid-1970s as well.

I travelled to New York City in 1973 to acquire over 20 volumes of all Jung's Collected Works in hardcover. I also read everything by Freud, Adler, Wilhelm Reich, and Otto Rank. Adler and his organ deficiency showed how people with heart challenges had inferiority complexes and unconsciously and consciously used their will power to overcome their impediment and birth challenge. I so needed to understand this in myself that I took Masters courses at the Alfred Adler Institute in Chicago, now the Adler School of Professional Psychology, via correspondence.

VIKTOR FRANKL, LOGOTHERAPY AND THE SEARCH FOR MEANING

When I was sixteen years of age, I went to hear Viktor Frankl speak at Massey Hall in Toronto. The place was so packed, the only chair left was on stage with rows of seats alongside Frankl. I ended up sitting on the right side of him, elbow to elbow.

Viktor, a Viennese Jewish psychiatrist, told his story about being in the Nazi concentration camps from 1942-1945. His father, mother, brother, and wife were killed there. He survived through finding meaning and purpose in every breath and thought.

Here is part of his speech:

> *"We stumbled on in the darkness, over big stones and through large puddles, along the one road leading from the camp. The accompanying guards kept shouting at us and driving us with the butts of their rifles... A thought transfixed me: for the first time in my life I saw the truth as it is set into song by so many poets, proclaimed as the final wisdom by so many thinkers. The truth—that love is the ultimate and the highest goal to which man can aspire."*
> **Viktor Frankl, Man's Search for Meaning**

It was that evening, having been in the midst of reading Frankl and Jung in my sixteenth year, that I decided the path of my life. I chose to become someone who was full of love, not revenge—and to become a specialist in the fields of medicine, psychology, psychiatry, and spirituality.

LEARNING FRENCH AND MEETING MY MOHAWK FAMILY

After Grade 13, in 1969, I went to Montreal to become more proficient in French, which is a language I love. I took a six-week course at UQAM, l'Universite du Quebec a Montreal. We were fined five cents for every word spoken in English. I learned quickly, afraid I would run out of money. After six weeks, I was able to retain a certain fluency in French.

It was at this time that I met a Swiss-German professor of French there. She hired me to do research and edit her English-language Ph.D.

for McGill on Mohawk Sociolinguistics. What a confabulation of languages we used!

In 1970, she took me with her for taped interviews with families in Kanehsatake, the Mohawk village near Oka, Quebec, which has been there over 8,000 years, according to archeological research. This is the same Oka that, from July 11 to September 26, 1990, had a handful of grandmothers, mothers, and grandchildren, along with a few Mohawk warriors holding off 700 Quebec Provincial Police, and the Canadian army, along with tanks and automatic rifles.

The professor's main informants were Samson and Ida Gabriel, and their only son David. I readily became fast friends with them; this deep loving connection lasted all my life. David and I fixed canoes; planted sacred corn, beans, squash, and tobacco; searched for wild garlic and wild ginger on the mountain; rode his small motorbike, and played. I was a few years his senior. We both taught each other so many things.

Samson was the spiritual leader of the traditional Longhouse; the physical building was situated in the backyard along with a sweat lodge. The Mohawk prefer to call themselves Kanien'keha:ka (k is pronounced as a hard g). The Longhouse is the Karihwiio.

Over the years, I learned Mohawk. I had to. The only language Samson spoke was Mohawk. Ida and David were both patient and diligent with me. They were pleased I wanted to put in the effort to learn the language, which is challenging, as it is all noun-incorporated and verb-incorporated words. I am by no means proficient in speaking, although I understand when I hear it.

I recall one time, when elders and members of The Haudenosaunee Confederacy were visiting our house—I had a bedroom in the back of the house. The men were joking—as Mohawks like to do—about roasting me over an open fire and how tasty I would be. As they smirked and pointed at me, they thought I didn't understand what they were saying. I joked back, saying in Mohawk, "Maybe I'm good, but I'm not as tasty as our famous corn soup or venison."

Within two years, I was requickened and adopted as a member of the Mohawk nation, given a clan, the bear clan, and a name. My name is Dehanakerehkwen. It means "he who lives in two worlds at the same time." When I asked Samson why he called me this, he smiled knowingly, and simply said, "You live in the Spirit and Earth worlds equally all the time; and you live in our Kanienkehaka world and the non-Native world; you are the messenger."

"Requickening name ceremonies" are given to those who are asked to carry the name of previous Mohawk warriors or chiefs. To this day, I still resonate with the ancient, deeper meanings of my given name.

THE HISTORY OF PSYCHIATRY

An understanding of mind and consciousness has been my lifetime goal. When I read Henri Ellenberger's The Discovery of the Unconscious: The History and Evolution of Dynamic Psychiatry (1970), I wanted to meet him. I rang him up and we had a chat. I was used to the Swiss personality, which can be very logical and straightforward.

His 932-page work covers early studies of exorcism, Mesmerism, and hypnotherapy, along with an in-depth analysis of the theories of Freud, Adler, and Jung. Nevertheless, I did not agree with his particular point of view or polemics. I am not a materialist. The understanding of Spirit, soul, higher consciousness, and the astral realms of consciousness and unconsciousness need to be interwoven into a strictly historical, reductionist point of view.

DR. MACKINNON PHILLIPS
PSYCHIATRIC HOSPITAL, OWEN SOUND, ONTARIO

This training set me on my own path, which synchronistically was a similar one to Jung's. At the age of 25, Jung began working in the Burgholzli, a psychiatric hospital in Zurich. His Ph.D. dissertation was based on observations of psychotic patients and was published in 1903 entitled, "On the Psychology and Pathology of So-Called Occult Phenomena."

At this time I was 26; I rented my brother's farm on the 11th Concession of St. Vincent Township near Meaford, Ontario. The farm, which became my place of great transformation, was right beside The Bruce Trail, where I hiked for hours, bathed in the streams in summer, and cross-country skied every day in winter.

I grew my own food garden and made fruit and vegetable preserves for the winter by drying, blanching and freezing my produce. I was very grateful to be able to co-produce with Mother Earth's support. The time will come again soon when we all will need to do likewise. In winter, I chopped wood for at least an hour a day to heat my home using the wood fireplace. Since the well pump froze, I boiled snow for drinking water and tea. Back then one didn't concern oneself so much with acid rain in the snow.

I was hired as a PNA or Psychiatric Nursing Assistant at the nearby Dr. Mackinnon Phillips Psychiatric Hospital in Owen Sound. It was originally built as a 250-bed psychiatric hospital in 1963. I soon discovered that the psychological conditions of the treatment of the guests there were like those suffered in the Salpetriere of Paris France, which in the 17th century was a holding place for the mentally disabled, criminally insane, epileptics, and the poor. It was also notable for its population of rats.

There were no rats at the Owen Sound hospital except for me, as you will see. The day staff was so poorly trained because most of them were farmers earning extra cash. The psychiatrists there were ones that apparently were not able to find employment in Toronto, and thus were sent north.

Day after day, I was shocked and disgusted to observe the reviling treatment the staff gave the patients. Police regularly brought street people, young local lads, itinerant workers, and others they disliked to the hospital for incarceration. It was very common for four or five big hulking guys to be called to the front door for an incoming emergency. They kicked, punched, verbally abused, and otherwise intimidated a young person who had been out late, perhaps drinking. They would take him to the back room, throw him down on the floor, pull off all his clothes (for protection against suicide was the common understanding,) and perhaps put him in a strait jacket. There was often no mattress, no blanket, no food, and no water. He or she would be left there overnight.

The shift staff, particularly at night, played cards the entire time. Inpatients, especially in the emergency ward where I worked initially, were supposed to be checked on every hour. There was often no check during an entire eight-hour shift. Once I came in for my morning shift at 7am; I walked around and peeked into every room and bay area to see how folks were doing. I found one person dead. I calmly walked back to give my report to the outgoing and incoming staff.

"How is everyone?" they queried me disinterestedly.

"Well, Mr. X is stone cold dead in bed," I blandly remarked, showing no emotion. "You might want to call the undertaker or the coroner." Fainting, a flurry of activity and a whiff of something in someone's underpants followed my remarks.

At the hospital, alcoholism and psychiatric drug abuse seemed common by doctors and staff. There were many times that inappropriate medications were given. The overuse and overdosage for patients of chloral hydrate and other strong anti-psychotics was often almost a daily experience. These heavy drugs were used to quiet people down, knock them out, "teach them a lesson," and give staff ample time to play cards, listen to country music, and chat about the latest local gossip.

To say I was shocked and appalled would be a gross understatement. Electroshock therapy, now known as Electroconvulsive Therapy (ECT), was used then and still is in Canadian hospitals. Then, as now, it is used for depression, mania, bipolar, psychosis, catatonia, acting out, and for sociopaths unwelcome in the community. Having spoken out about client maltreatment early on in my 15-month stay, I was quickly labeled and treated as the black sheep, the wrong one—a role I had been given early in childhood, so I was able to see through it.

Once, staff volunteered me for a training session in ECT; I went along with it for fun. They had me lie on the ECT table to show how the electrical plates were affixed to the temples of the skull. I was afraid they would actually turn on the electricity and start up the machine, so I had one male nurse friend make sure this could not happen.

On the acute intake ward, there were many young people aged 16 to 25 years who had a first or second psychotic break. When they weren't drugged up, I was able to speak with them, do some hypnosis, and ask them about their childhoods. The vast majority of these young people, perhaps 85-90 percent had been sexually and physically abused as children and teenagers, and this was the cause of their mental breakdown. They were good people; I felt deeply for each of them.

One young girl whom I will call Louise was 21 years old, anorectic and bulimic, and she was able to tell me her long history of sexual, physical, emotional, and verbal torture by her father, her mother, and her two older brothers. Telling her story was a big part of her healing, as is always the case. Eventually, I was able to find her a psychologist in town; we got her out of the hospital, and I know she was able to find her way in life.

My psychological and anthropological observations of the staff-client relationships there in the hospital community helped me to better understand human nature and our capacities for revenge, enforcement, restriction, harassment, intimidation, and so-called legal social justice. The projection of our own undealt-with personal and collective unconscious shadow is the cause of so much harm, hatred, murder, ethnic cleansing, and war in all societies throughout history.

Another young man of 25 years whom I will call Ron was admitted three times for acting out in town. He was wrongly labeled a sociopath and the staff greatly disliked him. He was treated so roughly that he was bruised from head to toe in ensuing scuffles when police brought him in again against his will. I befriended him and I found out that he was also deeply traumatized by sexual abuse, severe physical beatings, and being thrown out of the house as an orphan when he was 11 years of age. The third time he came in, he had razor-cut scars from his wrists to his inner elbows on both arms. I bandaged these for him. In our discussions, I realized that terrifying early traumas cause great lack of self-esteem; suicide often seems to be the only option and solution. With the mental, emotional, and physical kinesthetic memories, it is very painful to survive. I truly liked this man's soul; he was actually very gentle and kind. In the end after he was released, he ended up killing himself by bleeding himself to death.

There was a locked back ward there, which was for long-term psychogeriatric people and those with severe mania, catatonia, and depression. Many of the farmers in the area who got Parkinson's from the DDT sprayed on their farms in the 1950s ended up there where they eventually died.

There was one quiet, meek, middle-aged gentleman I met there in the back ward. He was a professor of philosophy from The University of Guelph, who unfortunately happened to be picked up for strolling along the street one evening. I contacted members of his University Department and we eventually got him released. Why he was in there in the first place still puzzles me to this day.

THE REPORT TO THE ONTARIO MINISTER OF HEALTH

Experiences such as these made me want to change the system. I decided to leave my job there, since I gained all the copied evidence and wrote a lengthy Report outlining all the maltreatment, overdoses, and deaths that I personally witnessed while at the Hospital.

I sent the Report by registered mail to Dennis Timbrell, the young Minister of Health in the Ontario Provincial Government. I never heard back from him.

Then I went on a four-week tour to the Art Galleries, Concert Halls, and pleasant sites of London, Amsterdam, Zurich, and Paris. This is where I was able to admire the great works of William Blake at the Tate Gallery in London. While in England, I visited the Roman Baths in Bath. Most enjoyable was the view of Salisbury Cathedral from the vantage point of where John Constable had painted it. The crypts and history of Winchester Cathedral were memorable for me as well.

While taking the train from Holland through Germany to various towns including Stuttgart and Munich, I found myself kinesthetically, psychologically, and auditorially trapped within the lower astral planes of the time-space warp that is World Wars I and II on and in that land. I could hear the incessant, high-pitched, very audible screams of terror and death of the soldiers, people bombed, and those cremated in all the concentration camps. The sadness and terror of these experiences in Germany nearly drove me to insanity. The enormity of the millions of dead that I saw and heard as I passed them while in the train made me severely ill. By the time I reached Lake Constance in Austria, I was delirious with a fever. I vaguely recall disembarking from the train, glad to be out of Germany. I lay down on my back on a public bench. Hours later, I found myself lying on a bed in the house of a sweet old Austrian couple. They nursed me back to health over seven days. It took that long for the voices, feelings, and astral ghosts of the 16 million dead ghosts to stop haunting me.

Following my trip to Europe when I returned to the farm, the psychiatric hospital was shut down. I went to visit my nurse friend at his home. When he opened the door, he grabbed me by my shirt, pulled me inside, and slammed the door shut.

"What are you doing here?" he demanded. Continuing, he shouted, "Do you want to get killed?"

"Why?" I stammered.

He continued, "When the Minister of Health came to shut down the hospital, everyone thought it was you who did it! Did you?"

"Well, yes, I did send him a Report," I murmured, somewhat defensively. "What happened?"

"He came, fired some staff, reassessed the facility, shut it down, and now is turning it into a General Hospital with psychiatric out-patient facilities."

This was what I hoped for—that the system would crumble and people would be free to make more of their own choices, and hopefully the staff would become more humane.

CHAPTER 7
ARCHETYPAL JOURNEYS TO THE
BOTTOM OF EVERYTHING, 26–30 YEARS

ARCHETYPAL DREAM JOURNEYS AT THE FARM

My European journey through historical global tragedy cracked open my psyche to the extreme and caused epic dreams of archetypal depths— dreams that each took 20 or more pages to write down. For the next three or four years I went to the bottom of hell; afterwards, I very slowly came back again with a renewed vision from Spirit of my life's story and roles.

My spiritual-psychological emergency lasted from ages 27 to 30. This was my deepest and most important Dark Night of the Soul—my whole life up till that point had been nothing but hell and dark nights, except for an innermost experience of love and light from Jesus and a few others. This time of the Saturn Return as we call it in astrological psychology is where one fully meets oneself and finds a path on Earth for one's future.

I saved enough money so I could just be alone at the farm. I spent all my time on my own and really could not bear to be with anyone. I needed my own space to process my ugliness, my darkness, my shadow, my potential for evil, and my crap.

For the most part, I read Jung's Collected Works again, and every Jungian book I could think of. In particular, a most promising, elucidative book that I read was Puer Aeternus, or Eternal Child, by Marie-Louise von Franz, a seminal book that described myself—the Peter Pan who idealized my father and mother when in reality I experienced them as vicious, angry, and hurtful. This Peter Pan and Wendy syndrome is a most powerful archetypal patterning of many of us living today and of any generation. Healing will happen when we discover the truth about our own inner feelings and childhood realities.

Infrequently, I drove to Toronto from Meaford to go to meetings of The Ontario Jung Society. We had many speakers from abroad, including Joseph Campbell. Jim Shaw was the President and we became good friends.

One day, out of sheer desperation and somewhat fearing for my sanity, I phoned Jim and said, "When is the first Jungian analyst coming to Toronto?"

"Well, Fraser Boa, who will be the first Canadian Jungian analyst, is flying in from Zurich next Tuesday to the Toronto airport."

"Great," I blurted out with much relief. "I'll pick him up at the airport. What flight is he on?" Jim promised to let Fraser know I would be there for him.

Thus I became Fraser Boa's first client and we instantly became great friends. Within two weeks of returning to Canada, Fraser, who is Marion Woodman's older brother and now deceased, rented the farm across the dusty backwoods sideroad from me. He came over to my home every other day for 8- to 12-hour Depth Psychology analytical sessions. If Fraser was not there for me, so close in proximity psychologically and physically, I might have lost the opportunity for great personal transformation; however, we must always perfectly trust in synchronicity and perfect love.

I walked the Underworld 24 hours a day, and I rarely surfaced over three years. My friends were very concerned because I never called or connected with them. My mother and brother were not involved at all except as past teachers prodding my psychic wholeness. Don Juan was right that our petty tyrants can be our greatest guides; and I was very thankful for them. As long as I paid the monthly rent, my brother was satisfied. At one point, I needed some money, so I asked my brother for a small loan; he gave it to me at 10 percent interest.

During this time, I dreamed, hiked, fasted, cleansed, wildly danced, sang, painted, played, and composed on the piano I bought second-hand (which I still have as my most prized possession.) I wrote hundreds of poems and several children's stories, some of which I illustrated. These were all the psyche and soma ways in which I learned to energetically deal with all the residue of my abuse. I was able to get out mountains of blocked emotions, feelings, and biochemical dregs from my brain, nervous system, muscles, blood, and bones. I experimented with every known type of energetic bodywork, energy medicine, herbs, diet, and exercise. I slept a lot.

Although I did quite a few oil paintings of mountains and lakes when

I was 10 to 13 years, I now spent three or four hours daily with acrylic paints, oil stick, charcoal, and watercolours. These were all emotionally expressive shadow paintings. During my therapy with Fraser, I did over 10,000 paintings, all in red and black with water-based children's paints on large pads of newsprint. I could do over 150 or 200 per day. I had so much volcanic fury and rage; oceans of sadness, grief, loneliness, bottomless mind-splitting fears, terrors, and dread inside me. It seemed endless. Three years is a long time to be in this shit. I just simply kept going, one hour at a time. One day at a time. Jungian Dream Analysis and Fraser's kind support were crucial.

During this time, I was most consciously aware of all the astral worlds. My attempts at dancing and hiking, growing and eating my own vegetables helped to keep me present and grounded. As my consciousness expanded towards Cosmic Consciousness in these astral worlds, I greatly struggled, and thus learned to surrender my ego to the larger truth of the Clear Light of Supreme Awakeness. I fought to find myself the victor, by processing all the victim mentality and experiences I perceived as a child.

All the archetypes of the collective unconscious, which are our magnetic fields of attraction for our psyches, came forward and seized me. I had to tame each one. There was the fierce snake-dragon 300-feet high who came out of the Meaford Harbour and asked me to conduct it with my musical wand so it could dance and be liberated.

One after another, I dealt with the unconscious and ancient elemental powers that rule the psyches of every one of us on Earth, including all our collective historical stories. These included the Innocent Child, the Orphan, the Inner Warrior, and the Caregiver, which all had been active since I was a baby; they actually kept me alive and stopped me from suicide.

Then there were the Seeker, the Destroyer of Lies and Fears, the Lover, and the Creator. These four realities gave me strength and hope to carry on and be a hero and adventurer in my own life.

Lastly, and most difficult to experience, tame, and to humbly become, are the Ruler King-Queen, the Magician, the Wise Sage, and the Holy Fool.

I searched for my Divine humanity. I honoured the diversity of my inner feminine soul, my masculine Warrior nature, my gayness, and my spiritual strength. Through these healing processes and techniques, I claimed my own personal life's mythology. I found my story. I began to more clearly and consciously live my true story—the reason why I came here in the first place. T.S. Eliot has a poem that describes my journeying process perfectly, "And the end of all our exploring, will be to arrive where we started, and know the place for the first time."

When we come from the unity world of Spirit into this third dimensional world of duality, we are always on the search for wholeness. Like the Buddha, balancing the opposites and finding the harmony of the middle way brings ultimate joy and divine I AM Presence to my daily experiences.

This needs to be done during each of life's stages. Human life evolves in seven-year cycles—spiritually, anatomically, physiologically, endocrinologically, emotionally, psychologically, and relationally. This knowledge enormously helped me. I am able to reflect and learn from my past cycles, and process the present life stage while I am going through it, thereby making the most of it, and fulfilling my destiny. I wonder how well I have completed the necessary evolutionary tasks of my last stage, and I plan to be open to the successful steps I need to take for my next seven-year cycle. In fact, whether from internal intention or external necessity, I have had joyous major ego breakdowns within every seven-year period of my life. This is what life is for! The ego cracks its walled shells, disintegrates, and is reborn and resurrected with more of the Soul and Self consciously and energetically running the show.

These essential personal issues for our time include the following: cracking all one's personae or false face masks, dealing with one's shadow, and allowing the inner feminine soul to fully come alive, thus finding one's own Holy Grail inside one's Self. This process I jokingly call becoming one's elf.

I had some masks to let go of when I was young, like putting on a brave face in the midst of terror, smiling when I felt sad, being friendly when I was raging, and pretending I was okay when actually I was conflicted, a mess, and falling apart inside.

Chapter Seven

SALVATION AND WHOLENESS THROUGH THE SHADOW

I have found that the only way to the soul and the Self is through the shadow. Spiritually, psychologically, emotionally, and relationally, there is no other way for any of us. Our greatest light is in our darkest shadow. Our greatest love is hidden within our greatest hatreds—for ourselves and for others. Our greatest hope, faith, and trust are within our greatest fears, terrors, and dreads. Our greatest joy is in dealing with our greatest sorrows and grief. Our greatest peace is within our greatest failures. Our greatest strengths are locked inside our greatest weaknesses until they are released and consciously transformed.

Only when we dig deeper layer-by-layer into the horrifying crap and conflict hidden within our psyches and physical somatic bodies can we become who we really are. Not until, and not unless we do this deep inner work will we find our meaning, purpose, life path and goals. I found I am the only one who can transform my own inner misperceptions and create experiences in alignment with the flow of the Great Spirit of Love in All That Is.

All day long, I transmute negative thoughts and feelings, and carefully choose the right attitudes and words to express to others the highest possible openhearted connections in life and myself.

When I did transformational Jungian Dream and Art Analysis with Fraser Boa for almost 3 years, I kept going deeper into my psyche and unconscious. Dreams of all my childhood torment and terrors came up. One by one, I processed the feelings of anger, hatred, searing sadness, mountains of tears, and underneath all this, hundreds of fears. Day after day, week after week, month after month, the crap and shit came up for conscious processing. Sometimes I felt dejected about how much there was, and I just kept going deeper with every dream.

I went back through my life to my birth, the womb, and back into the true world of Source beyond Earth life. On the Earth timeline, I travelled back 700 years, century by century, visiting all my relatives on the four family lineages of my grandparents from mother and father. I expunged, destroyed, and energetically and consciously transmuted all the pain of sad, lonely, treacherous lives of relatives from the Dark Middle Ages. Finally, I finished the work with my personal multigenerational family and relatives.

After this period, I dove deeper into the collective unconscious, and what emerged in my Dreamtime were mythological, fairy-tale style dreams based on the great cross-cultural archetypes. The major twelve archetypes that I have already mentioned that rule every human life on Earth pulled my psyche into a downward spiraling vortex. Powerful magnets that they are, they drew me here and there, ever descending and dropping deeper into the Underworld. I felt and knew I was in the collective unconscious inside the lower Earth realms. Visually and kines-thetically, I experienced the deadly weight of all the waters of the seven oceans. This imagery could have broken my mind into fragmented pieces of nothingness. However, my soul, will power, and one-pointed focus kept me going inwards, onwards, and downwards. It was the grace and love of the Spiritual Masters and the Source that kept me going, and eventually gave me my final ego death and full soul liberation.

DESTROYING THE NEGATIVE MOTHER COMPLEX, THUS FINDING MY FEMININE POWER

One of my most important tasks of my life's work has been becoming my full feminine energy and conscious feminine soul. All human souls are feminine with respect to the Creator. It does not matter whether you are in a male or female physical body in this life. In past lives, we have all had many lives as both women and men. The path to every man's Self-Realization is through his feminine feelings, emotions, intuitions, and instincts; it can only be this way for every man. Likewise, the path to every woman's Self-Awakeness is through her quest for her own lost femininity. This is often done hand-in-hand with transforming their psychological issues with their inner and outer fathers, husbands, and sons.

The goal for all men and women is the sensory activation and conscious actualization of all our feelings, emotions, sensations of the feminine physical body, and the opening of the spiritual-emotional heart. Individually and collectively, this is the only way human life on Earth can and will proceed. Through this inner gender equality, diversity, and openness to the feminine, as well as to our full range of spiritual-sexual orientation, each of us can develop into our highest and best Self. Within this search, we honour the diversity of emotions and experiences within ourselves—past, present, and future! This accomplishment will unite cultures and ethnic groups of the world, and reclaim a Living Global Unity Mythology for us and for 72 generations to come.

My major archetypal psychological complex in this life has been the Deadly Killer Negative Mother Complex. My mother and father not wanting me activated this in the womb. I was unplanned, unloved, and an object of derision, punishment, hatred, and fury. I became the whipping boy, the scapegoat, and they poured all their unconscious projections onto me.

The Negative Mother is likely the ruling collective unconscious projection and complex of our times for most of our world's families. It shows up in the way children are treated globally. They are unloved, beaten down, sent to war as children, prostituted worldwide, are shunned, abandoned, and killed by parents and society. All institutions, including churches, schools, and the legal systems punish, torment, and murder childrens' spirits and souls. The individuals, based in the toxic cultures of these institutions and societies, are caught up in the Negative Mother and Negative Father Complexes. You may rationally argue otherwise; however, lies are not to be believed. Truth knows otherwise. The movies, TV shows, books, comics, and advertising are all based on violence, murder, crossing personal boundaries, destroying the other, and making people amnesiacs. Think about how many movies and TV shows have the main antagonist as a hysterical or coldly calculating female or mother; two thousand years of patriarchy is only partly the cause. The collective inner devaluation and devolution of the feminine has caused a massive reaction of rage—both towards the masculine and the feminine.

The four main archetypes of my life are the Warrior, Seeker, Lover, and Magician. I am just a cell in the fabric of our collective psyche. Our society in this new Era of Dwapara Yuga, moving towards the next Golden Age of Meruvia, is leaving behind the "Victimizing Warrior" of the last 10,000 years. The patriarchy has fallen in essence, and its reductionist, unfeeling, selfish ways no longer support or comfort individuals. Personal freedom will overcome our desperate feelings of present nullification.

What is coming into being inside our souls? The Seeker will guide us to find our way into and through our own darkness and find the hidden inner Light that always shines there. The Lover shows us the only future we have is love—for All Our Relations. The Magician forces us to re-empower ourselves from the world's inner and outer vampires and entities, and to inspire the King and Queen in each of us. The once and future King-Queen is the Christ Consciousness that reigns in each and every one of us.

Being pervasive, the Negative Mother Complex is a tricky, slimy, deadly challenge to deal with. It is Medusa with a head of hundreds of snakes of needed transformation. Many times in so many dreams I was bitten by poisonous snakes; each time the shocking bite and poisonous toxins—through the trans-mutational power of highest love and wisdom knowledge—gave me and my blood greater power to move forward on my journey to my Self. I was knocked down, defeated, and wounded so many times. Often I lay in bed for days, unable to eat or get dressed. Then my resolve resurfaced from my heart, and I went into the forest of the unconscious alone again, where no one else had gone before.

THE NEGATIVE FATHER COMPLEX

My hatred and rage towards my personal father strongly came up. I had these feelings for the patriarchy as well. I felt like an orphan, an unacceptable man, partly because I was gay, partly because I came into the world with a wounded physical body creating a felt feeling of inferiority in my psyche. The masculine society had wounded me much and offered me little; I understood how this world is full of lies, illusions, and deceit, particularly in the outer world of men's competitions, subterfuge, and childish games. With my highly perceptive intuition, borne of my traumatic upbringing, I have always been able to see just how severely and tragically wounded most if not all men are; they respond as four-year old selfish, unfeeling masked beings, blaming, shaming, belittling, and abusing others around them in order to compensate for their massive inferiority complex. They have major compensatory superiority complexes that never make them feel good enough about anything in their lives. Then I watch their lives devolve; these individuals create personal life story tragedies of the highest order and draw down the collective. Very few seem to be manly enough or courageous and strong enough to do anything to get themselves out of their hellish abyss. Because I felt so bad inside about myself, I decided early on that I would do all and anything I could to improve the way I felt.

I have shared about my life with my father. When he died, I travelled with him through the astral worlds. People in the astral hells and middle realms are mostly focused on quickly taking rebirth so they can work out their karmas and elevate their soul consciousness. For this reason, I was only intermittently able to confront my father about the abuse and the various ways he had disowned, punished, and thrown me aside. When I realized that he was about to take rebirth on the Earth plane, I left him alone, and returned to the psychological processes of working with my feelings of the energies of our interactions while he was alive as my father.

EGO AND EVIL

Related to the abuse issues from my father and mother were the issues of my own internal capacities for deviant and powerful evil. I had dreams of being another Hitler and of being a Stalin or a Mussolini—any of the great totalitarian dictators the world has recently known. I knew I had the potential to become a hateful, murdering man, seeking revenge everywhere. I remember the group The Kinks had an instrumental song called "Revenge." When I was 12 years old, I used to play it all the time and imagine how much damage I could do to people, my parents, and those teachers and students at school who bullied and taunted me for being gay, quiet, or not adept at sports.

When I was 26 years though, going into my Saturn Return, I realized I had to make a final choice. I always felt I was a Lover of great proportions and abilities. I knew I could and would eventually befriend everyone I met on the planet. I did not need to like everyone; however, I can love everyone. At some juncture in my unconscious journey, I had to make friends with my "inner Hitler," my inner realization that it was entirely possible for me to become a tyrant. I embraced all my shadow figures, including all my inner parts that are despots, grand inquisitors, oppressors, and slave drivers. By learning from them, and listening to and loving them, I turned their perceptions and needs into becoming my lovers and friends. It took maximum effort and endless discussions and meaningful healing circles. I had many "parts parties," as Virginia Satir called them, where everyone gathered around the Round Table to hear what the ruling Self and Soul would say to bring all the parts together as a unity. These are among the most gratifying, meaningful, and remarkably evolutionary steps I have taken.

The psyche brought this process together in its own way and time. By the time I was 29½ years old, I journeyed to the very bottom of the collective unconscious. I vividly recall having a dream where I drank all the water in the seven oceans and transmuted it. Symbolically, this dream told me I had made conscious all the darkness in my unconscious, healed my past emotions, transformed my feelings into light, cleared all the toxic energies from my memories, and found some wholeness.

DESCENT AND FINAL DESTRUCTION IN THE NO-SELF

Jung teaches and instructs his analysts that clients are not supposed to go into the place called the "No-Self." This is a realm beyond dreams, symbols, and beyond the psyche. It is the final destruction where the mind, feelings, consciousness, and possibly even the soul no longer even exist and from where can never be brought back again by one's own will. It is the place of absolute surrender and requires 100 percent complete faith and trust. All hope needs to be thrown out the window in order for one to succeed. I had to go there. Fraser forbade it because he was fearful and had not been there. My dreams urged me to go into No-Self. I quit therapy with Fraser and went there on my own for a number of months.

Since doing all this inner shadow work, my hold on my sanity was remarkably better and I was very much more grounded and happier. My felt power came from my redeemed shadow, my earthy masculine, and my deeply compassionate, sensitized feminine. In the No-Self of the Void, I had dreams of giving up and surrendering all that I know about myself, and all that I ever could be. The Sufis call this fanaa, an Arabic word for dissolution and annihilation (of the ego.) Everything I knew about myself and held dear, I let Spirit destroy until there were no parts left—nothing but emptiness. No time. No space. No personality. No psyche. I felt empty but strangely full. I felt alone but not lonely any longer – whereas loneliness and depression had been my constant companions before. I felt dead to myself and this world and its lures, but alive to the Great Big Love of Spirit. I felt like I was nobody and wanted to forever stay nobody. During this time, Babaji reminded me that the biggest challenge on the planet today is that, "Everyone wants to be a somebody, and nobody wants to be a nobody."

Every night before I sleep, I take stock of my good and bad habits witnessed through the day. I transform my thoughts and feelings into better, more loving actions and words. Then I consciously burn up my mind, consciousness, psyche, and physical form with violet spiritual flames of transformation. The "Dying, Death, and Resurrection" archetype is the prime necessary three-step process for all Divine-humans. I die to personality and myself every night. Jesus reminds me that, "If anyone would come after me, let him-her deny himself-herself and take up his-her cross and follow me. For whoever would save his life will lose it, but whoever loses his life for my sake will find it." (Matthew 16:24-25). Yogananda constantly lets me know if I waver or forget this process. He tells me, "Whether a man is born in India or America, he someday has to die. Why not learn how to 'die daily' in God?"

In the I AM Presence of Source Light and Love, I always experience my full soul. This felt bodily flow of true life energy allows my mind, heart, and physical form to know that this world and the ego's outer perceptions or misperceptions are all illusion, and that someday this body will be thrown off like an overcoat. I practice this daily by imagining my physical body being burned up and cremated, and my ashes strewn over the seven continents and seven oceans.

Every day and night, my intention is to let Spirit take my imagination to a higher place where I have not yet been. I know that everyone I meet and everything we share is meant to be from a Higher Power and Higher Place. Rather than waiting for external circumstances to knock me over, I prefer to be open to Spirit and to be guided with my own surrendering to "whatever is." In this way, my life is perfect.

TRAINING IN NEURO-LINGUISTIC PROGRAMMING (NLP) 1974

I was present at the first training for Neuro-Linguistic Programming in May of 1974 at the Medical Faculty of the University of Toronto. John Grinder, one of the two founders, presented over a period of several days. I enrolled in every further program, eventually working through two Masters and the final Trainer's Trainer in NLP with Richard Bandler, the other originator.

These powerful techniques of deep vibrational healing of spirit-mind-emotions-feelings-biochemistry-physiology became one of the greatest lifelines in my healing. I released piles of emotional garbage, trauma, misperceptions, blockages, obstructions, hell realms, angers, sadness, and fears. I have since utilized this process on a daily basis to keep myself clear, present, focused, and joyful. It took me decades to finish clearing my emotional baggage, but once done, I have always been grateful for those who taught me this and for the work I did on myself. Although eventually I spent one-quarter of a million dollars on all my various trainings and therapies over many decades, I would do it all over again, even if it cost more money, just to feel the way I feel now—whole, complete, joyful, and overwhelming loved and loving.

EXPERIENCES AND TRAINING WITH REBIRTHING 1978

I heard about Rebirthing through Leonard Orr's and Sondra Ray's Rebirthing in the New Age, which I read when it came out in December 1977. Having read Otto Rank's work on The Trauma of Birth, and had my own very painful memories of my own birth. I knew this ancient Kundalini Kriya Yoga technique from India brought to the west through Babaji Nagaraj's guidance. It became the cornerstone for my ongoing healing process.

A note about Babaji Nagaraj, also known as Shri Maha Prabhuji Haidakhan Babaji: He is the Creator of the Universe, considered worldwide to be an incarnation of Shiva-Kali, and also Krishna. He has had innumerable Earth incarnations since the creation of planet Earth, and most recently incarnated from the Pure Light of Source as an 18-year young man in northern India, and lived as such from 1970-1984. It was during this time that many devotees travelled to be with Him in his Anand Puri Haidakhan Babaji ashram in the small Indian village of Chilianaula near Ranikhet in the north of the country. This is how the ancient breathing techniques of Rebirthing came to the west and the world.

Once I learned the basic deep diaphragmatic breathing techniques, done while lying flat on one's back on a mat, I continued to release my blocked emotional energies from my physiological tissues on a daily basis. I recall doing this wherever I was. It could have been while I was at the farm, staying at Kanehsatake, or with a friend in Montreal. I lay on my back on a bed, a floor, anywhere, and breathed deeply for one to three hours on my own. I cried, wept, thrashed, froze, and sweat for a while until I got to the state of final release for that session and became deeply peaceful, grounded and whole. Then I did it all over again the next day.

I continued Rebirthing for many years. Once, during a Jungian dream session with Dr. Roger Woolger, I asked him to sit while I Rebirthed myself. This was in 1979 on a friend's bed in Toronto. During Rebirthing, it was common for me to go into the astral realms during alpha, beta, and theta brainwaves, and meet up with old friends now in the Spirit world. In this particular session, I recall getting to the final peaceful inner experience. Then I saw my good friend, German composer Johannes Brahms. I asked him to come and gift me with greater musical compositional styles and invited him into my energy field. The experience was astoundingly powerful! I flew off the bed in massive waves from head to toe. I felt the power of Brahms's soul as electricity from a 100,000-kilowatt generator going through my nerves and body. I thrashed and levitated three to four feet off the bed. It was like a massive seizure. I could not open my eyes; my jaw was locked shut. Roger was panicking because he thought I was having death throes. He asked me what was happening. I could not speak at all. Brahms did a full download into me of all his musical knowledge and wisdom during seven or eight minutes. I was very thankful, though exhausted afterwards. I have had many experiences like this in unifying with soul friends in the astral worlds. In our Mohawk way, we call this the Requickening Process, when another great soul completely embodies with one inside their own physical form. This is one of my most dramatic and favourite experiences.

BABAJI NAGARAJ

My Rebirthing was necessary to enable me to transmute all the toxic energies I picked up from my parents, family, school, church, and my childhood. However, there is a more important reason. This is Babaji. During the reading of Rebirthing in the New Age, Babaji again started speaking with me in my innermost heart. Floods of memories of my childhood with him, past lives, and before coming into this life flooded my mind and memory with brilliant, sparkling Clear Diamond Light.

Babaji told me of our multitudinous lives together. One that I can share is as his primary student when He was Milarepa, the first and most famous Tibetan Yogi, who together with Marpa the Translator brought Buddhism to an animist Tibet when he lived 1052-1135 CE. Milarepa was a powerful energy and a prolific poet and composer of sacred music; he composed over 100,000 songs.

In truth, Babaji is the Great Divine Director and Creator of the Universe. I happily acknowledge this and feel so deeply blessed to be able to constantly communicate with him day and night, in waking and in dreaming astral realities.

TOM THOMSON TEACHES ME TO PAINT

One day in spring of 1976, when the farm's front quarter of an acre was filled with glorious, radiant yellow daffodils and white narcissus, a strong spirit came into my house while I was doing red and black therapeutic paintings on the living room rug. The power of this incoming presence knocked me on my side. I asked who it was.

"It's Tom again…" Tom, I thought, which Tom is this? Instantly I felt the very familiar presence of Tom Thomson, the great Canadian landscape painter who, early on, was part of The Group of Seven in the 1900s.

As a child and teenager, I loved to canoe through Algonquin Park. I first went there for a drive with my family when I was seven years old. After that, I always longed to be there. I was so taken with the beauty, splendor, and grandeur of the rivers, lakes, rocks, trees, and flowering plants. The animal spirits of the bear, fish, moose, deer, and birds communicated with my heart. While back in Toronto, all I could think of was how I could get back to Algonquin Park.

As a teenager of 13, I went there with some older male friends who were 17 and 18. We canoed around North Tea Lake, Opeongo, Canoe, Joe, and other lakes. I have been in just about every river and portage in the Park. When I was 16, I began hitchhiking upcountry to go solo canoeing and fasting for one or two weeks at a time. As a teen, I often went up every other weekend from early April until late October. In winter, I cross-country skied there, and stayed at the East Gate Motel.

During these early trips, I constantly thought about Tom Thomson and wondered what his life was like while he paddled and painted all those years ago. He was born in 1877 and died tragically in 1917 in the Park. I, too, enjoyed many drawing and painting excursions while canoeing.

At age 18, when I was dating a young woman whose family had a lease for their cottage on Canoe Lake, I spent long hours sitting at Tom Thomson's cairn high above the lake. There has always been a mystery as to the nature of his death or murder, and where his body is buried.

Tom Thomson became an archetypal personal hero for me. He was a solitary warrior, artist, philosopher, and wild man who loved the great beauty of nature, the elements and the animals. I visited the Victorian farmhouse near Claremont, Ontario, where he was born. Eventually I lived in the farmhouse beside the farm where he grew up in Leith, Ontario, just north of Owen Sound. While in Leith, I often visited The Tom Thomson Memorial Art Gallery in Owen Sound, as his artwork continued to inspire my own.

Two of Canada's best-known paintings are Tom's—The Jack Pine and The West Wind. They are iconic to Canada and found in airports and homes all over the country. Northern River is another of my favourites of Tom's, one that I have painted at least 12 times.

I often wondered how and why Tom had tragically died on Canoe Lake on July 8, 1917. His body was discovered in the lake eight days later. The official cause of death was accidental drowning, but there are still questions about how he actually died. It was reported that there was fishing line wrapped around his left leg and he had a head injury on the left side.

"What are you doing here, Tom?" it had been a few years since we had spoken.

"I'd like to make you a deal…"

"What's the deal?" I queried.

"Well, you need to learn how to mix colours and paint properly, and I need to be released from this ghost realm of the spirit world."

People who die accidentally and quickly most often remain within the astral ghost realms. Tom had been in the lower astral realms since his death in 1917. It was now almost 60 years later. But in these ghost realms, one can never be happy or settled; one is always confused and conflicted.

Tom sat in the chair in the corner and smoked his Sherlock Holmes pipe, of which he was very fond. His shock of long dark hair still covered his right forehead. I could see the gash on the other side of his head. He was so present, his body actually half-materialized. This could only be so because we knew each other really well, over the previous 13 years.

I was in the midst of my Jungian dream analysis with Fraser across the road, however I was intrigued with his offer, and did want to become a better painter.

"Alright," I pronounced, "we have a deal. You can live here with me, teach me to paint everyday, and when we're done and you're ready, I will help you to ascend out of the darkness of this purgatory realm and into the Greater Clear Light." I heard a profound audible sigh come from this great man.

Tom Thomson ended up living with me in the Meaford farmhouse for just over 2 years, from March 1976 to August 1978. I took him into the Light on August 5th 1978, his birthday. Taking people into the Clear Light is one of my services to ghosts and departing two-leggeds of this planet.

He slept on the couch in the living room, while I was in the master bedroom in the next room on the main floor. Every morning we would have breakfast together, astral eggs and toast, and talk about how we were feeling. Then we would get down to serious painting afterwards. According to Lawren Harris and other members of The Group of Seven, Tom was the renowned master of mixing colours into tones of his own creation.

We would get out books of reproductions of his colour paintings. He showed me the acrylic colour mix on my palette and I would copy his paintings as precisely as I could. Over the two years, he became more pleased with my progress. This process was very good for both of us—we both needed companionship and we became excellent friends, although there were times when we each needed our solitude. On brisk spring days, warm summer days and beautiful fall days, when the tree leaf colours were in their prime glory, we would go walking and hiking together along the Bruce Trail on the top of the Niagara escarpment, just 300 yards from the farmhouse.

Eventually I did multiple painting copies of many of his most favourite works, including Sunset, Northern Lights, and Lake and Red Tree.

Tom was a handsome, rugged man. He was noble, tall, slim, and walked like an upright bear. His nature was reflective, silent, and penetrating like a snake. When we looked at each other, we both felt the inner bond of masculine friendship. In many ways, Tom's presence helped me go deeper with my own inner psychological work. He was already in a bound place; I allowed my psyche to go down to where he was—into the dark lower astral realms where all the best psychological and emotional healing happens.

FEROCIOUS ATTACKS BY LUCIFER-SATAN AND THE DARK FORCES

Having opened the lower astral hell realms, I was a sitting duck for all the Dark Forces that exist and rule there. This includes Lucifer-Satan, Ahriman, Sorat, Mabus, their underlings, devils, apprentice demons, powerful elementals, orcs, ghouls, goblins, vampires, werewolves, and all the others. I am very serious about this; all these creatures exist, and most have for a very long time. Because we humans are mostly unconscious, all these Dark Forces laughingly rule us and the world through our ignorance, ego attitudes, arrogance, obnoxiousness, hatred, beguilement, mistrust, materialism, illnesses, mechanistic thoughts, lies, pure logic of mere rationality, heartlessness, selfishness, and greed. Because of where we are personally and collectively in our evolution, we give all our buried innate power to these Dark Forces inside us and all around us in the world and through our cultural representations. The Dark Side is very real. The Dark Force is everywhere and in everyone. It is not just in authentic stories like Star Wars, Star Trek, Lord of the Rings, The Narnia Chronicles, Stargate SG-1, Merlin (BBC), Supernatural, The Vampire Diaries, and so many others.

We were created with the potential for Great Love and Good, and also Forceful Hatred and Evil. True Love and Goodness is always way more powerful because it is the Source. Hatred and Evil is always just a minor force, however manipulative it can become within us. According to Carl Jung, "We ourselves are the origin of all coming evil." There are extant entities that try to rule our lives, companies, countries, and politics. What is our response to this? We have to fight and win at all times and at all costs. Otherwise, this world may not be here for our descendants to come.

As with my first few years of life, there were many months during my years 27½ to 29 when these Dark Forces tried to rub me out and get me gone by sorely attacking me. Honestly, looking back, I am not sure how I survived. I will chalk it up to the Grace of Source and the Love of my Great Spiritual Master friends.

Here is just one example. Tom Thomson and I had just had a full day's worth of painting. I was also deep in my unconscious dream process. I was exhausted so I fell on my bed about 3pm one late spring afternoon. Suddenly the house began to shake. The foundations were heaving; I could hear the windows rattling. I saw the walls waving back and forth in my main floor bedroom. Was this an earthquake? It was light outside, and the skies were clear, no wind. There was a deep hellish groaning roaring in the living room. A vast wind with hurricane force came blasting through from the living room, front door, and hallway into my bedroom. It threw papers, lamps, and other objects flying into the air, against the walls, and onto the floor.

I instantly knew that this was a major surprise attack by the Big Dark Guys. There is a terrifying Dark Force within and without that tries to break and shatter your mind, destroy your hope and faith, deaden your will power, and murder and kill your heart and love. If I had not gone into the depths of my darkest mind for myself by then, the Dark Force would have had me in its clutches and demonic grip.

Sam and Dean Winchester in Supernatural have nothing on me. I could definitely teach them a thing or two. Over the years, I have exorcised demons, entities, ghosts, walk-ins, bad ETs, elementals, and everything imaginable from friends, houses, places, planets, and myself. Having to deal with our evil nature and the real demonic forces existing outside on a daily basis keeps me and us on our toes. We always need to keep fighting until the very end, and then beyond. Surrendering to the Light means the end of our darkness.

Even if it takes us through the deepest hells, we need to go there with it. If we want to be alive to our life's adventure and the reasons for being in an Earth body again, we must transform everything we experience, and every Dark Force we meet, with the only weapons that work—pure true love, lasting trustworthy friendships, and our Christ Consciousness I AM Presence. We will never have inner peace and outer harmony in the world until we become this Magical Peaceful Presence of the One Source Light and Great Love.

TOM THOMSON'S SOUL RELEASE INTO THE LIGHT

When Tom finished telling me his full life story (which I will publish in a book,) teaching me his best strokes with the brush, and had me mixing colours to his satisfaction, I felt that he was getting antsy and wanted to leave his astral reality. It was July 8th 1979 when he first brought up the discussion about his leaving me; this was exactly 62 years to the day since his physical death. We sat and talked about it for a few days. We had grown very fond of each other throughout our lives together. He was my best friend. We planned his final departure to the higher astral realms of light for August 5th 1979, his birthdate.

We both had feelings of sadness and anxieties about our coming separation. When I kept feeling the coming deep loneliness of his eventual final liberation from the ghost realm I had to immediately recall in my heart that true friendship is indeed eternal. He would be with me everywhere I went and I with him. As I sit here writing about us all these years later, I feel Tom inside my heart and physical body. He is grinning, as he always did, about the things I am saying about him and us.

"That's it, Joseph, tell my true story; tell the world that I was murdered…" Yes, that's for another story in another book I have been writing since that time.

As I write this, I am saying to him, "Tom, our friendship is everlasting; I still feel your love and support inside my heart and being. I am so very grateful for our friendship."

As you will see, this is not the last "Tom" that I had to bid farewell to through death's portal. I will get to that part of my story in due time.

How did we prepare for Tom's elevation through the astral planes? We all have the innate, intuitive abilities to take souls from the dark realms to those of the higher light. One's own astral soul must travel with the soul to guide them. Demons try to prevent the soul from leaving hell. In Tom's case, they did not want to let him go. I had to fight them off with my inner psychic power and make them release his soul. I do not use Latin; I use English and Intergalactic, a language known to all beings in the universe. I do not use salt, fire, or holy water; although I do use lit white candles and bell ringing. These have the power to release and protect the soul on its journey.

There is one main and most essential process that must be engaged, or the soul will never get to the higher realms. It will only continue to wander around the vast wastelands of the inner mind of its lower-being consciousness. As in all cases, I called in the supreme power of "The Name and Blood of Jesus Christ." It matters not what religion or background you are. You must use this power to liberate the soul. This is because only Jesus the Christ has played a particular role on Earth throughout all time and space to free people from their own mental, emotional, and karmic fetters and prisons. Moses, Zoroaster, Buddha, Mohammed, Guru Nanak, and all other great spiritual elders have brought the same unifying teachings of love, inner Source wisdom, and showered us with Grace. Only Jesus had the singular role of dying and resurrecting, thereby wiping out a certain amount of individual and collective karma for good. Jesus gives all people, cultures, groups, and nations the chance to bow at the feet of the King of Kings, the inner Christ Consciousness we all share and are.

Living with Tom Thomson was a search for the Holy Grail for me. We supported one another in going into our deepest darkest places and finding the light, creative spirit, and insight, and the will to paint our lives with a brush of goodness, supreme earthly beauty, and truth.

ART TRAINING WITH OTHER PAINTERS

After he left, I sorely grieved for the loss of Tom Thomson for many weeks. Not wanting to keep him earthbound, I emotionally detached and I let him go. So many ghosts are earthbound because people and families do not know how to process sadness and loss; the living remain attached to the departed, holding them back.

I kept painting. During my dreams and daytime, I had visitations from other well-known painters. Over the next two decades, I had ongoing painting lessons and artistic discussions with these lovely souls who became very good friends—Lawren Harris, Vincent Van Gogh, Emily Carr, Wassily Kandinsky, Piet Mondrian, Marc Chagall, and Mark Rothko. My artistic leanings and master classes with these "Art Masters" took me further back to Renaissance times with John Constable, Raphael, Michelangelo, Rembrandt, Vermeer, and of course more communications with my brother William Blake.

LAWREN HARRIS, 1885-1970

After Tom Thomson went home to Spirit, Lawren Harris appeared in my living room; I studied and appreciated his paintings since I was a teenager. I used to always carry a postcard of his North Shore Lake Superior with me. Harris is the founding member of The Group of Seven. For years, he spent much time standing beside me while I painted. He gave me some of his previous lectures on theosophy, colour theory, symbolic natural imageries, composition, and the spiritual basis of Canadian space, nature, art, and our national cultural heritage as a result of this.

From Harris, I learned the importance of allowing the light in the painting to come from the upper left corner, as in North Shore Lake Superior. Other times it came from the upper right. There always had to be radiant light coming from the Spirit world into this Earth world. Nature is sublime, and reflects a representation of true Heaven in realms below: as above, so below. Harris often used thrusting phallic imagery to symbolize the power of the mind, will, and heart linked with Nature to pierce through chaos, confusion, and ignorance up towards and into the Light. For Harris, azure blue and golden yellow are the primary spiritual colours for painters.

As a result of my discussions with Harris, I began to study Theosophy more and read all his lectures. His interest concerns how Spirit works in Nature and our soul to bring light, beauty, truth, and goodness to the Earth, humans and the civilizing cultural process. Harris is a grandfather of Canadian spiritual painting. His brilliant mind, keen spirit, powerful visions, and kind nature were transmitted onto hundreds of beautiful canvases. My understanding of the spirit of art and the beauty of the etheric akashic realms on Earth owe much to my deep, abiding friendship with Lawren Harris.

EMILY CARR, 1871-1945

Harris was an early mentor of Emily Carr from Victoria, British Columbia. While studying with Harris, Emily often appeared in my living room as well. With her quirky, disciplined, and devoted way, I greatly respected her. She worked beside me on the art table. From her, I learned how to get the feeling, colour, and powerful symbolism of trees, forest, sky, and rock.

Her painting, Scorned as Timber, Beloved of the Sky, has always been one of my all-time favourites. It is symbolically a depiction for all Canadians of how we want to choose our future. All the issues concerning beauty, forests, ecology, and our future legacy are wrapped up here. Being Native myself, I resonate deeply with her fascination and depiction of totem poles, Longhouses, and First Nations peoples from her time.

Emily created a mystical feeling and sensation about Nature, specifically trees, in her swirling greens, blues, ochres, and browns. Her brushwork, upward sweeping flows and colours are what I learned most from Emily. Of course, I spoke with her about her poetry and prose, and read her Klee Wyck and Hundreds and Thousands.

Now I feel even closer to Emily Carr—for I live in the Highlands of Greater Victoria, exactly at the physical location where Emily had her wheeled summer carriage! Her monkey and dogs lived with her in this space; now I feel her energies around me more than ever.

Chapter Seven

VINCENT VAN GOGH, 1853-1890

Vincent was a tormented soul with far-reaching innovative talents using fantastic colours, brush strokes, composition, and his own impressionism. I knew he was in the ghost realms since I was a young boy, when I read about his life and art. In 1890, he had fits of despair and hallucinations during which he could not work. In between these states, there were long clear months in which he could and did create; these latter were during extreme ecstatic visions. On July 27th 1890, aged 37, van Gogh shot himself in the chest with a revolver.

While in Europe in 1974, I visited the Van Gogh Museum in Amsterdam. I was moved by these paintings in the deepest ways. It was here that I renewed my spirit and soul connection with Vincent. When I arrived home to the farmhouse in Meaford, Vincent was waiting for me.

From the library, I obtained a book of colour reproductions of his art. I set out the paper and acrylics and started in. Starry Night was the first one I tried. Vincent was not happy with my results. It took seven tries before he felt I had adequately learned the very unique style of paint application on canvas.

The truth is that Vincent put his own spiritual light from the energy of his Source visions into the coloured pigments, the brush, and the manner in which he rendered the paint on the canvas.

He said, "I want to paint … with that something of the eternal which the halo used to symbolize, and which we seek to communicate by the actual radiance and vibration of our colouring."

Irises is another painting I copied numerous times. Vincent's beauty for Nature, flowers, trees, sky, cypresses, and colours is a miracle of modern art.

The Dutch are a flower-loving country. In the 16th century, the Dutch traders brought tulips and other flowers back from Persia and Asia Minor through Constantinople. In the history of Dutch art, flower studies are common. Sunflowers is a perfect example of the exotic, breathtaking beauty of Vincent's feelings.

Between the ages of 24 and 30, I spent much time with Vincent. As Tom had done with me, Vincent spent many days sitting in my big armchair in the farm living room. Sometimes he was wearing his straw hat and had a pipe in his hand.

Vincent had a younger brother, Theo, whom he adored. While Vincent lacked almost all self-worth and was never really a successful artist within his lifetime, Theo was his life-long supporter and friend. While at my farm, Vincent encouraged me to read his Letters to Theo. These are sad, depressing, anxious, and emotionally conflicted missives that show great emotional and psychological self-flagellation.

Vincent was conflicted as a spirit being born into the challenges of the Earth world, as I was, and as many of us are. Vincent aspired to become an artist in God's service, stating, "to try to understand the real significance of what the great artists, the serious masters, tell us in their masterpieces, that leads to God; one man wrote or told it in a book; another in a picture."

Conflicted in a struggle between his spiritual visions and his earthly endeavours, Vincent became more mentally unhinged and emotionally desperate as he became older. I have certainly been there myself. For me, art, music, and writing are the processes that I engage in order to transmute the inner darkness, loneliness, and fractured nature of the illusionary Earth world.

While Vincent constantly used his immense talents to manifest his "longing for concision and grace," his poor diet, lack of sleep, and isolation eventually turned his hand against himself. In his last painting, Wheatfield with Crows, Vincent portrays his inner emotional landscape of melancholy and extreme loneliness through somber threatening skies and ill-omened crows.

While I enjoyed Vincent's friendship and artistic training, I coaxed him into leaving the ghost realms. When he was ready, we performed the ritual journey to the higher astral planes on his death date, July 29th 1981; this was 91 years after he left his physical body.

PIET MONDRIAN, 1872-1944

Another Dutch painter with whom I became familiar was Piet Mondrian. I witnessed the energies in his works firsthand while in galleries in the Netherlands. Likewise, he taught me from Spirit at the farm. Although I appreciate his later work of thick, black vertical and horizontal lines with interspersing solid primary colours, I prefer his earlier work. In 1912,

Piet experimented with cubism and created Gray Tree. This one image reminded me of a similar tree on my daily walks to the back of the property to see how the mixed grains were growing in our 73 acres, and to talk to the cows in the neighbouring fields that belonged to my Karate Instructor. This one solitary tree sits sweetly on a hillock that I loved as much as I have loved any tree.

I love so many trees; these Standing People are so honourable, resilient, joyful, and strong. They are the World Trees to save life's atmospheric lungs and supply us with needed oxygen. Over the years, I have planted over 7,000 white pine seedlings, and 1,500 red pine and jack pines, along with a few black walnuts. Where are they? They are on the roadsides of Ontario, and in fields throughout Haliburton.

WASSILY KANDINSKY, 1866-1944

Wassily Kandinsky is one of the most adept and erudite spiritual painters of the Western world. I viewed his paintings during my European tour of art galleries and I was closely drawn to his spirit. Wassily was another man who taught me more about the nature of art and its subtle and overt spiritual components than almost any other artist. I enthusiastically absorbed his Concerning the Spiritual in Art, and Point and Line to Plane. When I taught Myths, Dreams, Symbols and Self-Discovery as an "Experimental Art" class at the Ontario College of Art and Design from 1986–1993, I used these two books as texts for my students. When I founded The Academy of World Psychology and Creative Arts, 1989–1996 in Toronto, at my Snickers Art Gallery, 93 Parliament Street, on the corner of King Street East, the students loved the principles within Kandinsky's teachings.

Gentle Ascent shows the planes of the astral realms. 309 has an amazing effect on me. It portrays the psychological complexes within our unconscious and there is a harmonic balance to it. The colours are very healing and beautiful. Many of the hundreds of chalk pastel and oilstick drawings that I have done are inspired by this style of self-representation.

Composition VII (1913), according to Kandinsky, is the most complex piece he ever painted. It shows the dancelike, musical, and poetic nature of Wassily's soul.

MARC CHAGALL, 1887-1985

Marc Chagall, another Russian painter like Kandinsky, I loved for his stained glass creations. He influenced my symbolic flowing colour fields in my oil painting, acrylics, and paper works.

MARK ROTHKO, 1903-1970

Mark was the third Russian artist I trained with from Spirit while at the farm. I appreciate his strong, multi-layered, heavily coloured horizontal patches. Mark says, "The reason I paint… is precisely because I want to be very intimate and human." His intense, deliberate brush strokes carry his energy just as Vincent's works embody him. All Mark's works have scores of layers of paint on them, spreading his feelings into the paint and the process. There is deliberate power in his paintings, and this is his legacy to me.

His paintings are fugal and contain contrasting colours that appeal to harmony and balance. During his later life, Mark became quite depressed and his palette turned more somber, as in No. 61.

In later years and subsequent to his passing, his art fetched the highest prices at auction. Homage to Matisse sold for $22.5 million USD in 2005.

WILLIAM BLAKE, 1757-1827

Other than the novel techniques of plate engraving and his beautiful paintings, the essential aspect of my relationship with my brother William is the apocryphal and timely message of his visions of the spiritual-earthly challenges, changes, and catastrophes being visited upon the Earth. William's dire warnings and evolutionary choices he hoped peoples of the planet would heed. Whether or not they have, do, or will is an open question.

What are the key elements of his views of reality, the future of humanity, and connections to the Spirit world? There is the questionable concern of whether America will stay true to its spiritual origination and heritage. There are the aspects of humanity's understanding of the spiritual nature of history, human evolution, and global warfare. For

William, using a gnostic Biblical storyline, he shows us The Ancient of Days, Archangel Michael Binding Satan, the fractured lies of The Web of Religion, Good and Evil Angels, and The Last Judgment.

Perhaps the highest allegory Blake would like all to understand is how we are tempted and tortured by the Dark Forces within and without. The Old Testament Book of Job, with Job's story of abject misery, loss, illness, and degradation is an archetype for people for all time. Jung's Answer to Job is a marvelous psychological awakening of our human condition we share with Job.

William Blake has exceedingly helped me to understand the spiritual-psychological battle of "All Against All," which is presently heightening to its violent vortex, apex, turning point, and higher quantum resolution.

The only way forward for individuals, cultures, and our collective is to understand and to process our "inner marriage of heaven and hell."

Along with our acceptance of and being in charge of our own shadow and dark side, there is a need to recapture the glory, beauty and inno-cence of our personal inner children. William expertly depicted this in the cover for his book, Songs of Innocence and Experience. Our ongo-ing conversations inspire and direct my thoughts and goals still.

JOHN CONSTABLE, 1776-1837

I have always loved the serene, pastoral paintings of my friend John Constable. I searched out his works before my trip to England in 1974 and visited the very spots from which he painted. Dedham Vale, The Hay Wain, and The Cornfield are among my favourites. I have had these post-ers on my walls for years and have copied many of Constable's works as practice. It is the light and shadows, along with trees, clouds and a "New Jerusalem," almost Arthurian, sensibility about England that invokes the greater joy in my heart.

My all-time favourite of John Constable's is Salisbury Cathedral. I stood in the exact spot from which he painted en plein air and marveled at the beauty of the Gothic architecture, the glorious elms and other trees, and the rising spiritual evocation of his composition. John is a refined, noble, and remarkable friend for me.

JOHANNES VERMEER, 1632-1675

The Dutch artist Vermeer strikes me as unique for his bright colours, balanced light and shadows, humans in the midst of life, and floral displays. The Milkmaid shows a dutiful woman enjoying her chores.

The Girl With a Pearl Earring is the Dutch "Mona Lisa." The exquisite, lifelike beauty of the eyes, face, and posture evoke an angelic response for the viewer.

REMBRANDT, 1606-1669

The well-known Dutch painter Rembrandt van Rijn also spent much time with me during various periods of my life—from ages 14-19, 26-29, and especially from 54-59.

The Storm on the Sea of Galilee depicts Jesus calming the fears of Peter along with the waves on the water. The darkness is foreboding, while the light is emanating from Jesus's body.

The Mill gives a sense of home and groundedness for the boatman on glistening waters under darkening skies. It reminds me of the Dutch heritage of my mother's family.

LEONARDO DA VINCI, 1452-1519

The iconoclast Leonardo, the reincarnation of great scientists in both Lemuria and Atlantis, also became William Shakespeare (1564 – 1616) in his next life. This Italian gay Renaissance man was brilliant as a painter, sculptor, architect, musician, mathematician, engineer, inventor, anatomist, geologist, botanist, and writer.

It is Leonardo's humanist ideal that has benefitted humanity for centuries, and will for millennia to come. Leonardo's clear, etheric spiritual vision of the higher worlds give us glorious paintings like The Baptism of Christ. The androgynous John the Baptist points to the higher realities of Jesus and the Christ Consciousness.

Vitruvian Man has become the anatomical source for the human body within the circle of life and the "Flower of Life" imageries. The flying ships that Leonardo drew come from his recall of past lives in Atlantis.

Annunciation portrays Archangel Gabriel explaining to Mary about the birth of her child-to-come, Jesus. Leonardo's The Last Supper, here restored with original brighter colours, has become famous recently with the possibility that seated to the right of Jesus is his friend Mary Magdalene.

Leonardo's reincarnation in the 20th century has enabled me to have long discussions with him about the highest spiritual, Christed realities, the purposes of our past histories, and those of our coming millennia.

RAPHAEL SANZIO DA URBINO, 1483-1520

Raphael, the Italian High Renaissance painter, visually achieved the Neo-Platonic ideal of human grandeur and divinity. Saint George and the Dragon is now an archetypal iconic image of the need for each of us to kill our personality's personae or masks, ego, and shadows operating within ourselves, which bury our soul power and legitimacy.

Deposition of Christ shows the human agony of Mother Mary, Joseph of Arimathea, and others whose responsibility it was to take Jesus down off His Cross, and carry Him to Joseph's tomb. This image has been engraved in my mind for decades and for me it symbolizes the daily need we all have to sacrifice for one another and the loving friendship within this that is shared.

Transfiguration visually captures Raphael's spiritual and majestic knowledge of the two worlds, and the fate and future of every living soul who will pass into the higher real Spirit world.

Raphael's School of Athens is his masterpiece and the perfect embodiment of the classical spirit of the High Renaissance. Here Plato and Aristotle expound on the phrases, "Seek Knowledge of Causes," "Divine Inspiration," "Knowledge of Things Divine," and "To Each What is Due." Raphael has painted himself in the bottom right of the group of figures, with his back to us and wearing a golden robe. Some suggest this is either Ptolemy or Raphael.

SPIRITS I LIVE WITH AND COMMUNICATE WITH

HOW I COMMUNICATE

All of us are familiar with conversations we have everyday with dozens of people. One hundred percent of any relationship is great communication. Ninety percent of this is non-verbal communication—your love, eyes, smile, face, and body posture. The other ten percent is voice tone, inflection, emotion, speed, and volume. Each of us spends many hours every day talking to ourselves. Most people have a negative, castigating voice inside their head, based on an earlier poor relationship with a parent or teacher, and they continuously replay this hurtful tape over and over—sometimes for their entire life. Through techniques like NLP, positive self-talk, visualization, and internal auditory-kinesthetic feedback, you can entrain and replay these positive tapes to bring you greater self-confidence and self-worth.

My conversations with my Friends in Spirit are on a different level altogether. I have ongoing 24-7-365¼ fully embodied communications and daily conversations with thousands of Spiritual Masters. They are always present inside my heart-mind-body-spirit. They have all been "Requickened" within my bodily consciousness. Thousands of them are inside me within our one "I AM Presence" —continuously and eternally. When I wish to speak with any one or a specific group of them, I just call out silently in my heart and they are instantly there. If I have a question, I formalize it in my mind and intentionally think about it. Immediately there is a response from my Spiritual Friend or Friends. I see them, feel their personal energetic presence in my bodily sensations, know their responses in my heart, hear their voices, smell their unique soul aromas, and intuit the fullness of what they are sharing with me.

Even when I am not questioning, they will often come forward in my inner vision and hearing and share a suggestion, a protective warning, and a guiding choice about the synchronicity of being somewhere at a particular time down to the minute and second. They share with me whom I should meet, what I should say or ask them, and how I can inspire and support them. They carefully give the words to me, down to the last word, inflection in my voice, and the spiritual emotional energies I can send out from my heart. Everything is energy. Relationships and the love they send share the same vibratory field of a particular responsive meaningful frequency the other can receive and feel comfortable with and loved.

Since I was in public school, I always knew that it was up to me to adjust my heart's frequency to the vibration of the other person so that we can authentically connect. The message I send will then be received once I get around the other's own frequency fences, behind which they hide because of fear. It is up to me to run the ball around their defense lines and score the touchdown of having them receive my intended positive love message. I do this with everyone.

Although I have thousands of Spiritual Beings with whom I am constantly connected, I primarily discuss all matters with Babaji, Jesus, Dendreah, Yogananda, Metatron and Tashunke Witko (Crazy Horse). We speak of the how and what of each communication within every one of my human relationships—old friends, new friends, and strangers. I do this in person, on the phone, in emails, on Skype, in dreams and visions, prayers, and meditations all the time.

My life is built around this sure foundation—everything I think, feel, say, and do is at the behest or in unified conjunction with all these great Spiritual Masters. This is how I have learned to deal with my own bad habits, thoughts, words, and actions. Through these means, I have learned to surrender everything, always be open to and feel from Source the great unconditional love that I can be and give, and that others can feel if they choose.

DENDREAH – WHITE BUFFALO CALF WOMAN – GAIA

Here, for brevity's sake, I will only share with you about one of my best Spiritual Friends, although I could speak of so many that I love dearly, and with whom I constantly communicate.

What I would most like to share from my heart to the hearts of individuals now and in future generations for thousands of years to come is the knowledge of Dendreah, The White Buffalo Calf Woman, Gaia. The name Dendreah is likely unknown to most people. It is the name The White Buffalo (Calf) Woman gives Herself and has shared with me. It is Lakota Sioux for "(Wild) Desert Rose."

Who is Dendreah? She is the Mother of the Universe and thus has created all Matter from Spirit. She is the Divine Feminine, Sophia, Avalokiteshvara, Kwan Yin, Mother Mary, Mary Magdalene, Rabi'a and other great feminine inflections and manifestations of Her great divine nature. She is Gaia, the Earth Mother. She is the Creator of our Earth, Sun, and planets. She reigns and She rules all things divine and human. Along with The Masculine Creator Babaji Nagaraj, She is the Source of the soul, love, and all Created Light.

When one directly knows Dendreah, personally within one's own heart, one has come home. Come home to Source, Spirit, one's Holy Grail, one's heart, and one's purpose. Within this, one psychologically embraces the full femininity of the perfected androgyny that your soul is. All souls are feminine with respect to The Creator, whether in a male or female body. All souls are created equal, and each soul is equally 100 percent feminine and 100 percent masculine in our truest nature. Herein lies the goal of liberation through understanding and engaging this re-membrance of one's true nature.

ELVES, FAIRIES, LITTLE PEOPLE, AND ROCK, PLANT, TREE, ANIMAL, CLOUD, AND WIND SPIRIT BEINGS

Most people and cultures have long since forgotten the truth about other spirits who cohabit our beautiful Earth. Now, in this time of dense cluttered consciousness, most think that these living beings are just figments, fiction, or storybook characters from old mythologies. Well, for me at least, these ancient Spirit beings are real and they communicate, guide, heal, protect, and support our Earth and me.

Imagination is reality. We know this. All scientists—whether physicists, biochemists, or psychologists—must use their imagination, otherwise there are no theories with which to work. The world was once thought to be flat; now it is considered to be round and three-dimensional. Time was once precise and digital; now it is relative, bendable, and even non-existent in zero point. The same knowledge shift will occur in the future regarding space. All of space is enfolded within a grain of sand, your heart, and a thought.

Perceptions of reality are interesting. Usually the best we can do is be aware of 0.0001 percent of the actual reality existing in and around us—like our biochemistry, brainwaves, other dimensions, and what's going on around the multiverses. Perceptions are only filters of reality. They change and evolve over time when we are wise and open.

The same goes for knowledge about elves, fairies, and little people. Most people still think they're fiction. Unless you have had consciousness-altering spiritual experiences, you may never meet them. Historically, they were part of ancient Lemuria, Atlantis, and the Druidic, Tibetan, Turtle Island (North American) First Nations, and other post-Atlantean cultures.

In Britain a hundred years ago, Dr. Sir Arthur Conan Doyle, 1859-1930, author of the world-famous series on Sherlock Holmes, was knowledgeable concerning Spirits. He is part of a longstanding Celtic awareness of Spiritualism. Although he was a medical doctor, world-renowned author, and creator of the global archetype of the modern hero Sherlock Holmes—shadow and all—he was disregarded for his photos and knowledge concerning these Earth Spirits.

Since I was a boy playing by the Don River behind my house, making forts in the forest, and hiking and canoeing through Algonquin and other Parks, I have always heard, seen, and felt the presence of these ancient beings.

Within the global First Nations communities, it is a fact that all of them speak of the common heritage and communication with these Spirits and the rock, herb, plant, tree, animal, cloud, and wind Spirit beings. We get medicine, healing, wisdom, guidance, and joy from and with them. From the Mohawk to the Maori, the Aski to the Australian Aborigines, First Nations all know these Spirit beings exist in the fourth dimensional astral realities. Most of our cultures orally pass down the ancient stories concerning how two-legged humans and animal, plant, and tree beings shared the same language and could communicate with one another. When we have open communication and respect again, the world will be a much better place than it is now.

ELEMENTS, ELEMENTALS AND GIANT SPIRIT BEINGS

As a young boy and throughout my life, I have always connected with the four major Elements that the ancient Chinese, Greek, Roman, Arab, and Hindu speak of—air, fire, water, and earth. To this, I add and acknowledge the presence of ether or akasha, wood, and metal. When I became a chemist, biochemist, and microbiologist, I understood that I needed to have a conscious personal Spirit connection with every element of The Periodic Table of Elements—from Hydrogen (atomic number 1) to the densest Ununoctium (atomic number 118), which is the highest atomic number we know. Everything has life, energy, and being—even the atomic elements.

When I speak with and question any or all of the Periodic Table elements, I have a more conscious empowerment over my own internal biochemistry with the molecules that make up this biological body.

Elementals are ancient Earth Spirit Beings who may be millions if not billions of years old. They all exist within our collective unconscious, and now some of them connect within our collective consciousness, like Ramtha and Kryon. Each culture and civilization has its own Elementals. For instance, the Mohawk people have terrorizing and helpful Stone Giants, cannibalistic fearsome Flying Heads, Gahai evil spectral light guides, Gaha soft winds, and Hadui violent winds within their collective story; I wrote about their mythologies in my Ph.D. thesis, Kinship and Culture: A Study of the Kanesatake Mohawk.

Every culture has Giant Elementals—China, Japan, India, Rome, Greece, Sumerians, Assyrians, Jews, First Nations, and more recently Harry Potter, The Lord of the Rings and other cultural mythologies. The archetype of the simple, fearsome, helpful Giant of strong Earth energy is global.

ALL-OUT BATTLES WITH THE DARK SIDE

It was during my years of 26 to 29 while I was undergoing Jungian Dream Analysis, my own art therapy, learning to paint with the Masters, and taking daily hikes along the Bruce Trail, that I was constantly aware of the inner and outer presence of all the Dark Forces. It seems my mission has always been to understand them, to deliberate and debate with them, and to try to turn them back to the Light and Source. Some will and do while some will not. I refer to Lucifer-Satan, Ahriman, Mabus, Sorat, the dark demons and minions who are their helpers, along with Lilith, goblins, witches, werewolves, vampires, and ancestral evil collective spirits.

You might say this is in my imagination and you would be right. My intuitive sensors always feel when the Dark Side comes calling. It is not just in my head though; I feel the presences coming towards me from outside. I create an energetic powerful Light Circle around myself in all dimensions.

I have a longstanding agreement with all the Dark Forces, which I have instituted since I was two years of age. If and when any Dark Force tries to drain, capture, disable, or kill me, I do one thing. I always bless them with the much greater power of the Love of the Light from which any dark force must shrink. Then when I send them away packing, I tell them, "If you should come back again, only one thing will happen to you. I will send so much light and love into you, and have Jesus and the other Light Beings take you all the way back to Source to be rehabilitated. So it's your choice. I have told you what will happen. If you want the Light, I will send you there, either now or later when I see you again. If you don't want the Light yet, then you must stay away from me."

Between the ages of 26 to 29, this occurred on a daily basis. I multitasked throughout my days by sending demons into the Light while trying to focus on my artwork, piano playing, dream analysis, or hiking in the woods. My piano, ah yes, I bought a second-hand 1911 Heintzman Upright Grand in 1976, which is my favourite object of joy. I play it to this day, almost daily. I compose songs with Spirit for my friends, human and otherwise.

ENERGY STEALERS

Since Frankenstein and Dracula came on the scene in 1818 and 1897, respectively, we have witnessed a plethora of stories, movies, TV films, and shows on the topic of shadow creatures that need redemption and bring us redemption. This includes Beauty and the Beast, The Hunchback of Notre Dame, and so many others. Vampires, werewolves, and zombies are all the rage now. And rage they do—our hidden inner vampires, were-wolves, and zombies. Our inner vampire is the part that cannot find our own centre and energy source, so we suck power and energy, steal it, drink it, take it, and remove it from our willing or unwilling victims. Of course, our own inner vampire steals energy from our own Spirit, soul, mind, and emotions, until there is hardly any energy for living. That is when we become zombies. And most of us on the planet at this time are zombies—the walking dead.

Werewolves are gaining popularity now. The werewolf is the hidden unconscious inner teacher part of us. Wolf is teacher medicine. When we debase, ignore, and repress our wolf instincts, bodily needs, sexuality, sensuality, power, and truth, we become a werewolf, paradoxically becoming less human, more predatory, and more chained to our hidden inner full-moon feelings and emotions. When we deny our inner wolf nature, we become zombies.

Wolves are beautiful, and our fear and murdering of them is really our projection and fear of teaching and owning our own lessons in life. We need to become responsible for mistreating others and ourselves, and embrace our hidden instincts and animal natures within our higher humanity and divinity.

Collective ancestral evil spirits abound on every continent. These are not individual ghosts; these are the repressed collective unlived yearnings that have gone sour. They angrily live in our ethnic and global conscious and unconscious stories and actions, anxiously seeking revenge, human sacrifice, and death as atonement for being abused and thrust aside in our modern world. They started all the wars we have known. They are attached to and live in the lower fourth dimensional spaces and places. They are historical and timeless. They are responsible for murders, depression, suicide, hatred, and war.

Some of the best examples of this are the wars of the Vikings, Greeks, Romans, Chinese, Hindus, Germans, Mayans, and so many other societies. There may be a few exceptions—perhaps the Balinese and certain other Lemurian-based cultures.

I have felt these force fields while travelling through various places. I certainly feel them in Europe after all the centuries of wars there. Can they be transformed? Perhaps, once we all collectively agree to transform our own personal and group shadow thoughts, emotions, and actions towards one another and ourselves. We are moving back towards the next Golden Age, one person at a time.

Remember, as Babaji says, "There is more power in one person opening their heart to light and love, and transforming their past dark karmas, than all the atom bombs stored on the planet going off at the same time."

GHOSTS

Ghosts are another story. Every hospital, old house, graveyard, accident spot, funeral parlour, and crematorium has numerous ghosts. So do all the places where battles and wars have been fought and where people died. These are easy to work with. These ghosts typically mean no harm. They are seemingly dazed and confused, which happens when people die suddenly by accident or murder. I have spent my life helping these poor lost souls. I call upon Jesus and use the words, "the Name and Blood of Jesus Christ," I ask for the relatives and Spirit guides of these ghosts to come and fetch them, and I wait for them to arrive. I often use a candle or flashlight and a bell (because hearing is the greatest of the senses other than smell in the lower astral worlds.)

I intend and support the soul to release itself from its prison and go into the Light. As long as the ghost is willing, they always go into the light unless they have heavy karma to work on first. If so, then they are taken to a realm or planet where this can be accomplished. Several star systems have Christ Healing Temples for this, in particular, Altair, Arcturus, Alpha Centauri, Sirius B, and Sirius C. I astrally watch them while they go on their journey and confirm they make it through the veil into the fifth dimension.

WESTERN ASTROLOGY

My psychological training was balanced and anchored with a lifetime of learning Western Astrology. I took many classes with well-known Canadian Astrologers. I learned to use Natal Birth Charts to diagnose individual issues, complexes, possibilities, and karmas. Transit Charts delineate from the present for the next two or so years what issues and bad habits need to be faced. I learned that people experience illness, trauma, and life challenges at the age they are now based on illnesses and karmas in a past life at the same age. This is particularly true with unresolved fears from past lives that continuously resurface at the same age in this life as they did in a past life. So in their present existence, they have a golden opportunity to transform karma this time around in their cycle of rebirth.

I learned much about how I could better myself every day. Astrology, as any Buddhist or Hindu will tell you, is a necessary foundation for personal evolution and collective progress.

VEDIC OR HINDU ASTROLOGY – JYOTISH

Dr. Robert Svoboda and Hart de Fouw have been exceptional teachers for learning Jyotish. I learned how to read present, past, and future lives, and the karmic imperative for each soul. This proved to be invaluable for my future clinical and research work.

VEDIC PALMISTRY – HASTA-SAMUDRIKA

Hart de Fouw taught me Vedic Palmistry or Hasta-Samudrika over a period of 15 years. There is so much to learn about the life-, heart-, and head-lines. The left hand reveals past lives and the right hand the present life. I enjoyed reading the karmas of babies and telling parents of their child's future. I was astonished to see how quickly palm lines change when one does one's inner work.

VEDIC OR HINDU FACE READING – MUKH-SAMUDRIK

Something that life teaches me is to read faces, and we study this in anthropology as well. When I want to see what someone thinks of themselves and how they present their personae or masks to the world, I study their right eye. When I search for what they are hiding from themselves and others, I gaze into their left eye. One can always tell whether or not someone is clear, kind, and a truth-teller by watching their left eye. The eyes always tell the truth; they are the windows to the soul.

BODY READING – KAPAL-SAMUDRIK

In the Hindu tradition as well as in anthropology, we study non-verbal communication (NVC) as a way to understand an individual's personality, emotional state, body armour, and energy flow. I use this to assess and intuit people more carefully by observing every movement and tightening of body posture.

VAASTU SHASTRA VIDYA

I still utilize this 5,000 year-old science and art of the spiritual scientific use of space by humans. In my home, office, and garden I found I was more peaceful, relaxed, balanced, and harmonious when I organized colours, furniture, paintings, plants, and other objects to create a flow according to this valuable tradition.

WITH MILAREPA, TIBET'S GREATEST YOGI

One of my Hindu teachers told me something I intuited since I was a child—that I was the primary student of Milarepa, Tibet's Greatest Yogi. Milarepa, who is an incarnation of Babaji Nagaraj, was a wonderful sorcerer in pre-Buddhist animist Tibet, a culture directly descended from late Atlantis.

Marpa Lotsawa "The Translator" brought Buddhism from India to Tibet in the 11th century CE. He is considered to be the father of Tibetan Vajrayana Buddhism. Milarepa was his first convert. Previously, Milarepa gained great dark powers and could kill a whole village of people with one thought. He did this once because when his father died, his uncle stole the wealth of the entire family and left Milarepa and his mother destitute. His mother had asked him to study sorcery, which he mastered. When he found the Clear Light spoken of by Buddha, he transformed those powers 180 degrees into the power of love, patience, meditation, kindness, and charity. There are many great books by and about Milarepa. He is truly one of Earth's greatest treasured lives.

Throughout my life, especially in my training in world spiritual traditions and rituals in anthropology, Milarepa has been a constant teacher and companion. He is one of my very closest friends with whom I converse daily.

WITH VIVEKANANDA, 1863-1902

When I was very young, Swami Vivekananda always shared his God-centered wisdom in my heart. I heard his strong sweet voice. He seemed so familiar. I was with him on my way into my birth, and I recall sitting on the living room floor at ages three and four, listening to his soothing voice.

As a young man, Vivekananda travelled the length and breadth of India on foot, searching for just one teacher who actually knew God. Apparently, as today, they were few and far between. Eventually he found his guru, Ramakrishna. They became divinely in love with one another for the remainder of their lives and beyond in Spirit.

Vivekananda obtained a degree in Western Philosophy at the Scottish Church College in Calcutta at the age of 21. My Hindu teachers in this life told me that I was a student and colleague of Vivekananda's when we were with Ramakrishna and Sharada Devi, Ramakrishna's consort. This explains why I consistently had dreams, visitations and conversations with Vivekananda throughout my life. Many of the great choices I made in my life were made during talks with Vivekananda, particularly on becoming an anthropologist, which Vivekananda said he would become in his next incarnation.

Vivekananda's incisive, monumental mind and voice is so unique. He was the first Hindu to come to America; in 1893 he spoke at The Parliament of the World's Religions in Chicago. I love to listen to the audio version of this; it always stirs my heart with the hope for humanity and consistently brings me to tears through its majesty, truth, and wisdom.

Here is the full text of his speech, for which he was given the only standing ovation at the beginning of his presentation!

"It fills my heart with joy unspeakable to rise in response to the warm and cordial welcome which you have given us. I thank you in the name of the most ancient order of monks in the world; I thank you in the name of the mother of religions; and I thank you in the name of the millions and millions of Hindu people of all classes and sects. My thanks, also, to some of the speakers on this platform who, referring to the delegates from the Orient, have told you that these men from far-off nations may well claim the honor of bearing to different lands the idea of toleration. I am proud to belong to a religion which has taught the world both tolerance and universal acceptance. We believe not only in universal toleration, but we accept all religions as true. I am proud to belong to a nation which has sheltered the persecuted and the refugees of all religions and all nations of the earth. I am proud to tell you that we have gathered in our bosom the purest remnant of the Israelites, who came to the southern India and took refuge with us in the very year in which their holy temple was shattered to pieces by Roman tyranny. I am proud to belong to the religion which has sheltered and is still fostering the remnant of the grand Zoroastrian nation. I will quote to you, brethren, a few lines from a hymn which I remember to have repeated from my earliest boyhood, which is every day repeated by millions of human beings: As the different streams having there sources in different places all mingle their water in the sea, so, O Lord, the different paths which men take through different tendencies, various though they appear, crooked or straight, all lead to thee.

The present convention, which is one of the most august assemblies ever held, is in itself a vindication, a declaration to the world, of the wonderful doctrine preached in the Gita:

Whosoever comes to Me, through whatsoever form, I reach him; all men are struggling through paths which in the end lead to me.

Sectarianism, bigotry, and its horrible descendant, fanaticism, have long possessed this beautiful earth. They have filled the earth with violence, drenched it often and often with human blood, destroyed civilization, and sent whole nations to despair. Had it not been for these horrible demons, human society would be far more advanced than it is now. But their time is come; and I fervently hope that the bell that tolled this morning in honor of this convention may be the death-knell of all fanaticism, of all persecutions with the sword or with the pen, and of all uncharitable feelings between persons wending their way to the same goal."

CHAPTER 8
BACK TO UNIVERSITY, 28-38 YEARS

FINISHING MY FIRST JUNGIAN THERAPY

I worked with Fraser Boa for at least three years and was at the point of descending into my No-Self space inside. Fraser and I decided to amicably part ways.

THE KUNG BUSHMAN SHAMAN APPEARS

Luckily for me, I have listened to my dreams since I was a child. Most if not all my major life decisions have come from dreams and direct visitations. One night in early May 1978, I had a sharp twist of direction in my life based on a compelling visitation I had. At one point in my dream, I felt myself flying south across the African continent at nighttime with gleaming stars overhead. I suddenly felt pulled down to Earth and found myself sitting cross-legged beside an outdoor blazing fire in the middle of a mysterious black night. There was nobody around. Who had made the fire? Suddenly the body of a small, ancient, wiry Kung Bushman shaman appeared on the other side of this fire. He was knowingly glinting at me. Shocked, I just sat there waiting to see what he would do. With no warning, he thrust his arm through the fire's flames and pointed his right hand at my face, just inches away. In simple English with a direct command, he confided, "You must become an anthropologist!" Looking back, I feel it was likely one of Babaji's fun tricks to surprise me.

I was so startled by him and his non-burning body that I awoke with astonishment.

"Anthropology?" I muttered. "Why that?" I fell back asleep.

When I awoke the next morning, still feeling the power of the dream, I went to the phone book and dialed the University of Toronto Graduate Anthropology Department. I told the surprised Chairman that I had a dream last night of becoming an anthropologist. He did not find this too strange, and invited me down three days later for an interview.

At the interview, he went over my undergrad transcripts. I had only taken half of a course in Anthropology in Native Studies.

"You will need to do a make-up year to get into Grad School," he suggested. I enrolled on the spot. I did five courses in social-cultural anthropology.

TRAINING AS A SOCIAL-CULTURAL ANTHROPOLOGIST

After my make-up year, the next year I commenced my M.A. classes and requirements, and a whole new life emerged. Curiosity was the main reason why I went back to higher education. Wanting to be a universal synthesizer in a time of increasing specialization, anthropology is the one science that covers physical, chemical, psychological, social, political, linguistic, historical, archeological, and biological sciences. I learned enough of all these to piece together the puzzle of human existence on this planet. My mystical side gave me the direct intuitive knowing and the spiritual framework and overview; my scientific side gave me the data.

The second reason I entered anthropology focuses around my unusual life story. I knew that if people and humanity were to seriously accept me, I would need to appear credible and intelligent.

Thirdly, I came back to our Earth in a time of Great Upheaval. This is an era of Great Turning. We are in a devolving consciousness based on overwhelming materialist reductionism in thinking, society, and economics. By doing my due diligence in terms of academic research, I wanted to be able to refute anyone's ridiculous one-sided minimalist blinkered perceptions.

I was thirsty for everything. I read tens of thousands of academic books, reviews, articles, life stories, and biographies. My specialties in social-cultural anthropology became ancient and modern cross-cultural medical traditions, non-Western psychology, kinship patterns, ethnic family studies, First Nations studies, world shamanism, world religions and mythologies, and human sexuality, in particular homosexuality in bands, tribes, chiefdoms, and state societies. I found there was a lot of material concerning male-male bonding rituals, friendships, gay shamans, and gender options not yet available as lifestyles in the Western world. Some First Nations cultures have five socially accepted genders. In some cultures, androgynous gay males who are the medicine men and shamans are held in the highest regard in their community roles.

TEACHING ANTHROPOLOGY
AT THE UNIVERSITY OF TORONTO

My Level One Comprehensive exams on social organizational theories allowed me to understand how groups of people have come together over the history of hundreds of thousands of years. Anthropology gave me the timeline I needed to think about our Earthly human evolution. Finding out about other tribal realities and living these from the inside also gave me a non-Western experience to view my own Canadian socialization and upbringing with greater conscious and emotional detachment.

My ethnological fieldwork with the Mohawks and the Dogrib of the Northwest Territories over the years allowed me to escape the box of Western socialization with which I had been brought up. Being an anthropologist allows me to simultaneously be subjective and objective. Thinking as a participant in another language and culture allows me to be an insider. Watching as an observer makes me an outsider that can see the larger picture. This growing personal capacity allows me to start viewing other cultures, religions, peoples, and history in remarkable and highly insightful ways.

Some of the courses I taught were Introductory Anthropology, Native Studies, Kinship Marriage and the Family, and Sex Roles and Gender Identity. I gave graduate seminars on Psychological Anthropology, Medical Anthropology, and Spirituality and Anthropology.

RESEARCH FOR MY PH.D. THESIS

In May of 1980, I completed my M.A. degree, and carried on with my passion—Jungian Psychology. My thesis, which was agreed upon by my Thesis Committee, was "Jung, Archetypes, The Collective Unconscious, Anthropology, World History, and the Evolution of Societies." I wrote and published chapters as articles in our Graduate Journal. These included the psychological aspects of magnetic archetypes that have ruled individuals and societies since the dawn of time on Earth. I related how certain dominant symbols were key underpinnings of families, ethnic groups, religions, cosmologies, mythologies, rites of passage, medicines, and socio-political governance.

I dreamed of so many of these mythologies and archetypal symbols throughout my life. Now I was able to place them on a timeline stretching back 2 million years across all cultures. As I researched this, I was astonished to find similarities in the patterns of stories and histories about good and evil, light and dark, masculine and feminine, spirituality and sexuality, birth and death, and right and left. Most importantly, I wanted to uncover how people and cultures transform themselves through time and how we evolve and devolve in certain cyclical patterns. My understanding of philosophy of history changed from being a straight line to being a spiraling open circle with directional movement on an overall evolutionary timeline.

I finished all the chapters for my thesis. Committee members read these and agreed to them. Now, in retrospect, I suppose they never even read them. For when I went for the final approval, they out-and-out rejected the thesis as a worthy topic.

My supervisor said, "If you want to redo your entire thesis about Freud, we will accept it; Jung is just a mystic, not a scientist. We cannot accept your thesis."

This was cutting too close to the bone. Initially, I took it as a rejection of myself. However relevant Freud is—particularly with regard to identifying the id, ego, and life and death wishes—I was not interested. I taught the graduate students and faculty courses on Freud, so perhaps they thought I would be interested in doing my thesis on him. I absolutely was not. So I switched my thesis entirely to ethnography of the Mohawk village of Kanehsatake, Oka, Quebec, where I did research since the early 1970s.

HUMAN SEXUALITY AND THE UNIVERSITY OF GUELPH

Because I was still concerned with my own internalized homophobia and how to feel better about myself, I focused on sexuality across cultures and homosexuality in particular. This led me to find courses on human sexuality. I went to the Annual Guelph Conference on Human Sexuality. I met many great colleagues there. Several wonderful things came out of this. Sue Johanson, a Canadian writer, public speaker, and sex educator, periodically invited me on her live radio show, "Talking Sex with Sue."

Here we explored the hidden dimensions and attributes of living one's true sexual nature.

From 1980 – 1986, I took classes in The University of Guelph's Family Studies Department, receiving a M.A. Graduate Certificate as a Marriage and Family Therapist in 1986. I did over 10,000 hours of supervised clinical work with married couples and families there, which were usually videotaped. I became a Clinical member of the American Association for Marriage and Family Therapy (AAMFT), and the Ontario Association for Marriage and Family Therapy (OAMFT).

When Dr. Claude Guldner went on sabbatical for a couple of years in 1986, I taught his courses on Communications Theories, Group and Family Dynamics, Family Theory, Family Patterns and Cultural Change, Changing Gender Identity and Sex Roles, and Multi-Ethnic Canadian Families.

At Guelph University, I developed and taught a new course on Psychological Androgyny. In this class I brought in transvestites, gays, lesbians, bisexuals, and others to share their life stories. I recall one extraordinarily handsome and buffed 6'4" young Italian stud who was a football and soccer star. He was 26 years old and underwent sex change surgery and hormone treatments, for he had always felt he was a woman. All heads turned when he entered wearing a slinky red dress, high heels, perfect makeup, and beautiful long wavy black hair. He was gorgeous as a woman as well. It is stories like these that make the difference for equality, human rights, and evolving human social values and justice.

At this time, I was also asked to teach courses on Human Sexuality at Humber College in Toronto. The students here had only a passing interest in finding out more about themselves. So I was not as excited about teaching there as I was at Guelph University with the students there for whom I felt great affection.

JUNGIAN ANALYSIS WITH MARION WOODMAN

When I was 29 years of age, I moved back to Toronto and looked for a place to stay. My great friend, Michael Parke-Taylor, a retired curator at the Art Gallery of Ontario, told me about a room to rent in student housing with a friend of his, Tom Robson.

"You'll just love him," Michael said to me about Tom. And I did. I felt an instant attraction, mutual heart connection, and similar artistic interests. Tom was a 6'3" Welsh hunk who was training in architecture and landscape architecture.

So I moved into 22 D'Arcy Street in Chinatown. During this time, I really struggled with being gay, and my attractions for Tom exacerbated my inner conflict. Back then it was not as easy being out. For most young men today it is still a real struggle that often challenges gay men with deep depression and even to the verge of suicide. I felt this self-loathing and lack of self-acceptance. I needed a full-time friendship, and I needed to inwardly accept myself as being gay.

My first Jungian analyst was not accepting of my need to talk about my homosexuality. I went to see his sister Marion Woodman with whom I analyzed for almost three years. She asserted that I simply needed to be myself. So I really came out and Tom and I started a deepening loyal friendship.

MY RELATIONSHIP WITH TOM ROBSON, 1979-1985

Life has a way and a flow when I trust synchronicities. Tom and I were meant to be together from the start. He said that when he was very young, he knew he would end up his life living with a man he loved.

Tom's sister lived in the rental house with us. Most evenings, we had friends over for dinner and afterwards stacked all the living room and dining room furniture in the hall or on the front porch. Then we would happily dance to Motown music till midnight. And then go to class the next day. Tom "could dance as good as he walked."

There is much to say about our relationship together; it was extremely healing for me. I grew in leaps and bounds. Eventually, Tom and I bought a house together on 43 Marchmount Road in Toronto. A year after we moved in, Tom died. His diagnosis was an unknown adrenal cancer that had been untreated for years.

We spent great holidays canoeing and portaging in many of Ontario's Provincial Parks. As a harbinger of things to come, on one of our canoe trips to Lake Superior Provincial Park, I was stung by over 50 wasps while packing along a portage route; I inadvertently stepped into their sand bank nest. At the time I recovered quite easily and carried on. A month later in our backyard vegetable garden on D'Arcy Street, a wasp stung me between my toes, and I immediately went into anaphylactic shock. I did not have an EpiPen so Tom hastily called the ambulance. I was already dead and gone. My heart stopped beating. I recall my soul consciousness leaving the body, the planet, and travelling quickly off into the vast darkness of space. I was many thousands of kilometers away. I thought to myself, "Things are just getting good in my life… finally! I cannot die now. I refuse to die. I want to live with Tom."

This was my second Near-Death Experience. I moved so fast and so far away from Earth that it took me all the vast powerhouse of my will to stop myself from leaving, turn around, and head back towards Earth and my physical form. I wasn't sure that I had the mental strength to do this. I knew I was already dead. Back on Earth, just as the ambulance was pulling up, I forced myself back into my body. Coming back in with a thump, I groaned and struggled to open my eyes. Seeing Tom bend over me was all the inspiration I needed, for there was so much love and concern in his eyes. I declined the paddles of the emergency team, and within a month Tom and I were again using paddles of a wooden, non-electrical variety in the lakes of Ontario.

Death came to me and I beat it back. Tom was on his own journey and was unable to do the same. During these canoe trips of 1983 and 1984, it was evident that Tom's body was stressed. He lost weight, had to take water pills, and became more tired as time went on.

There are always moments from Spirit that foretell and inform us of what is pending. I remember driving down our Marchmount Road one evening; I was going to teach a course at Erindale College, University of Toronto. As I turned left at the corner, I noticed a man walking by who appeared to me as an ethereal ghost. Only farther down the road did I realize that man was Tom. His spirit was preparing to leave the physical.

Grieving is such a long spiritual, psychological, emotive, and biological process. If I did not work with Dr. Elisabeth Kubler-Ross in 1974 in Montreal, I would have had a harder time with Tom's death. I was his primary caregiver for at least a year. I gave him medication, needles, and tended to him in and out of hospital.

What I learned about my family members is very memorable. My mother, who liked Tom, left a message that she was sad about his death. My most shocking experience of Tom's funeral was when my brother approached me at the end of the service. In a matter-of-fact manner, he offered a brief platitude, and then callously asked me if I would loan him all the death insurance money I received. He whined that he needed at least $20,000 to put a new fieldstone fireplace in his Muskoka island cottage. I was so appalled at his uncouth, unfeeling rudeness that I uncharacteristically blurted out, "F…you!"

My brother's wife then angrily retorted, "Don't talk to your brother like that!" I rejoined with yet another expletive.

As Jesus says, "You can never trust your family members; so leave your family and follow me."

What I learned from Tom's death was remarkable. First, that no matter how hard you pray, if someone's time is up, then you must let them go and just keep loving them while they move higher into Spirit on their own soul journey. Don't keep them Earthbound. Second I realized that, because I received so little human love, tender holding, and comfort as a child, I was unconsciously projecting my needs through cloying attachments with Tom. When he died, I felt the loss so deeply that I was a basket case for at least four months. I was inconsolable. Going through my grieving helped me mature psychologically and find my own emotional bearings. I learned to receive more healing energy and superconsciousness from Spirit. Here was another gift, just as everything that happens in life can be experienced as learning. After Tom's death, I once again fully reopened up all the doorways and gateways to Spirit. I spent ample time travelling into every galaxy of our multiverse and reacquainted myself with great Love Beings there. Lastly and not least, I found that I could connect and relate to my need to be with myself and to be authentic and intimate with others. I treasured the caring friendships I already had much more.

My primary grace in losing Tom in the physical allowed me to focus on my own perfect connections with Spirit. His death ripped away all the veils between my daily consciousness and the highest Spirit worlds. Jesus, Yogananda, and Vivekananda were particularly tender with me. It was Vivekananda who reminded me about the microcosm and the macrocosm. After this, when looking up at all the stars in our Milky

Way Galaxy and the bazillions of galaxies beyond, there was zero-space and zero-time. There was a special moment when I astonishingly started experiencing all the universe-multiverse inside my own skin again—once and for all. As it was in the beginning, it was for me again. For me, there is no going outside to astral travel; my spiritual-emotional heart is the one portal that takes me anywhere across the multiverse in an instant! The speed of love is much faster than the speed of light.

I grieved profoundly and profusely when Tom died. When you lose a partner to death in mid-life in your mid-thirties, it destroys all your hopes, dreams, and plans. Although I allowed myself months and mountains of tears and biological grieving, the pain was so great. I unwisely took on extra teaching work. I taught full-time in anthropology at The University of Toronto, and started teaching full-time in psychology and family studies at The University of Guelph, while I tried to complete my second Ph.D. thesis on the Mohawk of Kanehsatake.

In 1985, I planned that Christmas to go alone to Varadero, Cuba for a holiday. Tom and I spent a great holiday there a few years earlier. I was marking my student's mid-term exams in mid-December at Guelph University and suddenly got Bell's Palsy on the left side of my face, the feminine and soul side. I went to my doctor and she said I should still go to Cuba and try to rest.

When you have Bell's Palsy, the nerves on one side of your face are immobilized and dying. I could not close my left eye. I could not speak out of the left side of my mouth. All my words were slurred and people had a challenge understanding me. My time in Cuba was absolutely horrible. The only blessing was that I found a local female doctor who gave me daily injections of vitamin B12. This at least helped the nerves to stay somewhat alive and hopefully eventually regenerate.

I returned to Toronto after my week in Cuba. In Toronto, I sought out a Chinese acupuncturist who gave me electro-acupuncture three times a week for a year and a half. Finally my speech was back, and my nerves healing. The pain of Bell's Palsy is excruciating. This suffering sent me deeper into myself, my mystical path, and my inner path of soul evolution.

INTERNATIONAL ASSOCIATION
FOR THE STUDY OF DREAMS, IASD

Because of my great and enduring primary interest in dreams, visions, visitations, the unconscious, and the superconscious throughout my life, I became involved in the International Association for the Study of Dreams (IASD). After Tom's death, I wrote an article on "Bear and Great Mother Symbolism of Upcoming Death" based on Tom's dreams. Poring through anthropological, shamanic, world mythology, and spiritual studies, I wrote an extensive 80-page paper using dreams of the dying to find meaning in dying and foretell death through Bear and Great Mother symbolism.

I was asked to give this paper at the 1986 ASD Conference in Ottawa. Giving this paper was a resonant relief for the grief I was feeling about missing Tom.

In the fall of 1986, I was asked to be the interim Editor of the ASD Journal. However, I was so swamped with my teaching at The Universities of Toronto, Guelph, and The Ontario College of Art, that I only took this on for eight months.

ROBERT MONROE AND HEMI-SYNC

Present at the Ottawa ASD Conference was Robert Monroe, author of Journeys Out of the Body (1971) and Far Journeys (1985). Ultimate Journey came out in 1994. In recognition of my own psychic and astral "Far Journeys" throughout my life, I labeled my first artistic productions company, along with the accompanying music, Far Journeys.

Robert and I delivered our papers the same day at this ASD Conference, and he and I became close friends. So much so that I went to visit him at The Monroe Institute in Virginia several times, doubling up this visit with my call on members of The A.R.E. as well—the Association for Research and Enlightenment, started by Edgar Cayce.

Through his own journeys out of the body, Robert is the founder of the binaural or "bilateral brain wave synchronization" of Hemi-Sync or "hemispherical synchronization." This is a patented audio technology claiming to facilitate enhanced mental performance, astral travel, and altered states of consciousness. By wearing headsets with alpha and theta brain waves alternating between the left and right ears, one quickly goes into a deep trance. I have used these tapes for many years and to great effect!

Robert was a visionary seer and leader of the unifying science of spiritual medicine, biochemistry, physics, psychiatry, and electrical engineering. I miss him and speak with him now and then in the Spirit world.

ASSOCIATION FOR RESEARCH AND ENLIGHTENMENT, A.R.E.

I have always been attracted to the life and abilities of Edgar Cayce, in particular his ability to give medical readings to so many thousands of clients, even when they were not physically present. My development in my clinical work as a medical intuitive was greatly enhanced by his thoughts and by the books his family and A.R.E. researchers published.

Cayce's interests match mine to a great degree, in particular Dreams and Dream Interpretation, ESP and Psychic Phenomena, Health-Related Information, Oneness, Philosophy and Reincarnation, and mostly Spiritual Growth.

SIECCAN, THE SEX INFORMATION AND EDUCATION COUNCIL OF CANADA

SIECCAN is a national registered charitable organization founded in 1964 to foster professional education and public knowledge about sexuality and sexual health. SIECCAN works with health professionals, educators, and community organizations to ensure that all Canadians have access to high quality sexual health information, education, and related health and social services. Members include sex therapists, professors, teachers, social workers, psychologists, psychiatrists, psychotherapists, and frontline care workers on the streets and in walk-in clinics.

I trained as a Marriage and Family Therapist, and Sex Therapist at The University of Guelph in the early 1980s, and I became friends with most of the members of SIECCAN. They are a wonderful group of human souls supporting the professionals and general public to learn more about sexual health and open-minded attitudes and values. I wrote articles for the SIECCAN Journal, the topics included AIDS, gay lifestyles, transgendered people, and bisexuality. In 1983, I was asked to be the interim Chair and take on the duties of publishing the twice-a-year Newsletter and handling the library. This I did, until 1986, when I moved out of the house that Tom and I bought.

STUDIES OF WORLD SPIRITUAL TRADITIONS, MYSTICISM, RELIGIONS, MYTHOLOGY, WITCHCRAFT

While I did my Graduate Studies at The University of Toronto from 1979 onwards, I also enrolled in the Graduate Department of Religious Studies on the 14th Floor of the Robarts Library. This was one of the greatest experiences of my life. I had a carrel on the 13th floor to which I carted crate loads of books from all over the world. I spent my lunch buried in my little closet memorizing texts from animism, shamanism, the Vedas, Upanishads, the Qur'an, Sufi love poetry, Zen Buddhism, Vajrayana Buddhism, ancient Egyptian books, Zoroastianism, and every religion known to humankind. These were actual ritual texts, as well as historical, theological and philosophical ones. Some of my courses were Judaeo-Christian exegesis, ontology, epistemology, and liturgies.

Within world religious and mystical cosmologies, there are often teleological truths and theories. Being fully mystic and a scientist, my personal task was to integrate my own daily experiences from before birth and throughout my life with the knowledge cultures had gathered over millennia.

I sat in my carrel and absorbed the energies of the mystics and religious specialists and felt their presences in my heart and soul consciousness. Once in a while, I looked up and gazed out the tall, narrow vertical window at Toronto Island and Lake Kanadario (now loosely translated from the original 8,000-year-old Mohawk tradition as "Ontario") beyond.

During this period, I engaged privately in ritual ceremonies, prayers, journeys, and conversations with Ancient Beings in all these traditions. Being an anthropologist allowed me to cross my wires between traditions, as Joseph Campbell used to say. These experiences were intense, original, and highly informative.

MY SUFI FRIENDS

I had years in which I read Sufi prayers and sacred poetry from Rumi, Hafiz, Attar, Al-Ghazali, Kabir, Ibn Arabi, Idries Shah, and others. I did zikr and created my own khanaghah.

I bought the collected works of Sufi Masters Hazrat Inayat Khan (1882-1927) and those of his son, Pir Valayat Khan (1916-2004). I learned much about the algorithmic fractals and mathematical theories of the universe, the solar system, music, and human consciousness from these gentlemen.

In Graduate Religious Studies there were professors of Chinese Buddhism, Zen Buddhism, Cambodian Buddhism, and Jewish Mysticism. I am so grateful for our many conversations. They pointed me in the directions that lifted my soul. I attended various Buddhist temples, Tibetan circles, Sufi circles, Zen sitting, and spiritual study groups.

DEEPER CONNECTIONS WITH CARL JUNG

Being back in Toronto was good for me in that I was closer to The Quaker House and OISE where The Jung Society of Ontario held its monthly meetings. Between 1978 and 1986, I spent a lot of time with other Jungians. I went to several workshops with Joseph Campbell, James Hillman, and dozens of other Jungian analysts who came. For the third time, I reread Jung's Collected Works, this time through the eyes of my deep personal experiences of three Jungian Analyses.

On a more personal level, I began dreaming of Jung and speaking with him more often during the daytime. He directed me to various pages in his works that were pertinent for my growth and evolution. I continued to write down my dreams and worked on my Ph.D. thesis on Jung, Archetypes, and Historical Cultural Symbolism.

Jung and I often connected about his past lives and the various times that he and I had been together over the centuries. This truly helped me understand why and what he brought to the world between 1875 and 1961. His previous lives led up to his life as Jung. I will write a book with Jung about his past lives and share what he wants the world to know.

As I continue, you will read about how a series of visitations from Jung at a time of great crisis changed the course of my life forever.

In 1982, I met another young gay man from Quebec who was starting to train at the Jung Institut in Zurich, Switzerland. I knew I needed to go to Zurich myself, although not to train as an analyst. I felt I already knew the inner workings of Jung's mind and soul, and my training as a psychotherapist and marriage and family therapist gave me enough confidence to not need to become a Jungian analyst.

In the spring and summer of 1983 I flew to Zurich and stayed with my friend in the pleasant countryside 20 kilometers away, and attended daily lectures and colloquia. Luckily I prepared by studying German and Dutch languages for two years at The University of Toronto to enable me to read Jung's original texts in German. I searched for materials from Jung on family and ethnic complexes, archetypes, symbols and human evolution over time. This was for the first Ph.D. thesis that my academic committee had disallowed, and which I fully intended to complete on my own terms. Precious little material was available in Jung's unpublished archives on these topics. Eventually, my direct communications with Carl were what stimulated our opportunity for me to write concerning these essential aspects of human nature.

While there, I studied with Mario Jacoby and others whom I got to know somewhat. There was a text in German by a German analyst on male homosexuality, projections, and bonding. I bought and read it. Eventually I developed my own theory and practice of why male-male gay relationships are most important spiritually, emotionally, and physically for soul evolution to take place. Jung himself has written on this topic, and esteems male psychological and spiritual growth through gay male bonding. This extended paper has yet to be published; it was a Master's thesis at Guelph University for my Marriage and Family Therapy Certificate and clinical recognition and registration.

AYURVEDIC TRAINING WITH DR. VASANT LAD

In the late 1970s, through my periods of great mental and emotional challenge, I received Pancha Karma treatments at the Maharishi's TM or Transcendental Meditation Retreat Center in Huntsville, Ontario. Although I have never been a member of the TM Group, they allowed me to come and do Pancha Karma there when I needed. In 1979, I spent two and a half weeks there where I watched 25 videos of Deepak Chopra speaking about Ayurveda. Pancha Karma (five actions) is a cleansing and rejuvenating program for the body, mind, and consciousness. It is known for its beneficial effects on overall health, wellness, and self-healing. The treatments balance one's constitutional doshas: rajas (anger) is subdued, tamas (lethargy, ignorance) is released from its depressive hold, and sattva or the "middle path" is created, which balances and harmonizes spirit, mind, emotions, and body. Stress and the aging processes are reversed. Self-reliance, strength, energy, vitality, and mental clarity are enhanced. Results also include deep relaxation and a boosted immune system.

Through absorbing all this material, as well as from my earlier training in Jyotish, I became fascinated with the 6,000 year-old Hindu medicine of Ayurveda, of which Pancha Karma is only a part. During my reading, I was aware from Spirit that I was an Ayurved many times in past lives.

Starting in 1982, I flew down to The Ayurvedic Institute founded and directed by Dr. Vasant Lad in Albuquerque, New Mexico. They just opened the doors of their Pancha Karma Treatment home for visitors, just around the corner from the center on Menaul Bouevard in north-eastern Albuquerque. I actually was the very first person to stay there and enjoyed several weeks of healing. Between treatments, I went home to rest, meditate, and write my dreams and journals. Pancha Karma is superb for releasing old toxic thoughts, emotions, and bodily obstructions and conditions.

I recall the very first clinical meeting with Dr. Lad. As part of training, other fellow students were invited to stay and listen. Dr. Lad asked if I minded if they were present. I said, "Of course they are welcome." He was dressed in his white medical coat and asked me to take off my shoes and socks, and sit on the side of the medical gurney. Dr. Lad looked at me quizzically and did not say anything. He tested my various wrist pulses. I could tell that he was telepathically and intuitively trying to figure just who I was.

After about three minutes of silence, he muttered, "Old soul... no, very old soul... no, ancient soul... no, very ancient soul... you were around at the beginning of planet Earth."

The students seemed astonished. I was humbled and relieved to be recognized for who I am, and who I was struggling to be consciously at the time. I was 32 years old.

Then he commented, "You have had lung operations and/or replacements."

I quietly corrected him, and said, "Well, actually, it's more my heart… I was born with a large hole in my left ventricle the size of a Canadian silver dollar. I was operated on when I was 8 years of age."

"Oh yes!" he rejoined, "Now I see, as a gift to your mother for giving you birth, you took all her karma into your heart to work it out on her behalf… and some of your father's karma too. This was a considerable gift to them."

As a child, I intuited this knowing. However, I was grateful to hear Dr. Lad say so. He is someone who could see these realities. I was grateful to know that the reasons for my heart birth challenge were true. Having this verified by a man like Dr. Vasant Lad increased my self-confidence and inner strength to carry on, and to understand more clearly how this would continue to affect my life and my goals here on Earth.

THE FOUNDATION FOR SHAMANIC STUDIES

Michael Harner, a fellow anthropologist who was one of the first Western people to study and write about First Nations shamanism, is the originator of The Foundation for Shamanic Studies. Studies commenced in 1979, and I attended many of Michael's workshops in Toronto. His training was excellent because he is the real deal and not a fake or a money-grabber. In 1956 to 1957, Michael studied with the Shuar (Jivaro) tribe of the Ecuadorian Amazon, where he trained as a shaman and got his Ph.D. His quiet, humble way of explaining and training us in ancient South American shamanism helped me to understand that my own previous mystical experiences were similar to the near universal and common practices across hundreds of cultures over tens of thousands of years. His trainings and rituals amplified and corroborated my experiences in reliving my own past lives in various cultures as a shaman in the world—the Three Americas, Lemuria, Atlantis, Druidic Celtic cultures, Tibet, Egypt, China, Siberia, Australia, New Zealand, and many African tribes.

I did the Basic Workshop, Advanced Weekend Workshops of Shamanic Extraction Healing, Dying and Beyond, Divination Training, Nature

Spirits, Shamanic Dreamwork, and Core Soul Retrieval Training. I took all of these from 1981 to 1985 in Toronto.

Michael Harner was one of the first to train others in our ancient Native ways. It has been said that, "What Yogananda did for Hinduism, and Daisetz T. Suzuki did for Zen, Michael Harner has done for shamanism, namely bring the tradition and its richness to Western awareness."

SWEAT LODGES WITH THE NATIVE SPIRITUAL MASTERS

One of my personal goals in this life has been to know about and master all the shamanic rites and rituals of all aboriginal peoples of all times. From 1971 until 2001, I was instructed by Spirit to give sweat lodges, usually on the Full Moon. We fasted for two or three days prior, and did rounds throughout the evening and night until sunrise. These lodges were in three locations in central Ontario. They were designed and built on the Lakota Sioux traditional size and shape.

The most important aspect of these sweat lodges, unlike other traditional lodges, was that they were not just mental, emotional, and physical healing lodges to reduce stress, bring peace, and find biological healing. Because of my personal inclinations and gifts, I brought in the Spiritual Masters to the lodge who spoke and shared healing spiritual energies with the participants.

These are the Native Spiritual Masters who attended from Spirit inside our sweat lodges. I extend the branches of love to them with all great honour, respect, and joy for their love, support and teachings. They are Dekanawideh (the Mohawk Christ, an incarnation of Jesus), Tashunke Witko (Crazy Horse), Tatanka Yotanka (Sitting Bull), Tecumthe (Tecumseh), Dendreah White Buffalo Calf Woman, Goyathlay (Geronimo), Cochise, Victorio, Hinmaton Yalatkit (Chief Joseph), Hehaka Sapa (Black Elk), Pitikwahanapiwiyin (Poundmaker), Isapo-Muxika (Crowfoot) and Ben Calf Robe of the Siksika or Blackfoot First Nation, Dan Taliesva and Thomas Monongye of the Hopi First Nation, and Geswanouth Slahoot (Chief Dan George).

Over the years, many of my friends, students, and psychotherapy clients came for weekends of training in the Medicine Wheel for Friday evening and Saturday, with sweat lodges on the Saturday evening during the night into Sunday morning. I have given over 290 sweat lodges in my lifetime. For some reason, I am able to speak and understand Mohawk and Lakota Sioux languages; so often I conducted the ritual opening prayers, requests for healings, and the ceremonies themselves in these two languages, sometimes with a bit of English. There were often particular lodges lead by certain Animal Medicine Spirits; typically these were the Eagle Spirit, Bear Spirit (I am Mohawk Bear Clan), Turtle Spirit, Wolf Spirit, Hawk Spirit, Otter Spirit, and Snake Spirit.

Over the years, I had the great pleasure of meeting many First Nations spiritual elders and medicine people. With Geezhis Mukwa (Sun Bear) and Wabun Wind, I did three weekend training workshops.

This is one of Sun Bear's prophecies from the 1970s for 2012 and beyond:

"Jesus Christ, in his prophecy, spoke of the end times most succinctly:
There will come a time of tribulation such as the world has never seen before
and will never see again. The sun and moon will not show their light… For
the sake of the few this time will be cut short otherwise no living thing would
survive.
When this shall be, no man will know. Not even the Son, only the Father."

It seems as if there is some psychic block. Even the Christian prophet Edgar Cayce, who made an astonishing number of accurate predictions, could not give a date or time. Jesus warns that no one will know, and that it will come suddenly, "at a time when you least expect it," he said."

Ojshigkwanang (Chief William Commanda), an Algonkian elder, spiritual leader and promoter of the environment, I met at his Kitigan-zibi Anishinabeg First Nation near Maniwaki, Quebec in 2000.

I listened carefully to Chief John Snow (1933–2006) from The Nakoda-Wesley First Nation at the Ecumenical Conference at Morley, Alberta in 1977. It was a wonderful time sleeping in a tipi on the buffalo paddock grasses for two weeks.

I travelled through every Canadian province and territory from coast to coast listening to many other powerful elders. I made several visits to the American Southwest. Here I visited many elders around Turtle Island,

and I am so grateful for these Wisdom-Keepers who passed on their knowledge and Spirit to me. They have all worked tirelessly on behalf of our peoples and All Our Relations. I would also like to mention Ernest Tootoosis from the Poundmaker Reserve in Cutknife, Saskatchewan, and Nick Black of the Dogrib from Fort Rae-Edzo in the Northwest Territories.

In 1972-1973 I spent the better part of six months travelling and sitting at the feet of many great Turtle Island Elders. One of my most revered teachers whom I stayed with in 1977 at the Morley Ecumenical Conference was Albert Lightning, a Cree ceremonialist and medicine person from the Ermineskin band in Hobbema, Alberta. He spoke of natural law and how the truth will always lead people to the Good Red Road of their life. He counseled that we must pay attention to our dreams and develop our spirits and our connections to the Spirit realms, and with those Masters on The Blue Road of Spirit. I remember Albert nodding in approval of Chief John Snow's comments, "Although people think the grandfathers have abandoned us… these spirits have always been with us. It is we who have forgotten about them."

I have always taken these words literally, and this is why our sweat lodges were always populated with scores of welcomed Native Spiritual Masters, the ones mentioned, and hundreds more.

TEACHING AT THE ONTARIO COLLEGE OF ART AND DESIGN, OCAD

The end of my physical earthly relationship with Tom Robson left me in emotional dire straits. When I get in this place, I process my feelings and spirit-mind-body responses through playing the piano, dancing, and painting. In January of 1986, there was an ad in the Toronto Globe and Mail looking for an anthropologist to teach courses in Liberal Arts Studies at The Ontario College of Art and Design for September of 1986. On a whimsical lark, I decided to throw my hat in the ring. They interviewed 13 people. I went in just to have fun meeting the professors. I was shocked when I was called back as one of three to be considered for the position. Unanimously, I got the job. I was overjoyed and daunted at the same time. Although I had been painting and drawing since I was about 11 years old, I never taught art, nor was I professionally trained, except for a few life-drawing classes with the great-granddaughter of Dr. Norman Bethune, the great Canadian doctor who helped Mao Zedong liberate China.

In the months of July and August, I was selected to be on a panel for interviewing possible new students for Year One. They had to write and tell us why they wanted to train in art and bring in their portfolios. I loved interacting with all these new out-of-the-box students. They had tattoos, piercings, hair colourings, and fashionwear that were so very creative and authentic. Black clothing was de rigueur. These young people were fresh, intuitive, open-minded, and in their hearts and bodies—much more than most of my academic students where I taught at The Universities of Toronto and Guelph.

While doing my own deep inner transformational creative process work from 19 years to 36 years, I developed many new techniques using art, music, movement, drumming, voicing, sounding, writing, journaling, and imaginal visioning therapies. They worked for me and I intuited they would work also for the OCAD students.

I devised a curriculum for a three-week, 15-day intensive summer course for 1986 as a segue to my fall classes, called Myths, Dreams, Symbols and Self-Discovery. Every student was required to have a Dream Book in which they wrote down all their dreams. They also had a Personal Symbol and Archetype Book where, in alphabetical order, they wrote down the most powerful symbols speaking to them from their soul, unconscious, and superconscious. They also carried an Unconscious Sketch Book with them everywhere they went, where they were required to scribble, draw, and do automatic writing with their non-dominant hand at least seven times a day. They made hand-made paper and a self-designed book cover for the Book of My Life, which was a timeline of their life story to date.

It was compulsory for each student to do one final painting in whatever media they chose; three masks that we did in class—one each of their personae-ego, shadow, and soul; and their finished Book of My Life. Also obligatory were group projects with seven others in four groups of eight; there were only 32 students allowed in class altogether based on space and the need for intimacy. Groups represented one of the four signs of fire, water, earth, and air. These massive projects were on large parchment rolls 32-40 feet long and eight feet high. They were done and assembled in the atrium of the college for all the OCAD students to witness.

The students were brilliant. I had students ranging from age 15 to 92 years. Some were OCAD graduates from the 1920s and onwards, well-known Canadian painters, jewelers, and sculptors. Some didn't speak any English—we had Japanese, Korean, Spanish, and German students; art and music are the lingua franca for all peoples. The language of art is the language of the heart, which is why I later created a private class called The Creative HeART Space.

Classes always started by arranging tables and chairs in a big circle to ensure equality and face-to-face interactions. I had a piano in my class-room in the far northwest corner of the College. I pulled out all the stops to get people to feel confident, awake, and experimental in their creative processes. When I was in Grade One, a teacher told us to draw a tree. I made my own version of a tree spirit.

She came up and said, "That doesn't look like a tree to me!"

Forever after, I felt ashamed about my seeming incapacity to draw and paint. I know the majority of young children have the very same experience, to which I say, "Listen to your heart and not other's people's criticisms and judgments of yourself and what you create!"

It took all my years of inner mystical, dream, and symbolic archetypal processing to undo this damage and create my own healed, personalized sensibility of what I choose to create.

I commenced each class by going clockwise around the room. Each student stated their first name, why they were in the class, and what they hoped to get out of it. I carefully memorized the first name of every student and developed a beautiful openhearted, supportive relationship with each one. Students always asked to see my own art or slides of my art. I always refused, telling them that I did not want to influence their own unique burgeoning styles. Honestly, part of me was also afraid of incurring criticism. Some Negative Mother complexes are hard to destroy and eradicate.

When we did Experimental Painting from the Unconscious, students wore a cotton blindfold bandana, and only used their non-dominant

hand while standing at their table with the lights off and the room completely dark. Meanwhile, I played carefully selected music to engage their
emotions and I played it extremely loud to purposefully create hypnotic
trance states, from which all true creativity comes. These songs were
typically fast, well-known rhythm and blues, soul, gospel, pop, and rock
tunes to energize their unconscious. I did all this to bypass their mental
ego judgments, visual misperceptions, and activate their kinesthetic core
body energies. We danced, boogied, jigged, swarmed, snaked, laughed,
and cavorted like wild hooligans on our safe, private island. We all loved
it immensely; we were stoked, jacked, and it was definitively awesome
and epic.

Daily, I showed them half-hour videos of Carl Jung's interviews concerning human nature, and Joseph Campbell's The Power of Myth (six
parts) and Transformations of Myth Through Time (13 parts). The
students ravenously took these concepts in and got out of their own
western boxes.

CLOWNING AND NATIVE EARTH PERFORMING ARTS FRIENDS

In the late 1970s, I was involved with the early origins of Native Earth
Performing Arts when they lived and workshopped up in the Beaver
Valley of Ontario, about two kilometers from the farm where I lived.
When I moved to Toronto in 1979, I was involved in the beginnings of
this theatre-music company. Tomson and Rene Highway became friends,
along with Alejandro Ronceria and Raoul Trujillo. Sometimes I brought
to my classes these First Nations musician and drummer friends to sing,
drum, dance, and stir up the Earth Mother and animal Spirits. We had a
ball.

I always locked the double doors of my classroom from inside, because many students, staff, and even the President of OCAD, Timothy
Porteous, wanted to know what all the ruckus and hubbub was about.
Once Timothy came in and thought it was a hullabaloo in the dark when
he saw the students gyrating to loud Native tribal music. Afterwards I
explained the psychological necessity of these processes for true creativity and he accepted my premises.

In 1983, in preparation for the Clown Trickster's Workshop, Ian Wallace, partner of Marc Connors of The Nylons, the Canadian a cappela singing group, asked me to come and channel Archangel Mikael. Ian Wallace, or Nion, is Canada's prime clown and teacher; he is one of the few Alpha Centaurians incarnate on planet Earth. I recall sitting on their studio floor, channeling words of inspiration, directions for productions, and enhancing lightning-like magnetic energies for the group of about 22 people.

RENE HIGHWAY, MY DEAR FRIEND

I spent many years as Rene's good friend, laughing, imagining new productions and sharing his stories about his childhood. When Rene was in Toronto Western Hospital with AIDS complications in October 1990, I spent time there smudging him and doing Snake Medicine healing journeys on the Rainbow Bridge to the Blue Road of Spirit. We once set the fire alarm off when smudging Rene and his room.

When Rene moved to the Hospice, he was blind, deaf, and no longer able to speak because he was in a coma. I used our deep telepathic heart connection to listen to him speak to me on our telepaphone from his big heart, and I translated in words to his brother and friends.

I received a call at 5am on October 19th. Rene was dying and we were going to hold a passing ceremony. I arrived along with Tomson Highway, Micah Barnes, and Marsha Coffey. Close to the moment of dying, I did an eagle feathering ceremony with Rene, brushing his soul energies from his feet to his head seven times. This allowed his soul to leave his body when ready. Telepathically, I told Rene to prepare for departure.

As I finished some smudging and prayers, Rene left his body in one big swoop of magnetic, electrifying soul energy. There was a whistling and roaring as if we were in the middle of a cyclone or near an approaching railway train. His soul-Spirit left the body and circled the room seven times counter-clockwise, the direction one needs to go when returning home to Spirit. The curtains flew sideways to the left with the power of his soul. We were aghast! His soul left through the closed window and immediately there was silence. Then the 12 crows on the top tree branches outside the window started cawing. I smudged the body and we traditionally washed it with Native herbs, and so prepared and honoured his physical form he left behind.

For 49 days afterwards, I connected with Rene in the astral planes and re-engaged him consciously with the Eagle Spirit, who took him to higher astral realities. His soul was purified and he is soaring with new imaginations for his next life.

STANISLAVSKI AND GROTOWSKI METHODS OF ACTING

At this time, I was involved with my Toronto theatre friends in studying and I physically embodied the kinesthetic feeling and emotional psychological processes and techniques of Konstantin Stanislavski. These powerful internal movement dynamics of psychophysiology involved, for instance, becoming the five Chinese elements in the order of transformation, from water to wood to fire to earth to metal and back again to water. I remember training with Jeff, a good friend of mine, on fully embodying these processes of nature.

Jerzy Grotowski took Stanislavski's methods and implemented his own version of internal and external investigative "paratheatre." Learning these techniques helped me to transcend the separation between performer and theatre. In his "Theatre of Productions," we learned to embody the elements of technique in the traditional practices of various cultures, such as African, Haitian, and other ethnic movements and dances.

These experiences enticed me to check out the dramas of R. Murray Schafer, Canadian composer and environmental theatre producer. He introduced the concept of the recombination and recontextualization of sounds woven back into their original source, or schismogenesis. Vividly I recall his Ra story set inside Union Station in downtown Toronto, and The Princess of the Stars wondrously captivated us on a wild northern Ontario lake at dawn. At 5am in early September 1997, we sat on wooden benches at the shore of a lake at Haliburton Forest and Wildlife Reserve listening to loons and wolves, while the Dawn Star and Sun peeked over the horizon, and huge alpine horns sounded from a cliff top across the lake. I still shiver with magical mystery when I re-experience these kinesthetic memories.

MYTHS, DREAMS, SYMBOLS AND SELF-DISCOVERY AT OCAD, 1986-1993

Continuing my earlier story, the summer course of 1986 was so positively viewed by my students that they told other students about it. For September 1986, there were over 160 students enrolled in the 32-person limit for the September to December course. The College asked me to simultaneously offer two versions of the same course from September to December, and another two from January to April 1987.

These courses were some of the most energetic, exciting, and hilarious moments of my life. Imagine 32 individuals crammed into a room 30 feet by 30 feet, in total darkness, with no shoes or socks on, pants rolled up, no tables or chairs, the entire floor covered with large sheets of white or brown "kraft" paper, tubs of red, black, yellow, and blue watered-down acrylic paints, and dancing to music like "I've Been Thinking About You" by the Londonbeat, or Sting's "Desert Rose," or "Living in a Box" by Living in a Box. We were wild, free, embodied, kinesthetically jacked, and stoked, and having the time of our lives. It is hard to imagine such creative freedom and psychological liberation at this or any Canadian art college taking place these days. The social educational boxes are sealed and the cycles of civilization have changed.

Over the 110-year history of The Ontario School of Art, I was told that my course, Myths, Dreams, Symbols and Self-Discovery was the most successful in terms of numbers of pre-enrollment. Over the seven-year stint I did there, eventually every session had over 400 hopeful registrants.

I developed and offered other important courses for my students. One was Creativity and The Artist in Experimental Art (Level Two of the Myths course) where we studied Goethe's colour theory, Kandinsky's spiritual in art, and related topics. Another was Aesthetics and the Artist (Level Three of the Myths course) where I trained students in the therapeutic use of music, art, movement, spiritual aesthetics, Jungian psychology, archetypes and symbols. Other courses were History and Philosophy of Design, Anthropology and World Art, Introduction to Anthropology, and First Nations Art—particularly Canadian, Australian, and African First Nations. I wish I still had the thousands of colour slides I used to show to my students.

Under my tutelage, I instigated with a number of First Nations students the OCAD Aboriginal Native Student Society in 1987. I had a dream of planning and holding a seven-day long Native Arts Symposium, which we held in 1989. All my Native Students showcased their paintings, drawings, masks, and sculptures. I had over 200 Native artists from coast to coast attend, including Daphne Odjig, Ioyan Mani (Maxine Noel), Carl Beam, and Michael Robinson. A Mohawk Elder friend gave the blessing ceremony for opening and closing the circle. Local Global TV interviewed Elders and artists. There were three-hour seminars morning and afternoon on pertinent topics. Through the Indian Art-i-Crafts, the Ontario Arts Council, and several corporations, we raised over two million dollars for the Native Arts Symposium.

It was so highly successful that we decided next year to bring our peoples together in a bigger venue where they could also sell their arts and crafts. Thus in 1992, we started the Annual Toronto Powwow, now the Canadian Aboriginal Festival, held mid or end November every year in the Sky Dome or Exhibition Place.

PART TWO
MID-LIFE TO THE PRESENT

CHAPTER 9
38-54 YEARS OF AGE

PH.D. AND GRADUATION

I was seriously emotionally challenged with Tom Robson's death and I struggled to get my Ph.D. thesis written. I was not making any headway with it in Toronto, so I took all my notes to the farm and kept writing until I finished it.

In May 1988, I had my final oral examination. Because of my Bell's Palsy, I could still hardly speak and enunciate proper English words. I thought of trying Intergalactic language but felt my supervisor and attendees would not understand.

I was so nervous that the only way I could get through the grueling two and a half hours was to write down all the questions I was asked and give myself time to think about the appropriate response. Perhaps they passed me because they felt sorry for me and just wanted to get it over with. I also wanted to get it over with.

Afterwards, they took me out for lunch. The chairman of The University of Toronto Anthropology Department, who had brought me into anthropology in the first place, was on my oral committee. A few years back, he hired Tom to do some renovation work on his house.

At lunch, he pleasantly inquired, "And how is Tom doing? I really appreciate the renovations he did for us!"

"Well, actually," I stammered, "Tom died two years ago."

"Oh my!" he blurted, "I had no idea!" He also had no idea that Tom and I had been lovers and partners.

SERIOUS ILLNESS AND LEAVING THE UNIVERSITY – CARL JUNG VISITATIONS

Once I had passed my Ph.D. oral, I passed my written French language examination and was granted my Ph.D. in late May 1988. It was not the thesis I originally intended, but it would do. I knew I needed a doctorate, mainly so people would think I was at least mildly intelligent and not be totally castigated because I was a modern mystic in this materialist reductionist culture. Many times in life, you have to prove you can fit in so you can at least be listened to. You must also go your own road all along the way by being authentic, honest, and truthful.

To my surprise, I was offered more teaching within the anthropology department for the fall of 1988. This was my dream. I climbed the academic ladder all the way to the top for over 20 years of my life. It had taken much psychological, emotional, and financial sacrifice to get here. I always wanted to be a professor.

Within days of receiving the gracious offer for more teaching, I fell desperately ill. I caught a cold, my back completely gave out, and I could not even move a muscle to get out of bed. It was terrifyingly painful to spend half an hour rolling over and sitting up, just to go to the washroom. This continued for two full weeks. My spirit, soul, and body were giving me a big message. I just did not understand what it was.

My mind still wanted me to be a professor. My heart, soul, and body obviously did not. I did not know where to turn or who to speak with. Thank God for Carl Jung. On about the sixteenth day of this, I started receiving visitations from Carl Jung, who was in Spirit. We were always close from many past lives together and certainly from what I learned from him in this life. I rejoiced over our ongoing conversations about spiritual realities of higher spiritual realms, human nature, good, evil, shadow, archetypes, symbols, and the unconscious—not to mention dream analysis!

For seven days and nights I dialogued with Carl about my future, and what my soul truly intended for my next stage. I followed many paths in my imagination to test them out on my future timeline. Very few seemed to work.

Gradually, through our discussions, I realized that my teaching days at the universities were over—for now. I wanted to test, research, and clinically experiment with all the techniques I learned. Although I had been seeing clients part-time since I was 21 years old, I now wanted to see clients in my clinic full-time.

I called the graduate anthropology chairman and told him I was leaving the University and teaching.

He almost shouted, "Are you crazy? You've spent your whole life training for this!"

"Well," I hummed, "now I see that the ladder to my success has been against the wrong wall. I am instead going to be a full-time psychotherapist."

"You're out of your mind," he said.

"Yes, perhaps," I admitted, "and I'm in my heart."

I rented a clinical space from some Psychodrama friends on the Danforth. After a few months, I took a lease in the commercial building at 226 College Street, near Beverley Street, in room 206. I hung up my shingle, and also started The Creative HeART Space.

THE PSYCHOLOGICAL SPIRIT-MIND-EMOTIONS-HEART-BODY MODALITIES THAT I OFFERED

MODALITIES FOR PERSONAL AND GROUP THERAPIES FOR INDIVIDUAL SOUL WORK

Individual soul work is a collaborative and confidential relationship between a therapist and a client. Treatment may consist of short-term counseling or long-term therapy, depending on your specific needs. An initial consultation can help you determine the best choice.

Individual soul work is dynamic and creative, and works well both with youth and adults. It can be used to address any number of issues such as depression, anxiety, work concerns, anger and shame, loss and grief, fear and trauma, abuse, relationship challenges, spiritual emergency, and low self-esteem. It can also be used to meet a desire for personal growth and to clear emotions to prevent illness.

There are a wide variety of approaches or modalities used in counseling.

The following modalities are offered to individuals, families and small groups for intensive inner work, personal transformation, and conscious integration.

FOCUSING is a technique to allow your consciousness to attend to what is happening in the moment within your physical body, your emotions, feelings, and your mind.

DIAPHRAGMATIC BREATHING is slow, deep, conscious inhaling and exhaling that relaxes, releases stress, depression and anxiety, and calms the mind and heart.

CREATIVE VISUALIZATION allows the mind to disengage from the "to do" list, opens up new possibilities, integrates the brain hemispheres and helps you to plan your life.

MEDITATION is the quieting and emptying of the mind, opening to and receiving from the universal Higher Mind, connecting to spirit, and accessing your personal destiny.

EMOTIONAL RELEASE is an energetic unblocking and outward flowing of held-in emotions such as anxiety, anger, sadness, and fear. The counselor does this through deep breathing, visualization, self-hypnosis, **meditation, and energy work.**

KRIYA YOGA is a set of ancient techniques of breathing, inner chanting, meditations, and mental and spiritual linking up with spiritual masters which brings peace, joy, certainty, confidence, full karmic release and conscious Self-awakening.

DREAMWORK allows one to tap the wealth of knowledge and energy trapped within the personal unconscious and brings direction, focus and personal integration.

ETHERIC HEALING uses subtle, high vibrations to clear blockages in chakras, meridians and organs, open the mind and heart, heal tissues and re-energize the etheric, mental, emotional, and physical bodies. This is advanced Qi Gong and Reiki.

ART THERAPY explores your unconscious thoughts, emotions, and impulses in order to heal the emotions, clear mental trauma, awaken the creative Self and find direction.

JUNGIAN DEPTH PSYCHOLOGY allows you to take off the masks or persona, depose the false personality or ego, confront your shadow, find your inner masculine and feminine, release your soul from prison, connect to the universal spirit, and Be Self.

EGO WORK removes old defense mechanisms and masks, deals with hidden pain, opens and resolves all feelings and emotions, completes mid-life crises, stops the ego from running and ruining you life, makes the soul and heart the living centre of you.

SHADOW WORK is essential for a full, vibrant life, for 95% of your energy and personality is locked in your unconscious. You find, transform and re-integrate the negative shadow that blocks your life, love, and work. You find the positive shadow and use its creative force for life, love, work, art, exercise, and enlightenment.

PSYCHOLOGICAL ANDROGYNY allows you to be all you can be and do more with life, and integrates full feelings and energies of archetypal masculine and feminine.

FINDING YOUR HIGHER SELF allows you to become your authentic nature, open to higher consciousness; be in an effortless daily flow of synchronicity, joy, and love.

SPIRITUAL MASTERS and Higher Beings constantly exist around you. To avail yourself of their love, guidance, and protection you need to know who they are, how to communicate with them, how to open to their energies and align your consciousness. Results include authenticity and spontaneity.

GESTALT approach takes into account mind, heart and body. You become aware of what is happening to you each moment. Results include authenticity and spontaneity.

PSYCHODRAMA allows you to connect with all your inner parts and let them have a voice. Conflicts resolve and you become more alive and integrated.

ANIMAL MEDICINES allow you to consciously experience becoming the animals in your dreams and inner world. Like our ancestors, we feel one with all creatures.

SWEAT LODGES purify body, mind, and soul, give your courage, strength, and will power, and help your consciousness travel to all worlds and connect you to spirit.

SOUL RETRIEVAL deals with split-off soul parts caused by abuse, incest, and past lives deaths; it is a spiritual, energetic shamanic technique to make the parts conscious and to integrate them into the core Self.

CREATIVE MOVEMENT allows your soul to move your physical, opens energetic meridians, releases tension in muscles, soothes the organs and brings spontaneity.

PERSONAL MYTHOLOGY makes you treat your life like a heroic journey, gives you a clear overview, presents trials to meet, tasks to complete, and goals to achieve. You learn to change the ineffective parental patterns and choose your own path in life.

LIFE ENERGY BREATHWORK AND BODYWORK™ allows you to release anxiety and tension, learn to breathe more efficiently, release old emotions, expand your consciousness, connect to your Diamond Crystal Heart, explore any lifetime, connect to the higher energies of spirit and open to the creative, loving Self.

MUSIC shifts metabolism, respiration, heart rate, and blood pressure, opens the imagination, clears and heals emotions, awakens the soul and body and brings joy and beauty.

PAST LIVES KARMIC HEALING finds, transforms, and heals negative core issues, thoughts, feelings and actions from any life, breaks old patterns in life and relationships, purifies the mind and heart, heals the physical body, and brings bliss.

NUTRITIONAL CONSULTATION evaluates your proper diet, exercise, breathing, sleep, and other health concerns. We offer nutritional products, readings, and analyses.

REIKI is a gentle transformational energetic healing. We offer you the Japanese, Hawaiian, Egyptian, African, and First Nations forms.

LIFE LINE THERAPY™ allows you to physically and energetically reconnect with the threads and patterns of your life, clear the blockages, reprogram, and open to spirit.

NEURO-LINGUISTIC PROGRAMMING (NLP) allows you to remove the negative, limiting filters and perceptions, expand your consciousness infinitely, explore new life possibilities, integrate mind, soul, and body.

STORYTELLING uses archetypal and mythological themes and variations to explore the blocks, tests, trials, options, and opportunities in your life, relationships, and work.

SPIRITUAL FENG SHUI is used when there are negative energies in your property, home, and office. It effectively reduces negativity, accidents, and promotes energy flow.

ABUSE, INCEST, AND POST-TRAUMATIC STRESS SYNDROME issues are gently healed through memory desensitization, self-hypnosis, art therapy, and journaling.

JOURNALING AND POETRY WRITING allows you to explore feelings, clear blockages, become creative, find life direction, and become more self-aware.

MARRIAGE AND FAMILY ISSUES are revealed, clarified, processed, and healed to give you personal freedom. Adlerian and Family Therapy techniques like family genograms, systems, solution-focused, **and brief therapies are used.**

TRANSPERSONAL PSYCHOLOGY creatively explores the truth of you being a soul with spirit connections, having an earthly incarnation to heal self-worthiness and relationships, to open your Diamond Crystal Heart, and to find personal freedom and realization.

CHAPTER 10:
BEING A FULL-TIME PSYCHOTHERAPIST

You get the idea of what I was offering to the many clients who thankfully, for themselves and for me, came through my door. It was a lovely, bright, windowed space with an interior door onto an open-air private deck. I had a large group and waiting room with a closed door entering into the alchemically energized private room.

From 1988 to 1992, I worked out of the clinic at 226 College Street. I had many unusual clients. Although I was a clinical Marriage and Family Therapist, I always preferred the one-on-one deep inner shadow work that I did myself. I held Native Animal Medicines Circles, Incest Survivors Healing Groups, Rebirthing, Kundalini Yoga, Psychodrama, Knowledge of Higher Spiritual Worlds, and other fascinating Process Groups.

MEETINGS WITH REMARKABLE PEOPLE
FROM PAST LIVES

What I would most like to share concerns the many remarkable clients I had. Without going into much detail, here is a list of some clients whose dreams revealed their past lives, and for whom I immediately recognized—Napoleon, Alastair Crowley, Anne Frank, Verdi, Respighi, James Morrow Walsh of the Northwest Mounted Police, Thomas the disciple of Jesus, and Judas Iscariot.

The hypnotherapeutic techniques of Dr. Milton Erickson, which I started using in 1989, came in extremely handy in healing these clients and also when dealing with the present-day survivors I analyzed who had been incarcerated in Auschwitz and Bergen-Belsen Concentration Camps during the Blitzkrieg of World War II.

Other than this, I saw hundreds of distressed people who were anxious about their increasing loneliness, depression, emotional blockages, angers, and serious childhood abuse. I treated all these with respect and love. Through word-of-mouth, my clientele increased weekly and I always had a waiting list and more than a dozen or so in each weekly group.

If I might add one caveat to those of you reading this—make sure you deal with all your childhood emotions, memories, and issues, for these are the bases of your healing, liberation, and personal happiness.

MEETING MY FATHER NOW REBORN AS MY OCAD STUDENT

In early September 1988, I had one of the most shocking, challenging, and intriguing experiences of my life. If ever you need proof of reincarnation and karma, here it is! This turns out to be one of the top seven greatest stories of my present incarnation. In the beginning of the new fall term at the Ontario College of Art and Design, it was the first day of class for Myths, Dreams, Symbols and Self-Discovery. I arrived early, and there was already one student sitting alone, rather sullenly and despondently just left of centre in the front row. Glancing at this tall, long-dark-haired, handsome, blue-eyed young man, a creeping sensation came over my entire body and nerves. In my mind, I uncannily felt something ominous, and so I prepared myself for what might come. It was verging on a sense of danger. Once in a while he and I glanced at one another. I pretended to prepare for class by shuffling my papers, and looking for something irrelevant in my light-brown leather briefcase. Over time as the classroom seats were filled, I began to feel more comfortable, though still somewhat wary.

As always, we went around the circle and introduced our first names and why we were in this class. When it came to this young man, he slowly and almost inaudibly said, with his head hanging down, "My name is Mark; art is my way of staying alive and this is why I am here.

It was a good first class and, as always, I was buoyant in order to raise the energy levels really high so the group as a whole would be inspired. At the end of the three-hour session, all the other students filed out except for Mark, who remained and was visibly uncomfortable and insecure in his seat. I looked at him again and recognized something very familiar in his eyes, so I peered more deeply into his soul. I now confirmed what my first intuition had been at the beginning of the class—Mark was my birth father reincarnated, and now my student in my art class.

I walked over to him, and for our first private conversation stated,

"You're my father reincarnated, aren't you?"

"Yes," he grimaced, "Yes, I am…"

"When and where were you born?" I questioned him.

"I was born in a small rural southwestern Ontario farm town. My dad was the Culligan Man who delivers water. I went to school in that town, and decided to be an artist. I knew you were teaching here, so I came to OCAD."

I thought of the synchronous symbolism of being the son of a man who sells water purifiers; metaphorically this means cleaning and transforming one's emotions and feelings, and washing and clearing one's karmas.

"When you were my father, you died on September 26, 1969. I supported you through the 49-day period of hell realms and knew you took birth immediately after that. The rebirth of the zygote would be November 14, 1969. Nine months after makes it August 14, 1970," I said.

Mark pulled a face and slowly pronounced the words, "August 14, 1970 is my birthday."

It took many months for Mark and I to communicate with open emotion. I was emotionally complexed with some leftover feelings about my angers and fears, even though I had done so much Jungian Dreamwork and body energy release around my father's punishment of me as a young baby, child, and teenager.

I realized I did still love my father and had been unconsciously deeply missing him, for I knew on some higher level we always still loved one another. I comprehended that my healing opportunity was here if I became truly conscious as a son, stop yearning for my absent father, and learn to authentically love my father as friend to friend—and thereby fully embrace my own spiritual, earthy, instinctual, sexual, and relational masculinity.

Therefore, I decided to befriend Mark and support his journey in his new life. Over the months and years, we spent increasing quality time together at his rental apartment above a store on Gerrard Street East and we often went for tea and Chinese food. Over the five years Mark was a star student at OCAD. He took all my five experimental art courses and my other courses. Our friendship deepened to the point where from 1989 onwards, he and I went up to my off-the-grid log cabin at my Lake of Two Suns on 350 acres near Wilberforce, Ontario. The solitude gave us time and space to confront and deal with many of our fears and issues, including the sexual and physical abuse.

While at OCAD, Mark never really released his melancholy, severe depression, self-hatred, angst, paranoia, and nihilist philosophy of his and all life. One of his main heroes was Antonin Artaud, the mentally challenged, self-hating, addictive French playwright famous for his Theatre of Cruelty. Mark's beautiful, haunting, strongly coloured, though ghostly abstract oil stick drawings symbolically showed cut-up body parts, mental splits, and emotional pain of incredible artistic intensity. I could feel the visceral troubled hurt from the expressed powerful self-hatred and guilt. Mark often gifted me with many of these drawings, perhaps as a way to expiate his guilt and perhaps to non-verbally ask for forgiveness.

Usually sullen and emotionally withdrawn, Mark sometimes burst into great fits of rage, often self-inflicted. I just held space for him and witnessed his grief and despair. There are no words for the volume, amplitude, magnitude, and range of his rage, shame, embarrassment, and inner terror. To some degree we did become friends, yet only to the level Mark would let me in. This is the way it is with all friendship—the level of surrender and trust on both sides always circumscribes it.

After his fifth year at OCAD finished, Mark vanished in May 1991, and I never saw him again… Until one day, the day before Christmas in 1995, I got a call on my home phone from an unknown number. It was Mark! All he said was, "I need to meet with you. I will be in town on Boxing Day… Can we please meet up?" He sounded petrified and extremely anxious and I had no idea what was going on in his life.

"Sure," I rejoined, "How about Toby's Goodeats at 542 Church Street, south of Wellesley on the west side?"

"Sure" said Mark. Stumbling with his quiet fearful voice, he added, "Can we meet at 1pm?"

"Yes Mark, that will be fine, I'll see you there in two days on Boxing Day at Toby's Goodeats at 1pm. Take care, and by the way, Merry Christmas to you."

"Yeah, thanks… you too," was all he could muster.

Christmas Day was a cold and blustery one in Toronto that year. I was very pensive and alert, and wondered why Mark could possibly want to see me on such short notice and with a desperate tone of voice. I had not heard from him in four and a half years. I had no idea what he had been up to.

I had questionable, apprehensive dreams Christmas Day evening. When I awoke late Boxing Day morning, a foot of heavy snow was falling in clouds on the trees and streets. I knew it would take me twice as long to arrive at the restaurant, so I left in good time. I got there at 12:45pm. One o'clock arrived, no Mark. I wondered if he would show up. Would it be the outer weather or his inner weather that was the challenge? Ten minutes after 1pm, Mark came in, his toque and the shoulders of his coat covered with heavy wet snow. It felt like he was carrying weighty dense blankets of shame and guilt.

He shuffled like a stiff, frozen salamander over to my table. Likely due to the inclement weather, Toby's was empty except for me, the chef and the waitress, so I was easy to find. I stood up, and went to hug him, but he just extended his right hand, so I took it and shook it. He undid his winter coat, placed it on the back of his chair, and heavily sat down across from me at the small table away from the windows and street. I wanted us to have privacy, but our years of emotional isolation and the fact that there was nobody else there anyway were sequestration enough.

I had the waitress bring some glasses of water, no ice. I wanted to order, and Mark gestured that he did not want to eat, so I let it go, and asked the waitress to simply leave us alone. I asked Mark how he was. He glumly looked up and held his face in a quarantined mask. There was a vacuum in his aura that suggested deep anxiety and grieving. Some kind of inner light needed to be let out, but his blocked body armour made him separate from himself, his mind and his heart, and withdrawing inside, seeking protection and relief.

His head and eyes looked down at the placemat and cutlery. Every time he lifted his head briefly to look into my compassionate eyes, he slightly opened his mouth and tried to mouth some words. In these moments, nothing audible ever emerged from the well of sadness pouring through his soul and body. I knew Mark was a very internal and shy private man, like many artists. I was patient and waited for him to share when he was ready.

This intermittent looking up and trying to speak went on for at least 20 minutes. He was bristling with fear and trying to jump-start the spark of his inner truth. Then he looked up, determined to continue, fixed on my eyes, and burst into heaving full-body sobs of sorrowful, doleful anguish. His frame wracked, lifted, then sunk into itself. What inner torment could he be going through? Why was he here now with me? What did he need to say and get off his chest?

Over the next 40 or so minutes, Mark tried to express his distress but the inner torment and wall of oppressive unhappiness and shame shut him down. His glumness and gloominess overtook him. There were bouts of showers of tears, followed by withdrawn isolation, heartsickness, and self-reproach. Sitting there, looking at my father in his new life and body, I remembered two songs that he listened to continuously in this life—"Shout Shout, Let It All Out" by Tears for Fears, and Sting's "Fortress Around Your Heart."

The crying waves cascaded down his face, shirt, and onto the placemat until it too was soaked in sadness. He took his hands and wiped the tears up over his long, thick, wavy brown hair that limply hung to his shoulders. I felt so much love and compassion for this man. I wondered what caused him so much troubling pain.

After an hour and a half of silence interspersed with tears, floods, and barricades, I offered Mark a pen and an overturned placemat. His way had always been to draw, sketch, journal, and paint. I asked him to briefly write what he had been doing over the previous years since we had seen one another.

Gradually, over an exhausting hour, Mark wrote about the fact that after art school, he read all the poetry of hip Buddhist author Gary Snyder. He lamented that his life had felt like a catastrophe, so he traveled to Vietnam and Asia to study with Buddhists. Eventually he stayed in one Asian monastery and took vows as a celibate Buddhist monk through one head abbot. Eventually, he travelled back to North America and lived and worked in The Buddhist Center in Chicago. The abbot there had been through many of Mark's past lives. This man saw the great karma that Mark had with me when Mark was my birth father.

This abbot requested Mark to clear his karma with me by personally visiting me in Toronto. Although Mark said he was in town to visit his family, I knew he was here to make amends with me. Finally, all the pieces of the puzzle came together. I had an opportunity in this life to forgive in person the father who had treated me so tragically and with such wrongful soul dismissal.

Knowing that Mark now felt the emotional karmic weight of all that he had set upon me, I felt deeper compassion and a necessity to be patient and allow Mark the chance to set things right with his soul and with my soul. Such wretchedness and heartache can stir the soul to salvation or to suicide. I knew Mark's past history with these melancholic thoughts, so I was determined to stay until he could get the words out and verbally ask for my forgiveness. I already forgave him years ago so that I could move on in my life with deeper kindness in my heart. I was an open door for Mark so that he could find his heart again.

It took three and a half hours of lamenting, stuttering, and stammering, wiping his tears with the back of his hand, and clearing his eyes, entrenched with mourning. I kept saying, "Mark, I am here for you, it's okay, take your time…"

Finally I simply stood up, went around the table, and put my arms around his shoulders.

"Mark" I softly said, "I forgive you and did so a long time ago; just tell me what you want to share. I am here for you." Then I went and sat down again in my chair.

As I serenely gazed out the window into the courtyard, the snow was now more heavily and softly falling in droves of white doves.

"I… I… I am…" more dejected sobs from Mark. "I am so sorry… for what I did to you… when I was your… father." I nodded and nonverbally welcomed him to continue. I knew how hard this request for repentance was for Mark's reactive, rebellious, and resistant ego.

"I'm listening Mark… take your time… I am here with you."

"I know and feel now what I made you suffer. It's horrible how I treated you. I am so sorry…" Then came more troubling tears of regret and misery. I felt and witnessed how the karma we put out will always return to us. It is ourselves that we need to forgive in such situations.

"I have already forgiven you years ago, Mark… it's your Self you need to forgive now… First and foremost, forgiveness and love are always really something we need and can give to ourselves; and then others can more easily forgive and love us back."

163

"Do you really forgive me?" he ponderously and incredulously asked.

"Yes Mark, I completely forgive you and will always love you, no matter what."

His lead-like load looked like it was lifting from his spirit-mind-body and soul. His eyes brightened somewhat; his countenance instantly became much lighter and more composed.

His eyes now brimmed with joyful tears, he smiled for once and faintly whispered, "Thank you... thank you so very much. I feel better now. I feel healed. You have been very kind to me." I thought he was going to add "my son." I felt the depth of his emotionally genuine words coming from his heart.

I wanted to complete this transformational circle of life, so I continued, "I will always love you, Mark. You know this. Wherever you are, and wherever you go, my heart and my love will always be inside your heart with your love. Please just remember this always." He nodded, somewhat happily, and rose from the table.

"Can I please have a hug?"

"Sure Mark, on the heart side!" We had one long hug standing there in the empty restaurant. That was a hug to remember forever.

We put on our coats, hats, and gloves. As we silently sidled towards the door, the waitress warmly smiled at us. I recognized her angelic countenance, witness to the great healing this day between Mark and me. It was as if her heart feelings were conveying, "Where there is great love, there are always miracles."

I opened the door for Mark and he gratefully walked through it. Out on the silent street, our boots steadily crunched the ever-falling snow. There were no cars and nobody was on the sidewalk as we slowly and meditatively glided south on Church Street. It was a rare supernal moment of transubstantiation and transformation.

I offered Mark a ride home and he declined, saying he would take the streetcar east from Carlton Street. We walked five blocks to the corner of Maple Leaf Gardens. I walked with my arm around Mark's shoulder because I knew he needed to find greater inner strength. As we continued side by side through this last chapter of our life, I consciously prayed for Mark to derive indomitable courage on his revolutionary evolutionary path.

"Even if we never speak or see each other again, Mark, I will always think of you with great love and send you my heartfelt compassion." He said he would do likewise with me.

I ruminated on how I could best give full closure to my final parting with my father. I only had a few minutes left. While I stayed in this life, my father purposefully returned into his next incarnation to meet up with me, become my student, then a Buddhist monk with vows, and finally freely liberate himself through his righteous request for forgiveness. Forgiveness and perfect love are the highest keys to karmic-emotional release.

We both felt pensively awkward. I knew the snowy streetcar would be here soon. What else could I possibly say and share? As it turned out, it took another ten minutes before the streetcar came east along the deserted streets.

What happened next still brings tears to my heart. Mark removed his knapsack from his back, and took off his toque and gloves. Then he went down on his knees in front of me, his hands held together as if praying, glad tears streaming from joyful eyes. Then he lay down fully in the deepening snow, and did a full Buddhist prostration to me on the sidewalk in front of Maple Leaf Gardens. He graciously and lovingly placed his fingertips on the tops of my wet boots. In his previous incarnation, these were the fingers and hands that had brutally hurt me. Now there was a peaceful resolution to all my pain, sadness, and desolation. Not a human soul was on the street except the angels present, greatly rejoicing.

I was jolted. "Mark, what are you doing? Get up, this is not necessary." With his face in the snow, his arms stretched up over his head, and his freezing bare fingers and hands touching the toes of my boots, he started crying all over again, this time out of eternal relief.

"Mark, really, just get up; you don't need to be doing this." He remained immobile, gently sobbing in full prostration for about three minutes while he offered Buddhist prayers. I let him have his comfort and necessary spiritual ablution and redemption. Then I helped him up, brushed the snow off his face and chest, and gave him the biggest kiss I had ever given him—in our previous life or in this life. He gave me the biggest grin and what a beautiful seraphic smile it was! The angels and the Christ visited us in person and embodied themselves in our Earth walk!

"My Buddhist abbot told me I needed to do this, and I wanted to. Thank you for my deliverance."

"Mark," I chided, "You have delivered your Self... You know I will always love you..."

We could hear three bells chiming from the streetcar strolling eastward from Yonge Street. In thankful easy silence, we stood arm in arm waiting for the streetcar to arrive. When it did, we hugged once more. Mark put his backpack on, and got on the trolley. As he climbed the steps, he turned, smiled sweetly, and waved before doing the hands-together Namaste gesture. I returned the Namaste, singing with his heart, "I see the god in you, Mark. All blessings." And I have not heard from or seen Mark since. Life is perfect.

One of my Ayurvedic teachers confirmed during my mid-twenties that my birth father was actually a student of the great Paramahansa Ramakrishna. In that incarnation, my father was called Kali or Abhedananda. He was an astute, devoted holy man serving Ramakrishna. In this life as my birth father, his shadow or "Kali" side came to work out some heavy karma. I was his willing and dutiful victim-servant so that my father could expel, learn, return, transmute, be forgiven, and consciously move forward in love.

Here is the only recorded voice of Abhedananda, and for that matter, the only recorded voice of a direct disciple of Ramakrishna, www.youtube.com/watch?v=D2HbdZsvCMc

KALACHAKRA TEACHINGS WITH HIS HOLINESS THE 14TH DALAI LAMA

In the late 1980s, His Holiness The 14th Dalai Lama gave a week of Vajrayana Tibetan teachings at The University of Toronto in Convocation Hall. Just to be in the presence of a laughing gentleman, a follower of the Buddha was a wonderful experience for me.

YOGANANDA AND I GO TO THE AMERICAN SOUTHWEST, SPRING 1989

I felt a calling to go and train with the staff at the Dr. Milton Erickson Foundation for Hypnotherapy. Training with Dr. Ernest Rossi, Dr. Jeff Zeig, and many others really solidified my earlier NLP training and gave me powerful skills with which to support my clients' endeavours in self-discovery through unconscious recall.

After my two-week training, I rented a four-wheeler Jeep Cherokee and drove into the Sangre de Cristo Mountains. While there, I was stuck in the spring snows and called on angels to get me out, which they thankfully obliged. Driving across the trackless Painted Desert in Arizona was a Spirit journey I undertook with Paramahansa Yogananda beside me. The landscape we traversed had no markers, no roads, just hard and bumpy red Earth. Before starting, I meditated under the last tree on the horizon and found some valuable knowledge I needed in order to expand my Native spiritual rituals.

After 4 hours of driving due east, I ended up in a small Navajo community of two hogans. I met a medicine man there that knew I was coming, and shared some ancient stories of Our peoples. These stories have become part of my hozho way of balance and beauty in my life—a harmonious continuous internal state of wonder, flow, and order.

I partook in a Navajo ceremony called the "Beautyway Blessing." Beautyway connotes perfection, harmony, goodness, success, well-being, blessedness, and happiness. Typically, the ritual is done seated on a healing sand painting of gorgeous colours and is meticulously crafted. The Tibetan Kalachakra Mandala is another cultural representation of this, only people do not sit on it, they receive the healings through vibrations. Here is our Navajo chant sung during the ceremony. I often sing it or pray it to the world and myself:

The Navajo Beauty Way Ceremony

In beauty may I walk
All day long may I walk
Through the returning seasons may I walk

Beautifully I will possess again
Beautifully birds
Beautifully joyful birds
On the trail marked with pollen may I walk
With grasshoppers about my feet may I walk
With dew about my feet may I walk
With beauty may I walk
With beauty before me may I walk
With beauty behind me may I walk
With beauty above me may I walk
With beauty all around me may I walk
In old age, wandering on a trail of beauty, lively, may I walk
In old age, wandering on a trail of beauty, living again, may I walk
It is finished in beauty
It is finished in beauty
Anonymous (Navajo)

IN ANCIENT EGYPT WITH THE GURDJIEFF GROUP, 1989

There are many historical spiritual groups that interest me, although I have never joined one. The Gurdjieff Group is one. Some of my closest friends growing up were in "The Work."

Starting in 1988, the "Group" of 21 of us took classes in Egyptology from a professor at The Royal Ontario Museum. We hired John Anthony West to take us on tour up and down the Nile in Egypt. We visited all the ancient sites and discovered a different time-line than previously accepted. In preparation, we pored through West's The Traveler's Key to Ancient Egypt: A Guide to the Sacred Places of Ancient Egypt. We went in the summer of 1989. The weather was often over 50 degrees Celsius, so we were glad to have pith helmets that we could drench with water.

Since I was a child of five, I read many of my past lives in ancient Egypt. I also remember, as Edgar Cayce had, that those of us who sailed reed boats to Egypt were one of five post-Atlantean "root races" who travelled far and wide when Atlantis and Poseidia went down for the third and last time. I often still dream of and envision these times. The other root races from Atlantis went to Tibet, Switzerland, British Isles (the

Druidic Celts), South America (Olmecs and Maya), and North America or Turtle Island (all First Nations).

Archeologists have always wondered how a full-blown civilization could come to the Nile River and Basin when there were only small groups there previously. The answer is Atlantis.

The theories of Sphinx water erosion in geology presented by Robert Schoch allowed John Anthony West to put together greater background on Atlantis than heretofore was amassed by scholars. Schoch found weathering evidence on the Sphinx dating from 10,000 to 5,000 BCE, farther back in time than was previously accepted as 2500 BCE. Extensive flooding and rainfall between 10,000 to 5,000 BCE caused the water erosion.

There were many memorable moments in Egypt. One was staying at The Mena House with its grand architectural sensibilities. Perhaps the most spiritually engaging and powerful experience was walking inside the Serapeum, where ancient Apis bulls were sacrificed and entombed in large red granite sarcophagi. Inside the Serapeum it is quite dark with an ancient musty smell of bovine. Each tomb is over 20 feet long, 10 feet wide and 7 feet high inside.

While meandering through this underworld, one of my fellow compatriots, while standing on wooden steps and looking down into the depths of darkness, dropped her flash camera inside the tomb. Foolishly, I told her I would simply jump down and retrieve it for her. I did, and then I could not get up and out. The inside of this black granite sarcophagus was as smooth as glass. I could not get a grip. I was down there for a while trying to find a way up. This was not to be. Memories of my past lives being entombed during our ancient rituals of The Egyptian Book of the Dead Initiation rites flashed and coursed through my body-mind.

My friend left me in the pitch-black darkness to find help. Thirty long minutes later, the Arab security guards came with rope. I grabbed onto it, and they pulled me up. It was a heavenly experience to be out of a possible hellish death once again.

Inside The King's and Queen's Chambers of The Great Pyramid, we were allowed one hour on our own. We meditated in silence, chanted, and prayed together in the two chambers. I had a feeling of recognition of many previous past lives experiences when inside The King's Chamber.

Below this massive pyramid, there is a most ancient tunnel that leads to a Subterranean Chamber. One crawls backwards on one's hands and knees over lateral boards down into this small space, buried many metres below the immense weight of The Great Pyramid. It is stiflingly hot down there with little oxygen. There are many ghosts there as well—workers who sweated and died building this monumental wonder of astral-physiological projection and transduction.

THE SINGING TEMPLES OF MADINAT HABU, DENDERAH, EDFU AND PHILAE

By accident and synchronous luck, I stumbled open a sound quality with which many of The Great Temple and Tombs of Egypt were built. Many of the great architects of this ancient culture, such as Imhotep, "the one who comes in peace," had their own mathematical note from the 12-tone scale. Imhotep soul tone is the note A. The A above middle C has a frequency of 440 Herz; it is used as the general tuning standard for musical pitch.

Since I was a child at the piano, I recognized the resonance of each note that I had previously used in my past lives. When playing in the key of A major or A minor, I reflect on my Egyptian past. For me, composing in the key of D major or D minor is a Celtic Druidic energetic. B minor is very much Russian. C major is definitely a glorious sacred Renaissance music feeling, such as Bach might compose, including his Prelude and Fugue and Flute Sonata. Playing in this key reminds me of my past lives as Giovanni Pierluigi da Palestrina and Jean-Baptiste Lully. And as Serge Prokofiev says, "There are always great melodies yet to be composed in the key of C major." This includes his superb third movement of his Piano Concerto No. 3, which is in C major.

The vibrational resonances of the 88 notes of the modern piano, in alignment with the Schumann Earth Resonances of between 3 Herz and 60 Herz, have major feeling and sensation effects on humans world-wide. Schumann Resonances modulate with changes to the ionosphere and lightning activity. When people hear songs in different frequencies, they collectively respond in accordance with the thought-form of the note itself and its vibration. There are harmonics naturally occurring as higher octaves, and these harmonics also create multiple awarenesses. There may have been a conscious intention for the following composers to create mystical experiences through their music—Bach, Gurdjieff, Scriabin, Messiaen, Vaughan-Williams, Ravel, Debussy, Poulenc, Faure, Rachmaninoff, and others.

No doubt music is the best international mode of communication used regardless of language and culture. My goal in future is to create many more beautiful melodies. If I can leave the world with at least seven entrancing, soul-opening riffs, I will be eternally happy.

In the ancient Egyptian temples of which I speak, I was vocally toning the 12 notes of the scale, sliding up and down. In many of the temples, when I toned A 440 Herz, amazingly the entire inner space of the building resonated with multiple harmonic overtones at over 50 times the volume. The architects mathematically had created the sacred geometry of the length, width and height of the temples. They placed their own soul's eternal tone into the fabric, structure and materials of their buildings. This causes a musical sonic expansion that is exponential.

While in the temples of Madinat Habu, Denderah, Edfu and Philae, I would tone with one of my friends. The harmonics were instantly bellowing from the innermost sanctuary and holy of holies to the outer entranceway and hypostyle hall. Seven guards once came running from the entrance to a temple to the inner sanctum. They looked around, stunned and bewildered.

"Where are the hundreds of people who were just chanting?" they demanded.

"There are just the two of us and we were singing; that's all." They did not believe us and went looking for more people hiding in other rooms.

G.I. GURDJIEFF, P.D. OUSPENSKY, MAURICE NICOLL, JOHN G. BENNETT

During the late 1980s and early 1990s, I spent many hours poring over the collected works of Gurdjieff, Ouspensky, Nicoll, Bennett, and many of their followers. Their mystical views of Western and Eastern thought, ritual, and history greatly influenced me in my own development and evolution. Great stars come to this planet, and I have always been a stargazer and admirer. I enjoy travelling on their star to distant inner worlds. As with Joseph Campbell, my life has been a Journey to the farthest Inner Reaches of (Human) Outer Space.

TRIP TO THE DOMINICAN REPUBLIC, 1990

It was during my second trip to the Dominican Republic that I found my medicine dog, Snickers. She was a perfect dog for me—a wild Egyptian pharaoh hound who accompanied me on all my shamanic and astral journeys, and she was present for all the sweat lodges I facilitated.

The reason for my visit was through my connection with the Toltec Don Juan and the nagual Masters I work with. In a dream, Don Juan directed me to fly to Sosua in the Dominican Republic and meet up with another fellow nagual traveller whom I met many times in my astral journeys yet never in my physical body. I have already covered the story of meeting her at the airport.

She took me in her car to the small town of Sosua in the Puerto Plata region. We were walking down the very small main street of town when a dog came running towards me from quite a distance in front of us.

My friend grabbed me, saying, "This is an abused street dog that does not like men! Watch out!"

This open-spirited creature was loping at such a quick pace towards me and did not stop when she reached me. I braced myself. She jumped into my arms and started licking my face! This dog always proved to be smarter than me, and she intuitively and psychically recognized people and places before I did.

From that day on, this scent hound followed me wherever I went. At the end of the day, she ran behind the car up the hill outside of town and slept on my bed with me. We were fast friends.

She had been the pet of a Toronto businessman who left her locked in the house when he went back to Toronto. It took her almost two weeks to claw her way through the wooden slat window in the bathroom. When she freed herself, some people in town took pity on her and fed her scraps and gave her water; eventually her emaciated body became lean and healthy again.

The owner of one of the few restaurants in town fed her burgers at his door almost every day. The other young street boys were jealous of her because they did not receive free handouts. I gave her food at my friend's house.

My fellow Don Juan student and I planned to do a sacred mushroom experience, just the way that we had been taught. We picked dozens of fresh mushrooms on her farm at one of her two orphanages. While reading relevant scriptures from the Old and New Testaments, we prepared our honeyed concoction. Then we rode our horses to the nearby private beach and spent an amazing 32 hours alone being blessed by the grace of the Sacred Mushroom Mother Spirit. I have never done psychotropic drugs or entheogens before or since.

During this experience, I revisited full flashes of thousands of my previous lives, one after the other, as if watching videos on fast-forward. In my vision, my friend's physical body disappeared, and all I experienced and sensed were her bones and rainbow colours streaming from her eyes, heart, and hands. Sitting on the rock, listening to the lapping of the Great Mother's oceanic lullaby, my soul was ecstatic and serenely quiescent throughout. It is possible to have this experience any time you choose. My feeling is that, should you choose to take entheogens, it's best if you always do this for vertical higher spiritual enlightenment, never for horizontal recreational kicks—otherwise you might attract many different kinds of human and non-human negative entities.

Snickers was with us during our journey, as were our horses whom we fed and watered. The beauty of the physical, white sandy beach cove was exquisite and perfect. Ever the "medicine watcher," Snickers presided over our safety and our journeys together.

At the end of my sojourn I departed for Toronto by plane. My friend asked if I could take Snickers with me. I still had my then-present dog companion, Otsitsa Elhar or "Flower Dog" in Mohawk. So I could not bring Snickers home with me.

A few weeks after I returned home, my elderly dog was getting ready for her own journey to our one spiritual home. Her back legs would not work and she could no longer get up on her own. With a heavy heart, I called my vet and he came over. I held her head and felt her heart with my hands while she took her last breath, and her glassy eyes showed that her soul went onwards. I followed her soul, as I want to do with all souls leaving the physical, and made sure that she would come back to me. Of the dogs I have had since I was six years of age, it has been the same dog soul reincarnated each time with a mixture of other dog and human souls I have previously known.

Three days after I let Otsitsa go home, I got a long-distance call from Sosua. It was my Don Juan friend.

"You've got to help us get Snickers out of town. The heat is on her!" was how she started the conversation.

"What's up?" I blurted out.

"My husband, the local vet, fixed her up. We have her in our compound."

"What happened?"

"When you left, she was wild with anxiety and missed you terribly. She kept going up and down the main street looking for you. The restaurant owner felt badly for her, and kept giving her burgers. Some local young teenage boys became even more jealous of her; they jumped her, tied her up, and dragged her to the ocean. They tried to drown her. As you know, she is so wily, squirmy, and agile that she wriggled loose and got away. That didn't stop the boys. One of them got a gun and shot her. It just missed her heart and spine, but went through part of her liver. We operated two weeks ago, and she seems better now.

"The whole town is in an uproar. Three-quarters of the town want the boys to be punished. The boys' families want the dog to be put down because she tried to bite the hand of the boy who shot her. She did this once she got out again; she was only courageously trying to warn the boy to leave her be. I'm afraid that they'll try something again, and kill her this time!

"Will you take her? We will give her all the shots, papers, put her in a cage, and pay for her plane trip. All you have to do is pick her up at the Toronto airport Sunday at 4:30pm. Will you do this for her? She has to get out of town."

"Sure I will! What flight is she on? Are you sure I can't pay for some of this?"

"No, it's our pleasure; she is such a great medicine dog!"

When I picked Snickers up at the airport it was early April and there was a bit of fresh snow on the ground. When she jumped out of the car, she had no idea what this was and kept leaping in the air to get out of it. Eventually, she learned to love it. I spoke with her in English and Spanish because she was perfectly bilingual, more than me.

This is how my medicine dog Snickers, who is also part human from lives in Egypt and Lemuria along with spiritual psychic abilities from the Pleaides, and Sirius B and C, came to live with me. Because she was greatly loved, and we roller-bladed, biked, hiked, and walked daily for at least one hour, she lived to be 27 years in human terms, which makes it about 189 years in dog years! She was a most remarkable and loving dog in so many ways.

I remember the first time I took her to my cabin at The Lake of Two Suns. I wanted her to acclimatize to the environment slowly, so I left her in my truck, while I unlocked the cabin. When I came back, she climbed through the open sliding window in the roof of the truck. She was wildly running around, even frothing at the mouth. I realized that she was actually emoting an entity that I had hitherto not felt; entity aggregation in human and animal auras is common among dogs and people in the Dominican Republic, as in every country. I caught her in my arms and did a depossession of the entity, and immediately she was calm, meek, and attentive. Thereafter, for many fine years, she ran about the 350 acres at will, always coming back at the end of a day, feeling very satisfied with herself.

At the Full Moons, when I held the 13 annual Spiritual Masters Sweat Lodges, she lay outside the lodge all night, keeping away bears, wolves, raccoons, beavers, and other critters. Dogs are not allowed in sweat lodges. However, to have a medicine dog such as Snickers was indeed one of the greatest blessings in my life.

MARC CONNORS AND THE LIFE AFTERWARDS

Marc Connors, one of the group members of the a cappella singing group, The Nylons, was a very close friend of mine. Marc did his inner spiritual-psychological work with me for three years before moving into the Spirit world in 1991. Through his dedicated search of dreams, personal symbolism, and earthly endeavours, he plumbed and found great depth in his soul.

A revelation that appeared often in his dreams was that he had been Marcus Aurelius, the Roman Emperor, 121–180 AD, and author of the great all-time classic book Meditations. Marc gave me copies of his daily writings and musings on his life and dying. I have a manuscript I am writing in which I link several of Aurelius's Meditations with Marc's writings. It is uncanny just how similar the themes, sentiments, and outlooks are between the two documents.

FOUNDING THE ACADEMY OF WORLD PSYCHOLOGY AND CREATIVE ARTS, 1992-1995

In February of 1992, in a cold, wintry, minus 40-degree windy solitude alone at my cabin at The Lake of Two Suns, with the lanterns gleaming in the night mystery, I had a full-out vision from Babaji Nagaraj about starting a unique Academy. It seems it was the first of its kind in Canada. Perhaps the easiest way to share the program is to give you the outline:

The Academy of World Psychology and Creative Arts
Founded and Directed by Dr. Joseph Martin in 1992, offering Diploma and Certificate Programmes and Workshops

DIPLOMA PROGRAMMES

1. **Transpersonal Psychology Counselling**
   3 year full time diploma / 5 year part time

   Courses:

   • **Principles and Practices of Western Psychology Levels I - III**
   Freud, Rank, Adler, Jung, Skinner, Perls, Moreno, Frankl, Rogers, Satir, Hillman,   Maslow, Grof, Erickson, NLP and beyond. Dealing with recovery issues of healing the Inner child, adult children of alcoholics, co-dependency, interdependency, incest survivors, love and romance survivors, substance and sex abuse survivors.

- **Companion Weekend Workshops for Western Psychology
Levels I - III**
Embedding Self-Trust in the Four Bodies
Transforming Beliefs & Identity, Dynamic Learning Restructuring
Exploring Your Dreams and Personal Mythology
Healing the Inner Child, Discovering and Healing Inner Parts
Releasing Co-Dependency, Reconnecting with Your Self

- **Principles and Practices of Eastern Psychology,
Levels I – III**
Vedanta, Buddhism, Zoroastrianism, Jainism, Taoism, Judaism,
early Christianity, the Essenes and Gnostics, Islam and Baha'i.
Practices of Raja Yoga, Kundalini Yoga, Kriya Yoga, Kabbalah and
Sufism (Rumi, Kabir, Rabi'a, Hazrat Khan, Pir Vilayat Khan).
Vajrayana Tibetan, Mahayana, Theravadan and Zen Buddhism.
Studies of karma, reincarnation, soul, spirit, and higher energy
bodies.

- **Companion Weekend Workshops for Eastern Psychology
I - III**
Past Lives Theory and Therapy
Meditation, Raja Yoga and Yoga Psychology
The Essence of the Chakras
Heart Ways of Knowing and Being

- **Principles and Practices of Tribal Psychology I – III**
Global tribal wisdom from the Americas, Africa, Asia, Australia,
Siberia and Scandinavia. Learn to honour the medicine traditions
of all creation: minerals and rocks, plants and herbs, animals, birds,
the elements, planets, constellations and star beings. Techniques
of healing, journeying, story-telling, drumming and medicines.
Connection with the Spirit Ancestors. Traditional vision quests and
sweat lodges.

- **Companion Weekend Workshops for Eastern Psychology I - III**
Music, Sound and Soul Psychology
Spirit Gift of The Eagle
Empowering Your Inner Shaman

Comparative Religions and Spiritual Practices
Goddess Wisdom Traditions
World Shamanic Principles and Practices
Holistic and Systemic Approaches to Psychology
Counselling Practicums
Jung and the Archetypes
Anthropology
Spiritual Science
Mythology and Symbology
Transformational Rituals
Earth-Gaia Consciousness
Life Studies of Spiritual Masters
Philosophy
Body-Mind Techniques
Meditation and Yoga

2. **Expressive Arts Thereapy**
3 year full time diploma / 5 year part time

Courses:

- **Myths, Dreams, Symbols, Self-Discovery Level I**
Artists derive much of their creative imagery from their inner world. Dreams are the Reservoir of this wealth of knowledge which comes in the form of archetypal, collective and personal symbols. Mythology is the collective dream. Creativity is the aim of the course. Through music, feelings, spontaneous drawings, colour, number, journaling, painting and creative writing, one delves into the dialogue and creates.

- **Aesthetics, Creativity and the Artist Level II**

The aim of this course is to understand and experience how the mind and soul of the Artist can work, play and explore artistic expression through visual, auditory, and kinesthetic pathways. As in Level I, we study mythologies, arts and religions of the world cultures. Archetypes and Jungian psychology are explored in more depth, particularly the shadow. Creative blocks are worked. Deeper emotions open up more meaningful creative expressions. Each develops their personal mythology.

- **Multi-Modal Creativity and Strategies of Innovation Level III**

Special class in creative theory and practice for artists and teachers. We explore Archetypal themes of death and rebirth, the creative masculine, the lost feminine, good and evil, light and dark, the Holy Grail, the inner quest, balance of opposites, the romantic quest, angelic realms, and universal creation. One's personal mythology embraces the Self, anima, animus, trickster, fool, wise old person, shadow and others. Methodologies include performance art, ritualistic art, kinesthetic art, kinetic art, improvisational music, voicing and drumming, and primordial sounds. A study of creative artists like Blake, Kandinsky, Mondrian, Klee, Harris, Thomson, Carr, O'Keeffe and Michael Robinson.

Spontaneous Drawing and Painting
Creative Writing
Voice Work
Dance and Movement
Drumming and Rhythm
Music and Sound
Mask-Making
Holistic and Systemic Approaches to Psychology
Sculpture
Psychodrama
Story-Telling
Counselling Practicums

3. **Expressive Arts Therapy / Transpersonal Pscyhology**
   3 year full time diploma / 5 year part time
   A major / minor or double major combination of aforementioned topics.

CERTIFICATE PROGRAMMES

- **Basic Counseling**

2 year part time

Courses:

Communication Skills
Focusing
Psychodrama
Personal Mythology
Creative Visualization
Roles and Group Dynamics
Dream Analysis
NLP (Neuro-Linguistic Programming)
Gestalt
Jungian Psychology
Archetypal Psychology
Transpersonal Psychological Skills
Marriage and Family Systems and Therapy

- **Transpersonal Counselling (Advanced)**

1 year part time

Courses:

Transpersonal Psychology
Rebirthing and Breathwork
Spiritual Science Techniques
Advanced Shamanic Traditions
Advanced Meditation

Deepening Intuition
Emotional Intelligence
Chakra Energising
Body-Mind Techniques
Archetypal Psychology
Deep Self- Hypnotic Ericksonian Trance Work

I started to offer the following workshops and courses in 1992 through
The Academy. Later in 1995, when I inaugurated ~The Soul Initiative~
Coach Training Program; I beefed up the material in the Energy Medicine
Trainings, as well as the spiritual heart workshops which, eventually came
to be entitled, "Heart Ways of Knowing and Being" when two business
partners and I, Miriam Sanua and John Ryan started Source Co-Creations,
the company Miriam and I still co-run for our books, workshops, music
CDs, art, and blogs.

WORKSHOPS AND COURSES OFFERED

Energy Medicine Levels I - IV

- **Energy Medicine I**
Quantum Mechanics, Adamantine Particles, the Four Energy
Bodies according to Ayurvedic Medicine, Natural Medicine,
Homeopathy, Naturopathy, Traditional Chinese Medicine,
Advanced Complex Homeopathic Remedies, UNDA Numbers,
Spiritual Realities, the Soul's Source Template, the pineal and
pituitary-hypothalamus, breath techniques, mantras, intention, kinet-
ics, the sacred heart

- **Energy Medicine II**
Cosmic Light particles and waves, advances in the Four Energy
Bodies, the sixteen chakras according to Ayurveda, blockages in
the chakras, Structure of the personality, the four rites of passage
stages of healing, further breath techniques, meditation, mantras,
intention, surrendering, kinetics, the soul's template, universal web
of light in creation, opening the heart, spiritual masters' techniques,
source healing techniques

- **Energy Medicine III**

Everything in universal creation is Light, research on Adamantine Particles, breath, skin, prana, Qi, Ki, DNA, gravity, electricity, magnetism, advanced mantras, inner six senses, sun, moon, planets, stars, dextro-rotatory and laevo-rotatory cellular and bodily energies, the sacred heart and the Spiritual Masters, Earth Healing meditation

- **Energy Medicine IV**

Dedication, Source healing, experiential healing, self-love Remedies, DNA, human evolution, miasms and energetic bodily frequencies, metabolism and regeneration, ego and soul, transpersonal psychology, etheric healing

This Academy of World Psychology and Creative Arts was a full-time program that lasted three and a half years. By then I was worn out from seeing psychotherapy clients from 9am–6pm Monday to Friday, and having two classes Mondays to Thursdays from 6–8pm, and 8–10pm. I had many guest lecturers come in for various topics, such as Dr. Robbie Svoboda on Ayurvedic Medicine, Hart de Fouw on Ayurvedic Astrology or Jyotish, along with talks by friends who are in the Baha'i, Zoroastrian, and Muslim faiths.

WORKING WITH BABAJI, JESUS, YOGANANDA WITH EACH CLIENT

During my time as a clinician, the main focus of my listening was to be aware of the Spiritual Masters inside my heart and consciousness who instructed what questions I asked of each client and when to ask them. I have been doing this all my life, starting when I was in public, junior, and high school; Jesus had me focus on the sphere of astral light a foot above everyone's head and draw their consciousness up into it, and shower them with love.

With decades of practice, my clinical work became much easier. The experience of having Jesus, Babaji Nagaraj, Yogananda, Mother Mary, Archangel Mikael, Metatron, Melchizedek, and Sananda, consciously support my own intuition about a client's deepest needs and issues was priceless. By the end of each day, I had more energy than when I started—and this was because of the love energy from each and all of the Spiritual Masters pouring through me.

As I did clinical processing in this manner, I was able to easily, naturally, quickly, and incisively pinpoint the deepest emotional, psychological, and karmic issues of each person, couple, and family. I was also able to energetically link the individual with their most appropriate Spiritual Master, a Source Being of the highest caliber. The results were magnificent in that people always came away feeling loved, whole, positive, and heartened, knowing there was a Great Light at the end of the tunnel and in their heart.

Sitting in my comfy emerald green Victorian wing-back chair observing and listening to my client in a similar chair seven feet away, I often felt the kundalini rush of energies as one or more of the Spiritual Masters made their I AM Presence felt within my body. Ever since I was a baby of two years and onwards, I always felt these kinesthetic thrills rushing through my body from head to toes, and from toes to head. These kundalini experiences always give me love, peace, joy, hope, courage, strength, commitment, patience, and knowledge to share with All My Relations.

To psychotherapists and other practitioners reading this, I highly recommend that you consciously and energetically link up with some or all of the Spiritual Masters you feel close with, in particular Jesus and Babaji. You will find great healing for yourself and your clients through these experiences, even ecstatic joy and fulfillment! You will be doing your clients a great favour in supporting them to take back their own powers of love, choice, and liberation. The therapeutic process will be assuredly and extremely heightened, shortened, and more focused. The long-standing emotional karmic issues of angers, sorrows, and fears will be released from the client's very first past life where and when the issues originally occurred, and then they will be healed along their past-present-future timeline. Offer your clients the best healing. As Jesus says, "I am the way, and the truth, and the life."

If your chosen spiritual path is to support others in finding their own healings, then I would greatly suggest that you as the coach-facilitator undertake Rebirthing and your own karmic emotional psychological healing before you start connecting with clients. It will do you a world of good and your clients even more so.

EMPOWERMENT OF THE UNIFIED FEMININE – MOTHER MARY, MARY MAGDALENE, DENDREAH, RABI'A, KWAN YIN, AVALOKITESHVARA, DURGA, DEMETER-PERSEPHONE, KALI

Once I learned to transmute all the negative and destructive energies from the Negative Mother Archetype and complex that infected and rattled my soul consciousness, I felt the need to bring to my clients the Positive Mother Archetypal power of pure love and unconditional friendship through listening and supporting. All the world's children are born into this Negative Mother destruction that diminishes our holds on our lives, and creates great lack of self-worth including self-hatred, guilt, shame, and self-destructive tendencies.

To accomplish these chosen ends, I have spent my life engaging in a personal experiential connection with as many Positive Mother beings as possible. These include and are not limited to Dendreah, Mother Mary (Jesus' Mother), Mary Magdalene, Rabi'a, Kwan Yin, Avalokiteshvara, Durga-Gaia, Demeter-Persephone, and especially Kali. The positive side of Kali is the most useful energy I have ever explored and utilized. I am so grateful for Her knowledge, wisdom, and guidance. The positive side of Kali, the Hindu Mother of All Destruction of All Negativity, has allowed me to access and command Kali's Sword of Truth that destroys any and all negativity from the Negative Murdering Mother, the Dark Forces, demons and entities; and to create positive healthy boundaries with other humans who are energy vampires. God-Goddess bless always these positive Feminine and Mother figures. Without them, I would most certainly not be where I am today.

EMPOWERMENT OF THE UNIFIED MASCULINE WITH MERCURIUS-HERMES, BABAJI, SHIVA, KING COBRA

On the masculine side, I knew early on that I needed to transmute the childish, arrogant, psychopathic-homoerotic side of my personal father and the Collective Negative Father. My father was totally caught up in this toxic blend of psychopathology, from birth, his family of origin, his father, and the masculine side of his mother. Like my personal father, these kinds of fathers feel the unconscious and conscious compulsion to control, dominate, and disempower the masculinity of their sons, and thereby castrate their sexuality and masculinity, and disembowel the will power of their male offspring.

My ongoing psychological-spiritual-emotional progress has led me to Mercurius, Hermes, Hephaistos, Shiva and the King Cobra. Mercurius, for me, is the full Source masculine spirit, alive and well and living inside my earthy, instinctual body and sensuality. He teaches me, trains me, guides me, and empowers me. Hermes is another name for him. Hephaistos is the wounded lame god of healing and the fiery forge. Every son and male is wounded in some ways; I was multiply wounded and knew I needed all the help I could get. Hephaistos helped me through my early wounding for the first 35 years of my life.

After that, I had an intuitive impulse to move on and work with the Powerhouse and Central Source of all masculinity, Shiva and the King Cobra. Babaji Nagaraj, Creator of the Universe, Krishna and Shiva incarnate, has taught me to become the all-out masculine male I am today. This has come through serious, sincere, and difficult inner processing. This struggle has resulted in an ongoing sense of personal liberation and clarity. Shiva destroys all the negativity, arrogance, greed, totalitarian evil, and patriarchal force of the old Negative Father and Male Archetype. I fought against the world and won for this. In the old patriarchal system of homo economicus patriarchus, men are mentalistic, non-feeling, robotic somebodies climbing the ladder of competition and intrigue. Lying, cheating, and soul murder is their way. Babaji Nagaraj as Shiva gave me the conscious power to destroy all this in myself. I found my life when I became nobody within the outer world of descending patriarchal force; I found my own path of individuation. Babaji as King Cobra gave me the necessary internal snakebite poison that became my antidote to the allure and domination of this outworn, man-killing Archetypal system. Gradually, over the decades, I have won the battles, although I always keep the search and journey. The journey is the joy and what it is all about! I keep using this Shiva power of destroying the inauthentic in order to keep metamorphosing into a real living human being with heart.

HALIBURTON SWEAT LODGES WITH
THE NATIVE SPIRITUAL MASTERS

CRAZY HORSE, GERONIMO, SITTING BULL, DENDREAH, TECUMSEH... MOHAWK AND LAKOTA LODGES... EAGLE, BEAR, WOLF, SNAKE LODGES, 1989-2001

I have been giving sweat lodges since 1971. I have built sweat lodges in various places in central Ontario. Starting in 1989, when I became the steward of The Lake of Two Suns near Wilberforce Ontario, I held sweat lodges virtually every one of the 13 full moons of the year until 2001.

I built the sweat lodge according to the Lakota tradition. The size, shape, and materials were just as our Ancestors have been doing for millennia on Turtle Island. The differences within our sweat lodges we held were several. Often sweats are given to heal the mind and physical body of individuals, and to heal emotional losses, troubles, and relational separations. These were also central to our lodges. Above this, and more key, was the fact that these sweats were organized, run by, and inhabited by many of our greatest Native Spiritual Masters. Spirit's instructions to me were to make these sweat lodges focused strictly on spiritual openness and connection to the Native Spiritual Masters.

While the participants, Fire Keeper, and myself fasted between one to three days beforehand, we ritually called in by name over 60 First Nations Spiritual Great Ones. Some of the most significant ones are Tashunke Witko (Crazy Horse), Goyathlay (Geronimo), Tatanka Yotanka (Sitting Bull), Tecumthe (Tecumseh), Hinmaton Yalatkit (Chief Joseph), Chief Dan George, and of course, Dendreah (the White Buffalo Calf Woman). The prayers and recitations to the Upper World, Spirits, and Animal Medicines of the Middle and Lower Worlds were given in Mohawk, Lakota, and English languages.

Those participants attending were a combination of my trainees in the shamanic way, personal psychotherapy clients, many with cancer and other serious illnesses, and some of my adopted Native sons.

While walking about a kilometre and a half from the log cabin to the sweat lodge with eyes closed while drumming and rattling, we sang ancient traditional medicine songs from the world's First Nations. Scores of red-hot "Grandfathers" or healing stones were brought into the lodge. Our Fire Keeper started the fire early in the morning, so that we would have scorching heat by sundown. He endeavoured to make each lodge hotter than the last. Eventually we had upwards of 100 red-hot "Grandfathers" stoking our lodge with Spirit and rock medicine powers. And man, did we sweat! Individuals were often encouraged to bring their head down to the ground in order to breathe more easily. Essential oils of the great medicines of cedar, sage, fir, pine, and sweetgrass were offered to the "Grandfathers" and the Spiritual Masters throughout the sweat.

We started with prayers of thanksgiving to all the Spiritual Beings from "Below the Earth, On the Earth, to Above the Sky," in the traditional Haudenosaunee Uhkwehuh:wenehah way. One by one, the Native Spiritual Masters arrived from the Spirit world and entered through the top of the lodge. Their presence was palpable and unmistakable. Each Master has their vibration and emotional-spiritual expression. Those present for the first time were floored at "seeing, feeling, and sensing" the astral presences of these Native Ancestors who graced our lodge.

All individuals got the healing they needed. Since illness, to a large degree, is the result of hidden unconscious fears, sadnesses, and angers, these were transmuted with the support of these Masters. The sweetness of Dendreah's soul, the beauty and mystical awareness of Tashunke Witko, the clarity and strength of Tatanka Yotanka's energies, and the powerhouse, cunning, humility, and hilarity of Goyathlay embraced those seeking opening and healing. While each of us surrendered to the experiences, there was great relief, rejoicing, and silent honouring of the process. Respect for these Spiritual Masters brings greater self-respect and self-worth. May these Ancestors always be blessed for their roles and presence in our lives! I feel truly blessed to have been able to co-participate with them.

We offered various lodges that were aspects of Animal Medicines that would support the greater healing of individuals—Eagle, Bear, Wolf, and Snake.

THE JOURNEY TO THE WORLD'S BIGGEST POWWOW, 1993, AND DREAMS OF RECEIVING THE MEDICINE PIPES FROM ELDERS

In the winter of 1993, I had many unusual and powerful dreams about some of my Native Ancestors in the physical in the American Southwest or the Four Corners of New Mexico, Arizona, Colorado, and Utah. Living elders visited me in the astral plane for many nights from January through to March 1993. I saw their faces, heard their voices, and listened to their suggestions. They wanted me to come down to The World's Biggest Powwow or Gathering of Nations in Albuquerque, New Mexico that April. It is held in The University of New Mexico Arena called "The Pit."

I went to powwows across Canada since the early 1970s when I had spent time in every province, territory, and state in Canada and America sitting at the feet of great elders and listening to their teachings. However, I never considered going to this Gathering of Nations in Albuquerque, even though I had spent many months training there in Ayurveda with Dr. Vasant Lad.

My visitations at night were unusual. I was told that I was to come down to the Gathering and would meet up with seven different elders who had gifts for me that I needed. These elders were from different tribes—an Acoma Pueblo woman elder who was a potter and jeweler, an elderly Dine or Navajo medicine man, an androgynous male medicine man from Taos Pueblo, a Zuni maker of animal fetishes, a grandmother of the Tohono O'odham or Papago tribe, and a middle-aged Ojibwe man who is a pipe-maker from Pipestone, Minnesota, and Ron Sunsinger from the Oglala Sioux and a descendant of Hehaka Sapa (Black Elk).

I travelled alone to Albuquerque. The Grand Entry was the longest I was ever a part of; it lasted two and a half hours for all the Elders, Grandfathers, eagle lances, veterans, and dancers to come into the arena. Through my intuition and "Inner Voice," I was asked by the Spirits to go and sit in various seats. One of the first I went to was in the nosebleed section. Here I met the very elderly Navajo medicine man that spoke only in Navajo and yet we understood each other through spiritual heart knowing.

One after another, I was led to each of the seven people who had appeared to me in my visitation-dreams. The gifts I received were bowls, silver jewelry, fetishes, and pipes; in return I offered sacred tobacco. Among the most important was a Walking Bear Medicine Pipe from the present male of the Ojibwe family, who hereditarily mine the red catlinite in Pipestone, Minnesota from where all sacred pipes have been made for over 5,000 years in the three Americas. Another was the exquisite Eagle Medicine Pipe with an orangewood pipe-stem, which was offered to me by Ron Sunsinger.

BLESSINGS OF THE MEDICINE PIPES

After the Powwow, I felt Spirit's nudging to go and have the Pipes blessed by the Spirit Ancestors in Mesa Verde National Park in Colorado. There I met the Chief Ranger, Bill, who is Lakota Sioux. From the moment we met, we commenced deep spiritual conversations about our many experiences. Bill told me about his contact with Ancestors in the Park and in particular the kivas or ceremonial underground circular sacred ritual sites. I told him that I came down from Canada to be gifted with several Medicine Pipes and would like the Ancient Ones from Mesa Verde to bless them for me.

Although by law, one is asked to leave Mesa Verde Park by sundown every day due to the sacredness of the site, Bill asked me if I wanted to sleep overnight in a kiva. I said, "yes" immediately without thinking what might be involved. As I drove out with Bill in his flatbed truck to make sure the front gates at the highway were locked after the last visitor departed, he told me that I could take some water and my sleeping bag and head down the trail and sleep in one of the reconstructed kivas overnight, and that he would make me some fried eggs the following morning when I came to his lodging.

I packed up the pipes in my bag and headed out for a truly remarkable and stellar night of profound visitations. That night I drifted in and out of visionary Dreamtime and was powerfully visited by many Ancestors. Most of them thanked me for coming, blessed the Medicine Pipes and myself. In a deeply mystical Medicine Ceremony They asked me to carry on their old ways and spiritual truths through Medicine Wheel Teachings and Sweat Lodge healings.

In the morning after sharing with Bill, I told him that the Old Ones asked me to spend the day perched on the top of a rock cliff in the Park. I was to lie on my back for eight hours and let the Sun's rays and Ancient Medicine Powers of The Four Elements, Eagle, and Ancestors continue to bless me. Bill suggested I lie on a small flat rock just off the cliff near Pipe Shrine House. While suspended there in time and space, I went in and out of visions outlining my future and how to use these Pipes. To this day, my experiences with the Ancient Ones in Mesa Verde still impulse my sense of oneness with All My Relations.

RELEASING IRISH SOULS FROM BATTLEFIELDS, 1995

A good friend of mine, John, and I went in 1995 to The 10th International Transpersonal Psychology Conference in Killarney, Ireland. We travelled to Ireland a month earlier and stayed with good friends in Dublin, a husband and wife who both attended my Academy in Toronto. We were so grateful for the loan of their four-wheel-drive vehicle that allowed us to journey to every county in Northern and Southern Ireland. I used some of the time to visit areas where my father's relatives grew up centuries ago.

As it turned out, we were most excited about visiting the sacred sites of ancient Ireland—those connected with the Druids, the Celts, and the early Christians. Among the places we slept overnight were Newgrange, the fascinating burial mound 5,000 years old aligned with the winter solstice, and Skellig Michael, a dramatic offshore rock where hermit monks lived in tiny beehive huts from 588 to 1100 AD. We felt the presence of the ancient ones there in these places. Other sacred spots included Glendalough, Clonmacnoise, The Hill of Tara, Knock Shrine, Monasterboice, Dowth, and Gallarus Oratory.

The most influential on my psyche were The Hill of Tara and Clonmacnoise. The Hill of Tara has been a sacred site since prehistoric times, with the earliest known monument—The Mound of Hostages—built between 2,500 and 2,100 BC. In the Iron Age, roughly spanning the 1st through 5th centuries AD, The Hill of Tara was the ceremonial center of the Celtic high kings of Ireland. The kings appear to have abandoned the site in the 6th century. Perhaps this had something to do with St. Patrick visiting Tara in the 430s AD and lighting his "Paschal Fire" on the nearby Hill of Slane. My friend John and I opened the locked entrance to The Mound of the Hostages and slept there overnight. We were kept awake all night by the constant visitation of many ancient deceased souls, to whose stories we attentively listened.

In the middle of a large flat grassy field stands The Stone of Destiny, a phallic coronation object, symbolic of the right of ancient Celtic high kings. While the Stone is about four feet tall and quite slippery, particularly in the rain, both my friend and I were able to perch atop this Stone creating a magical experience, though hilarious at the same time.

St. Ciaran, the son of a master craftsman, founded Clonmacnoise in 548 AD. The settlement soon became a major center of religion, learning, trade, craftsmanship, and politics, thanks in large part to its position at the major crossroads of the River Shannon (flowing north-south), and the gravel ridges of the glacial eskers (running east-west). We spent several days living in an old thatched hut, heated by a peat fire, and astral travelling with the founders of the community, including St. Patrick.

RELEASING THE GHOSTS OF ANCIENT KINGS AND WARRIORS

Perhaps the main reason for visiting my ancient birthplaces in Ireland was to release the ghosts of ancient kings and warriors that have existed in the lower astral realms of the land since 2,500 BC or earlier. My friend and I journeyed from one crossroads, battlefield, and ancient graveyard to another throughout Northern and Southern Ireland—whether city, town, or land. Looking into these astral realities, I spoke with all these bodiless souls, told them whom I was, where they were, and then proceeded to take them all en masse back into the Light. For many lives I have offered this transitional soul process to dead souls; I do so always with Jesus and the Christed golden-white light, which makes the process so easy, natural, and quick.

Over a period of weeks, over 10,000 souls were released back into the Clear Light and they are now able to choose rebirth when they are ready.

~THE SOUL INITIATIVE~
COACH-FACILITATOR-TRAINER PROGRAM, 1995-2001

In 1995 I initiated a new Coach-Facilitator-Trainer Certificate Program in Toronto, called The Soul Initiative. Some of these were clients from The Academy of World Psychology and Creative Arts, and most were new people who heard about my other programs and wanted to train as Coaches.

The Program was an individual and group process for about 12 people each year. It was a one-year training, although most carried on for the second and third year. It was a very comprehensive program, incorporating all that I had done and learned over my lifetime.

The first year of the training has been compiled as a self-help process book entitled "Travelling Light: A Call to Great Power Through the Nine Inner Places of Truth, Freedom and Love Consciousness," (537 pages) by myself and Miriam Sanua, and available through www.SourceCo-Creations.com. Volumes II and III cover years two and three and will likely come out within the next few years.

Here is the brief outline of the course.

~ The Soul Initiative ~ Coach - Faciliatator - Trainer Certificate

A Path to Self-Actualization and Remembering the Love You Are

A three-year course offering the following eight modules each year in advancing levels:

THE DIVINE PHYSICAL
THE DIVINE EMOTIONAL AND INNER CHILD
THE DIVINE MENTAL
THE DIVINE SPIRITUAL
THE DIVINE UNCONSCIOUS (Split off soul parts) AND DREAMS
THE DIVINE CREATIVITY, VOCATION AND PROSPERITY
THE DIVINE PERSONAL MYTHOLOGY
THE DIVINE SOUL RELATIONSHIP

Chapter Ten

BELL'S PALSY A SECOND TIME

When Tom died, I had Bell's Palsy the first time in my mid-30s. In 1995 I had it a second time. I was working in my Toronto clinic with a group of about 12 young street kids who had been severely sexually abused. During one of the treatments I gave them in the healing circle, my neurological energy systems were over-firing and I instantly got Bell's Palsy—only this time on the right side of my face! Again as with the first time, it took me two full years of twice-weekly electro-acupuncture stimulation to get over it, to the point where I could close my eye, talk, and smile again. As anyone with this condition will tell you, the pain is excruciating. Minor painkillers were all I took, although the doctors offered me heroin.

I saw Dr. Paul Ho at The Toronto Pain and Headache Clinic. He set the 24 needles, attached the electrical wires to a central device and left me for half an hour. Ever the card, one time I stiffly and jerkily walked into the waiting room that was filled with clients and said, "Dr. Frankenho, something has gone terribly wrong... the bolt came out of my neck and the wires are frying my face." We still chuckle about this after all these years.

MY HOMEOPATHIC TRAINING WITH SEROYAL INTERNATIONAL, 1993-2002

Between 1993 and 2002 I attended dozens of weekend workshop trainings in Homeopathic Medicine, UNDA Numbers Complex Homeopathic Remedies, and the treatment of all the common ailments known to humanity at this time. The courses I took were invaluable for the treatment of my psychotherapy clients. I have always had an interest and done major self-study in Homeopathy, Naturopathy, Anthroposophical Medicine, Chinese and Tibetan Medicine, and of course Ayurveda.

Some of the courses I took were Clinical Patient Evaluation: Miasms, Temperaments, and Constitutions; The Immune System: The Cause and Solution to Chronic Disease; Individualized Nutrition: Addressing Biochemical Individuality for Optimal Health and Wellness; Reclaim the Brain: Holistic Assessment and Treatments for Key Endocrine Disorders; Improve Clinical Outcomes with Gemmotherapy, Phytotherapy,

Oligo-Elements, Tissue Salts, and Biotherapeutics; Successful Case Management of Chronic Disease; and Clinical Applications of Biotherapeutic Drainage and UNDA Numbered Compounds.

The most advanced series I took was with the late Dr. Gerard Guenot on the spiritual, psychological, karmic and biochemical causes of illness. Dr. Guenot recently came to me from Spirit and asked me to write some texts with him on Health Regimens.

CHAPTER 11
MY LIFE AS AN ANTHROPOLOGIST
28–39 YEARS

LIVING WITH THE MOHAWK OF KANEHSATAKE

Since the age of 19, I was living intermittently with my Mohawk family in Kanehsatake near Oka, Quebec. As mentioned, once my Jung Ph.D. thesis was disallowed, I switched and used my ethnographical fieldwork experience in Kanehsatake on cosmology, mythology, spirituality, history, marriage and the family, art, and symbolism to attain my Ph.D. in 1988.

I often wondered why I was so drawn to the community and the connections with the Mohawk people. While there, it came to me in dreams, visions, and visitations just what had gone on there previously for me in past centuries. It was clear to my body sensations and astral memories that I had been the Mohawk Chief Augneeta, living in the village in the mid-1800s. With the pressure from the Sulpician Church and local French people, our Mohawk lands were gradually decimated until there was hardly anything left. As Chief Augneeta, I trained with the Jesuits and learned their languages of Latin and French. Through many confrontations, I stood up for the rights of my people and this was not taken well. Finally, on a journey to Chocha:ke or Montreal to state our grievances before a higher council, I was poisoned by the priests and died. My present life here with the Mohawks is a remedy, redemption, and a reminder that the liberation of people is always through our own struggles for justice, respect, kindness, and entitlement.

From my lengthy discussions with many elders in Kanehsatake, I realized that nefarious deeds had been going on here for centuries. During The American Civil War priests and their henchmen had gone down to the Northern Union camps that were filled with men dying from smallpox, and brought back infected blankets, giving them to the needy Natives for supposed comfort in the cold winters. At this time, many Mohawk died from the illness. As well, rats and poisons were surreptitiously placed in the daily soup that the Sulpicians doled out in front of their riverside church in Oka.

Again, Mohawk men, women, and children died from this ethnic cleansing.

While there, Kateri Tekakwitha became one of my guardian saints, and she is now recognized as such by the Catholic Church.

In other dream visitations, many Mohawk chiefs from the 1600s and 1700s came to me. One chief actually told me where his Medicine Bags were buried on the side of the mountain; I retrieved the energetic contents of his Medicines, and he instructed me in their proper use.

THE DOGRIB OF FORT RAE-EDZO

This is a story of a deadly serious attack I underwent while being in the Northwest Territories in 1977. I travelled north through the polar bear country of the Eastern Arctic to be the best man at my friend Patrick's wedding to his wife Gab, a beautiful Dogrib woman. After flying in to Yellowknife, we took a 12-hour bumpy ride in Patrick's old red pickup truck to a small cabin on the tundra in the small-lakes district north of YK. We got there very late that night and bunked out in the small cabin. Patrick and Gab took the loft and I slept in my sleeping bag on the wooden floor.

Shortly after midnight, I was in my Dreamtime astrally wandering the flat landscape in the moonlight. I was suddenly viciously attacked and thrown on the ground on my back. There was an old, evil-looking witch-man sitting on me, glowering nastily in my face. He felt and looked demented, crazed, and demoniacal. His force was so powerful I could not get him off me. Then he dragged me over to the nearby cold stream and threw me down underwater on my back. He sat on me, pushed my shoulders and face down so that I was completely submerged and could not breathe. I panicked and awkwardly tried to throw him off, first to the right and then to the left. Nothing seemed to work. Sensing that I would soon run out of oxygen, I managed to fake to the right and threw him off to the left. In doing so, I woke myself up, and sat up in the sleeping bag panting and exhausted. I let my friends sleep after our long journey and quickly bedded down again myself.

Within a few minutes, I was thrust underwater again by this dark, long-haired, unkempt, and witchy figure. This time he had renewed intent and energies; I felt his murderous gaze through his eyes, sapping me of my courage and strength. The force of his arms and body atop me left me pinned and extremely worried. Even though I have trained for many years in martial arts like Karate-do, Tai Qi, Qi Gong, and Aikido, I knew that I was no match for this man. Where did his strength come from? He had the power of ten men! Was he still living in a physical body? Fainting from the lack of oxygen and panicking at my impending death, I fought tooth and nail; I scratched, punched as best I could, spit, screamed, and threw my knees at his back. Nothing worked. I was going unconscious. With one strong movement of my lower body I threw him off over my head, turned myself over in the water and sat up, drenched. Then I woke up stunned once more, my sleeping bag ripped open and a mess.

Now I was terrified to go back to sleep. I quietly opened the cabin door and went outside to wait for the dawn. It was far too cold, and being severely chilled, I went back inside, and tried to fall asleep. Being exhausted from my flight and long drive, I did finally sleep. The third time in my astral dream, I found myself again underwater with this creature riding me and pushing me against the sharp stony gravel on the riverbed; now he had the power of 100 men. Suddenly my kinesthetic martial arts training and my Don Juan nagual training kicked in. This was a spiritual battle to the death. One of us had to die. I spun my internal energy around my dantien and forced it up through my eyes, voice, hands, and feet. I meekly struggled to free myself twice, pretending like I was dying and giving up in fear. The third time I did not wait that long, and pretended I was fainting and losing consciousness, I focused all my spiritual energies on one big push and threw him into the sky about forty feet. There, Jesus and Babaji were waiting to take him into the Clear Light so he would never bother anyone again. The plan worked. These "petty tyrants" are our best teachers. They force us to find all our innermost courage, strength, focus, and spiritual power to protect ourselves and destroy what would destroy us. This was a most powerful lesson that I learned at the age of 27, and I have trained myself far beyond the capacities I had to very good positive effect.

THE BALINESE

One of the blessings of being trained as an anthropologist is being able to divest myself from my social-cultural trappings and childhood socialization as a Westerner, and delve fully into other cultures as a participant. I did this earlier with other religious traditions. I love other symbolic cultures of the world that attempt to hold together heaven, earth and hell within their own historical worldview and cosmology.

The Balinese have always fascinated me, in particular their wonderful melding of Animism, Buddhism, and Shivaite Hinduism, while surrounded by the Muslim cultures of Indonesia. Their respectful personalities of great silence, presence, kindness, and tolerance are evident in their daily attire, activities, and spiritual-cultural representations such as their temple food offerings, Lagong dances, and lengthy ritual ceremonies to Mount Agung and the Nagas of the ocean.

THE ARANDA OF NORTHERN ARNHEM LAND, AUSTRALIA

These indigenous First Nations, whose ancestors date back 40,000 years, are an important world culture for their abilities to live and work in the fourth dimensional Dreamtime where they still contact Ancestors, Creator spirits, animal medicine beings, rock spirits, and the elements. They constantly astral travel along the kunapipi lines of their longstanding human and animal Ancestors.

While training as an anthropologist, I learned some of their language, art, culture, mythology, worldview, and ethos. I planned to make an ethnographical trip to their territory, including Alice Springs; however, too many other inner and outer journeys took precedence and this was not to be.

CHAPTER 12
OWEN SOUND, ONTARIO, 2001–2004

Through many intuitive and synchronous events I was asked by Spirit and the Spiritual Masters to close down my Toronto psychotherapy clinic in June of 2000. At this point, all the members of The Soul Initiative graduated, and I felt the need to stop doing psychotherapy, which I did part-time since 1970 and full-time since 1989.

My inner indications also moved me to sell my house in Toronto and to move up to Owen Sound, Ontario; this occurred in August 2001.

I moved to Owen Sound, and lived with my two good friends Miriam and John when a month later 9/11 occurred and my ongoing quest to understand the corruption and denouement of the old civilization and the coming-of-age of our next civilization consciously increased tenfold. 9/11 was a turning point in all our lives, an explosive new exclamation to the 20th century of massive World Wars.

As a clinician and anthropologist, my work is cut out for me. I constantly analyze the outer repercussions, historical events, and personal outcomes and fallout from the split-off psyche we all have individually and collectively. The only answer to this conundrum is to embody our awakened soul, embrace the paradox of spirit and matter, heaven and hell, good and evil, light and dark within our own consciousness, and thus find harmony and balance that will lead to inner and outer peace.

PSYCHOTHERAPY

I love the land around Owen Sound—the rolling hills, the creeks and waterfalls, the trails through nature, and of course swimming and body-surfing in Georgian Bay at the Meaford and Sauble beaches. I lived up in the Grey-Bruce area in the mid-to-late 1970s, so I longed to go back to be out of the big city to hike, ski, and swim at my leisure every day with nature.

Although I gave up my clinic at Parliament and King Streets, I journeyed one day a week to a clinic on Yonge Street in Toronto that I shared with other practitioners. After a few months, I realized the trek was taking its toll on me energetically so I started seeing local clients in a friend's clinic in Owen Sound. I did this from 2001 until 2004.

NATIVE HEALING-TEACHING GROUPS

Over the years, I have met and become friends with quite a few Native people in the area, and those who wanted to learn the First Nations Medicine teachings. We held circles in the back of a local Health Food Store, and on flat rocks at the edge of Georgian Bay waters near Dyer's Bay, south of Tobermory.

We spent wonderful times at local summer powwows and daily swims at Sauble Beach on Lake Huron. This is one of my favourite beaches in the world, with its miles of white sand and gently rolling waves on a warm Lake Huron.

NLP TRAININGS

Miriam and I gave two NLP Basic Trainings and Intermediate Masters NLP Training at the local Owen Sound Health Club. Many of our attendees went on to become great public speakers, teachers, musicians, and writers.

HEART WAYS OF KNOWING AND BEING WORKSHOPS

At a Chiropractor's office in town, Miriam, John, and I gave our first Sacred Heart Workshop where we did process work to enable individuals to retrieve their souls lost in the astral realms and open their emotional and energetic hearts.

ENERGY MEDICINE TRAININGS, FOUR LEVELS

Miriam and I also gave four levels of Energy Medicine Training to yoga teachers of the major yoga studios in Toronto. We based this on Ayurveda and the wisdom of The Bhagavad-Gita. We held a group in Fergus Ontario as well.

SWEAT LODGES

In the spring of 2001 and spring of 2002, we held two sweat lodges at a friend's lodge on the Bruce Peninsula. We also held sweats at our Fire Keeper's lodge in Bolton Ontario over a number of full moons. We did a winter sweat in Bolton in February 2001, in minus 20 degrees with three feet of snow!

SELLING LAKE OF TWO MOUNTAINS CABIN, SPRING 2002

At Babaji's request, I sold my cabin in the Highlands of Monmouth Township near Wilberforce Ontario in the spring of 2002. Closing up the cabin was a sad time for Miriam and myself. We were buoyed and grateful for all the scores of Sweat Lodges we had given there, along with Medicine Wheel Trainings, and simply all the quiet personal time swimming, sailing, canoeing, and reflective meditations in the hammock.

As we left with our full load and crossed the homemade bridge constructed from the metal base of a railway car, the metal side of the U-Haul truck got hung up on the metal side-rail of the bridge. I hoofed it five miles into Wilberforce on a Sunday and found all the garages were closed. I finally procured a friend with a tow-truck and winch to pull the U-Haul off the railing and across the bridge. It was a hilarious endeavor that still makes me smile.

MOVING TO THE FARM NEAR LEITH, ONTARIO, 2003

In 2003 Miriam sold her house in Owen Sound and we rented a beautiful hill-top farm just opposite Ainslie Woods Conservation Area on Georgian Bay, a few kilometers north of Leith on the east side of the Bay. This was a century-old Victorian farmhouse with 100 acres and cattle. Just to the south of this property was the farm home where the great Canadian painter Tom Thomson lived from age four until his untimely death. My relationship with Tom had come full circle from canoeing in Algonquin Park as a teenager, living with him at the Meaford farm in the late 1970s, and now living next door to where he grew up. Here he had roamed the local forests and landscapes and established his amazing painting skills.

SHINGLES AND PAIN, 2003

One of the last workshops Miriam and I gave was on NLP. On a friend's small picturesque island in Lake Huron near Sauble Beach, we spent the day outside in the full sunlight. By the end of the evening, I had a fever, blistering headache, and pain like I had during my two previous bouts of Bell's Palsy. When I went to the doctor, I realized I had a bout of Shingles, also caused by the same Zoster virus that causes Bell's Palsy. The condition is caused by extreme fatigue, adrenal stress, and liver toxification.

During many long months I experienced excruciating pain in my head, back of the neck, and spine. My whole body was on fire. Most people take heroin injections for this unbearable pain; I simply took Tylenol and found a natural remedy of the First Nations from the American Southwest called the Creosote Bush or larrea tridentata. I took these capsules daily for over a year and eventually the pain subsided. During these many months of rest, I spent much time in meditation, reflection, and resting. As a direct result of this condition, I decided I needed to radically change my lifestyle and living situation.

CHAPTER 13
DRIVING TO VICTORIA
SEPTEMBER 2004

My good friend John moved to Victoria in 2003 and Miriam returned to Toronto in April 2004 to be with her four young men, her sons. I decided to move to Victoria, a place I always loved since playing there in our musical group in 1972.

Over the summer of 2004, I had multiple "Give-Aways" in which I divested myself of nearly all my material goods. I gave away brass Buddhas, furniture, a sailboat, clothing, and other effects. Hundreds of books went to friends and the local Owen Sound Public Library, particularly my books on psychotherapy and issues of co-dependence, shame, guilt, and the need for healing.

I moved all my other books to Miriam's garage in Downsview. The day after Labour Day in September 2004, I packed some clothes, my computer, my art supplies, and easel, and together with my wonderful medicine dog Snickers, I headed west. On a drizzling fall day, we took the ferry to Manitoulin Island, where I had spent so many days camping, swimming, and hanging out with my First Nations friends. We drove north to Espanola and took the Lake Superior Route.

Snickers and I camped in provincial and national parks all along the way. Some of my favourites were Lake Superior Provincial Park, Batchawana Bay, Pancake Bay, Agawa Bay, and Crescent Lake.

One of the most mystical ancient shamanic places in Canada is Rainy River District and Lake of the Woods. I spent many summers there canoeing and watching lightning come across the lake towards my tent. Once, a frightened skunk joined me during a thunderstorm. Another time a rat visited me in my sleeping bag. I was familiar with this region, because as a teenager I went canoeing in Quetico Provincial Park and canoed down into Minnesota and enjoyed Nature for three to four weeks at a time.

In Manitoba, Snickers and I wandered in the woods with buffalo in Riding Mountain National Park. The Qu'Appelle Valley called us, so we rode west in our "Zion Horse" vehicle.

CYPRESS HILLS CAMPING

Cypress Hills Provincial Park, in Southwestern Saskatchewan and Southeastern Alberta, is one of my most sacred places in Canada. It is the rolling hills, the small lakes for swimming, the pine trees and the gentle breezes of Nature and the great beauty. Historically, it is the site of one of the final encampments of Tatanka Yotanka or Sitting Bull when he journeyed north of the "Medicine Line" (the 49th Parallel) to escape the marauding American cavalry. We stayed here for a week, camping out on the site where Sitting Bull had placed his tipi, on a knoll overlooking the valley. For me, the Fort itself still resonates with long-gone battles, struggles, intrigue, and hardship. Being a powerful "sensitive" means I get so much more out of my personal experiences and memories.

Driving through Alberta, it was a beautiful site to see row upon row of the large wind power machines perched atop ridges near Pincher Creek. When the flat plains and golden fields turn to rolling hills and one glimpses the first visuals of the foothills of the Rocky Mountains in the western distance, it is like reaching the elven land of Avalon, and the higher Spirit lands into the west. These are our heavenly mystical mountains, similar to those of Tibet, Nepal, and Peru. These Canadian "Himalayas" are our Mount Kailash.

WATERTON NATIONAL PARK, ALBERTA

From the relative warmth of the prairies, Snickers and I drove through increasingly colder weather and a bit of snow to Waterton National Park in the Southwestern area of Alberta, into British Columbia, and into Glacier National Park in the state of Montana. Here we stayed four nights at The Bayshore Inn, located on the banks of the beautiful Waterton Lake. I took many day-trails and hiked up into the hills and mountains nearby. One of the reasons we departed Ontario after Labour Day was to avoid all the congestion in the parks of Canada. For me, it is always more of a delight to be quiet, serene, and alone on a mountain trail, observing a Stellar's Jay, Ravens winging and croaking, and Bears off on the scree of a rocky slope.

JASPER

Jasper has always been a sweet spot of mine since I hitchhiked out west four times as a young man. The town itself and the Columbia Icefields Parkway are especially majestic in the fall. The golden colours of the aspens, poplars, and tamaracks heighten my spirit and give my soul a sense of the eternal beauty of Mother Earth.

OSOYOOS

Driving through the BC interior mountains haunts me still with the millennia-old feeling of Ancestors hunting, fishing, trapping, and guiding here. The strength of their spirit moves me deeply in my body. I recognize and feel their presences at every turn. We owe so much to our Native Ancestors, more than modern Canadians might know. From Golden, we made our way down to Osoyoos, a treasured place in my heart, for it is one of the few Canadian landscapes that remind me of the American Four Corners in the Southwest, definitely a Lemurian place where my soul resonates deeply.

CHAPTER 14: ARRIVING IN VICTORIA

On September 29th of 2004 I took the Vancouver ferry to Vancouver Island's Schwartz Bay terminal on the Saanich Peninsula and was thrilled to feel I was finally home. Through John, I procured a room for four weeks at the Admiral Inn on Belleville Street, right on the harbour in downtown Victoria.

SITTING BULL HELPS ME FIND MY HOME NEAR GOLDSTREAM PARK IN THE HIGHLANDS

While I was thinking about where I would like to live, and had briefly flown out to Victoria to scope possibilities out for a few days previously in June 2004, one day Tatanka Yotanka Sitting Bull said to me, "Get out your map of Victoria."

Having spent most of my life with him, I obeyed him immediately. He always has my best interests at heart, and in fact he and I have written some beautiful poetic discourses about the healing future of Mother Earth and All Our Relations. I laid the map on the table.

"Now, let me use your index finger of your right hand," Sitting Bull insisted. I did, he led it to a road off Finlayson Arm Road in the Highlands down near Goldstream Park called Emerald Road.

"I like the sound of that road," I proclaimed, "it reminds me of the emerald colour of the heart chakra!" Sitting Bull continued, "Now, get in your truck, drive out there, and stop at the house where I tell you." I did just what he commanded.

Emerald Road is a tiny lane off another small road off Finlayson Arm Road. There is really only one house on Emerald Road, with another smaller cabin down closer to the inlet of the ocean.

"Pull in the driveway and go knock on the door," Sitting Bull insisted. I had reservations about this, and followed his directions anyway. A strong middle-aged man opened the door and I told him I was looking for a house to rent and had just driven across Canada.

"Wow, that's amazing, my family and I are leaving on a trip for Mexico for 8 or 9 months, and need a house-sitter. How would you like to stay here?" Steve said.

Within a few minutes, it was settled, and so I lived on the ocean with Snickers and had my 55th birthday party there on the deck overlooking mountains and water. It was extraordinary and the setting unparalleled.

Throughout the first few months there I met many new friends in the spiritual community that I was directed to connect with. Many of them were in the TM movement, energy workers, and Complementary MDs and NDs. Within a few months I did spiritual energetic group hypno-therapy for these medical professionals.

I also met with Jock McKeen and Ben Wong, founders of The Haven Institute on Gabriola Island. I knew these gentlemen in the 1980s at the Sexuality Conferences we hosted at The University of Guelph, Department of Family Studies (FACS). They invited John Ryan, my business partner from Ontario who had earlier moved to Victoria, and I to come and give workshop-playshops at The Haven on Heart Ways of Knowing and Being. John and I gave a similar workshop at the Kingfisher Oceanside Resort and Spa in Courtenay, up-island from Victoria.

From 2006 to 2008, our Heartways Playshops became well attended from folks across Canada; Miriam flew out from Toronto to join John and me. These were miraculous experiences for all because Jesus, Babaji, and Dendreah, among other Spiritual Masters and Archangels, presented themselves in person to group members who received heap-big healings. It's all about the heart and perfect love. Being human in the third dimen-sion, we "need all the help we can get" —a motto and mantra I have used for myself since childhood. We also presented a Heartways Playshop once at Hollyhock on Cortes Island, farther north off Campbell River and Quadra Island.

THE INTERNATIONAL INSTITUTE
OF INTEGRAL HUMAN SCIENCES, IIIHS

Jock and Ben mentioned that attendees at the annual Montreal confer-ence of The International Institute of Integral Human Sciences (IIIHS) would appreciate and get a lot out of the process of the Heartways Playshop. I presented there three times between July 2005 and July 2007; I did the first two alone and Miriam joined me for the last one.

At these IIIHS Conferences were all the world's scholars and practitioners in Energy Medicine and Unified Mystical Holographic Fields. Here I met and became friends with Bruce Lipton, Native Elder Grandmother Sara Smith, and many others, including specialists in crop circles, military psychological operations, the role of the Illuminati on the planet, ETs, flying saucers, mind-spirit medicine, and other intriguing topics. Human consciousness is definitely developing towards a unified theory of Spirit, soul, superconsciousness, the unconscious, atomic physics, and universal cosmology.

I participated in leading some Native Drumming and Dreaming Workshops where we envisioned personal, Earth, and global healing for All Our Relations. The directors suggested I close the Conferences on the last morning by having about 200 people, including the presenters, lie on the floor in the main hotel conference room, and lead them through a cosmic-earthly astral journey to Source to find their life's highest purpose and connect with all the Spiritual Masters of Clear Light and Pure Love.

During these amazing group energizations, all had profound emotional energetic healings, superconscious revelations, and heightened senses of the internal presence of the I AM Masters. These were also a lot of fun. It is all about clearing the fears from around your heart, mind, and in your unconscious body, opening to "Being the Great Love You Are," and surrendering to the will of Spirit and showering people with love.

SHARING THE HEART WAYS PLAYSHOP IN VICTORIA

The three of us, John, Miriam, and I, offered the Heartways Playshop in Victoria to our new friends and colleagues. This included three times at a local Healing Centre, which we rented, and also three times at The Church of Truth in James Bay. We typically had from 15–20 participants, and found many traditional Native and cosmic methods and techniques to open our hearts—such as drumming, individual and circle dancing, Ericksonian Hypnotherapy for deep guided visions, and inner heart experiences. Through playing the piano, I conveyed the guided Spirit messages. Since a child, I have been able to express individual and group "musical soul portraits" to engage energies for people that are highly transformational, protective, and energizing. Music shifts people's hearts and consciousness like no other modality.

WEEKLY NATIVE SPIRITUALITY HEALING AND TRAINING GROUPS

For over four years I facilitated Native Healing Circles every Thursday night at the home of some dear friends in Oak Bay. During these experiences, members learned to listen to Dendreah, Crazy Horse, Geronimo, Sitting Bull, Black Elk, Chief Joseph, Tecumseh, and many more Native Spiritual Masters, Teachers, and Healers.

When I arrived in Victoria in the fall of 2004, I spent several months alone astral journeying underneath the rock of the island, through the deeper ocean depths off the island, up the coast to Bella Bella and Bella Coola, and over to Haida Gwaii. Giving respect to the Ancestors, shamans, and medicine people is an essential sign of protocol, kindness, and learning to work together from the world of Spirit to this challenging always-changing illusion of the third dimension. During these times, I came to know and work with several great Spirit medicine men of Haida, Kwakwaka'wakw and Coast Salish traditions. I studied and taught this wisdom in my First Nations classes at The University of Toronto during the 1980s; my growing personal experiences working with them for healing purposes of All Our Relations is truly gratifying.

With these medicine people I spent much time healing the dark and desolate energy fields on the land, under the land and ocean, and within people's minds.

CHAPTER 15
THE DEATHS OF THREE OF MY BEST FRIENDS

Three is a sacred number, although four is more healing, grounded, and transformational in cosmic-earthly ways. Four is the number of our Native traditions with the four directions and four energy bodies. As many know, events in life happen in threes. Within the space of a few years, I lost three of my greatest and dearest friends to Spirit.

SNICKERS THE WONDERFUL MEDICINE DOG

In September 2007, at the ripe old age of 27 years, I lost my medicine dog Snickers. Snickers had been with me throughout this life. Earlier in this book, I told you the story of how we met. Snickers is a progressive and complex soul. As a child of seven, she was there as my Beagle dog Champ. Then during my late 20s and 30s, her soul transmigrated into my dog Otsitsa Elhar (Mohawk for "Flower Dog"). When Sitsa passed on, the Buddha took her soul for me and merged her soul with Snickers who came to me in Toronto soon after Sitsa passed over. So my various dogs have been a progressive soul for me throughout my life. Dogs are among my most beloved creatures and have always been my familiar.

Snickers is a composite soul of the highest medicine nature, a human Egyptian priest from ancient Egypt, and a Spirit being of enormous spiritually psychic healing abilities. Snickers was always with me during my many years of clinical counseling, and she was often the vehicle for the miraculous healings that many of my clients experienced. I often felt that she was the healing therapist and I was her sidekick.

Snickers was always present as the guard-dog at the entranceway to the scores of sweat lodges we gave in various places in Ontario. She actually looked like Anubis, the ancient Egyptian god-dog of the Underworld, who tested people's hearts and took them over to the Other Side—The Blue Road of Spirit as we say in the Native way.

Not only was she uncannily psychic and intuitive, she also knew exactly how to heal my own and others' emotional issues. Her love is immense and unconditional. I still dream about her and see her in visions, and I know one day she will come back to me as a wolf dog.

For all the years I had Snickers, she was not really ill. Twice previously I had cured her of serious kidney issues with homeopathic remedies. She had bacterial spondylosis when I found her, which I treated with garlic, blue-green algae, a special raw and sometimes cooked diet, and by myself giving her massage, Reiki, and acupuncture. Only in the last few weeks of her life was she failing physically. During the last three days she was preparing to journey to Spirit, so I played Buddha's mantras and songs for her while we prepared for her to transition to the Other Side.

My veterinarian came over with an assistant the day we auspiciously planned for Snickers's departure. John and I prepared her comfortably on a pile of folded rugs in the living room. She knew her time was come, and I assisted her soul into the higher astral realms before she was even given the injection to stop her physical heart from beating. Her heart was so strong she required two injections. Once the vet left, I journeyed with her to complete her successful appearance at the highest levels beyond the astral into the causal planes.

Anyone who has lost a dog or pet to death knows that the grieving is similar to or even greater than losing a spouse, child, or parent. This is because dogs give us perfect unconditional love, something we rarely if ever receive from another human being.

Until Snickers comes back to me as a Husky-Wolf dog, we have fun running, roller blading, playing, and cavorting in the fourth dimensional Dreamtime just like we always have!

ALIEDA, MY MOTHER, PREPARES FOR HER JOURNEY

Before I moved out west, my Dutch mother Alieda and I completed our transformation from mother and son; we became equals and really good friends. This was only accomplished as a direct result of my inner emotional and psychological process, my giving her unconditional forgiveness for the dark roles she played in my childhood and young adult years, and by co-creating a new spiritually based deepening friendship of mutual support, loyalty, and pure love.

This truth of the revolutionary relationship that my Mother Alieda and

I went through is one of the greatest inspirational stories I would like you to take to heart and hopefully manifest in your own relationships with your mother, father, siblings, children, colleagues, and friends.

Although it took upwards of 50 years to accomplish this evolutionary journey, I hold it as one of the most remarkable, worthwhile, and uplifting experiences of my lifetime. I know Alieda feels the same. She is smiling over my shoulder from Spirit as I write this about us. Love is the only and greatest healing power available to humans—and to any species within the entire universe, for that matter!

Alieda changed from a traumatized, war-torn, emotionally shutdown ice-queen when I was a child, to a remarkably intelligent, intuitive, open-hearted, prayerful saint by the time she passed over. Part of this came from Alieda opening her heart to Jesus in a most personal way, and from being initiated into Babaji's and Yogananda's healing Kundalini Kriya Yoga, meditations, mantras, and prayers. I say to you my friends, always highly consider the infinite power of spiritual love consciousness for those you care about.

From about 1998 onwards, Alieda constantly prayed for all the participants that we had for our various Heartways and other Workshops-Playshops. She was mostly bedridden for the remaining years of her life, and so focused her attention on her heart, her brilliant mind, and her intuition. For Miriam, Alieda finally found the daughter she always wanted. They were as close as sisters, confided in one another, and always had fun. Alieda loved the shrimp and avocado meals Miriam brought weekly to their visits.

When I moved to Victoria in 2004, I had weekly visits with Alieda on the phone. We laughed, we smiled into each other's hearts, we shared our journeys, and we supported each other in every way possible. As the time drew near for her passing during her 91st year, I made sure that she always had what she needed for medical, nursing, dietary, and friendship supports. In the end she was in so much pain from scoliosis and physical degeneration that she just wanted to go.

Over the years, Alieda and I had hundreds of conversations about the Spirit world realms, about Jesus, Babaji, Yoganandaji, the Spiritual Masters, and what it is like to leave the physical body behind and pass into Spirit. Because her mind is so strong and sharp as a tack, and she has indomitable will power, she found it hard to know how to let go of her physical body. She could hardly move in bed, let alone wash herself and feed herself. Even before I moved to Victoria, during my regular visits, I spoon fed her. In the end, she desperately wanted to leave the pain-body behind, and fretted about her inability to do so.

On her last day here, September 13th 2008, we had our final conversation on the phone. My close friend Jo-Anne called me on the phone; she was in the room with Alieda. When the phone was put to Alieda's ear, she raspily, softly, and slowly moaned, "I just want to leave and I don't know how to do it."

"Just surrender, and let go, and trust Jesus," I gently offered.

She still did not know how to complete this. I was there in astral with her, and prayed that Jesus, Mother Mary, and Archangel Mikael would just simply take her home. Alieda said all she could muster and we hung up.

Jo-Anne went down to the nursing station for a couple of minutes to talk with the nurses. When she returned two minutes later, Alieda had left. Jo-Anne called me back right away.

"It took her some time to be able to engage into the final surrender, however, she just left, she just let go while I was down at the nursing station. Her face looks very peaceful and calm."

That is how Alieda passed, with love in her heart, friends at her side, and me on the phone.

I called Miriam back, who had left just before noontime. She raced back and performed the necessary astral and physical ablutions I prescribed she do. In the astral planes, I helped Alieda journey for the requisite 72 hours to make sure that every last vestige of astral emotion, mental thoughts, and will power had left the physical overcoat that was thrown aside.

She said she wanted to be reborn in Jerusalem. In speaking with her upon her release, I assured her that it would be more prudent for her to go into the heavenly Jerusalem and stay there for some time, in order to rest, recuperate, learn, grow, and perhaps to continue to support myself and friends while I finished my own Earth walk. She agreed. Most days, I feel her I AM Presence with me, and during my Dreamtime. She is a valued, loving, and kind supporter and nurturer, just as I am with her. Alieda is now a powerhouse of love, kindness, and insight. I hope you find the same with your mother once you transform all that needs recognition, reparation, forgiveness and perfect healing with pure love.

THE "WALKING-OUT" OF JOHN RYAN

John Ryan has been one of my dearest, though short-lived friends for my life's journey. I first saw John on a video in 2000 in Toronto. He was talking about a book he ghostwrote, entitled Love Without End – Jesus Speaks. He and Mary Cole had edited many dozens of audiotapes by Glenda Green, an American portrait painter, who met Jesus in her bedroom over a series of nights when Jesus asked her to paint His physical and light-body portraits. Although not much credit for the book was given to John and Mary, much of their high spiritual insight, love, and direct connection with Jesus is the source of the beauty, love, and grace of this exceptional book. If there is no other book you read for the rest of your life, do read Love Without End – Jesus Speaks.

Upon seeing and hearing John speak of his participation with Jesus in the writing of this book and the workshops he was giving on it in Mississauga, I decided to phone his number. Nobody answered, so I left a message that went something like this: "John, I just watched your video about Jesus. I feel such a Christ kinship with you and your heart. Never have I felt another love Jesus as much as I do. Please give me a call and we can talk and perhaps meet."

I heard nothing from him for two weeks. Then I got a message from his soon-to-be ex-wife. She said that John was away for two weeks, "That was a wonderful message you left, and I will save it and have him call you when he returns to the city."

A few days later, John called. He said his birthday was the following Tuesday. I told him we could meet and I would take him out for his birthday lunch. We did. Over two months, we walked daily for hours on wooded trails in Mississauga. The intense sparkling and lightning-like spiritual etheric energy field between us kindled a divine fire that will always reign and rule over our world.

He is a man like no other that has walked through the world. He is an incarnation of the apostle Peter the Rock, Leonardo da Vinci, and

William Shakespeare, among others. To be in his presence was to be burnt to one's core by the strong eternal and infinite love of Jesus and the Christ Power of indomitable Clear Light and Purity of Heart Love. You cannot escape his blazingly intense blue eyes and spiritual power. I have yet to meet a man of his masculine power and single-mindedness. Having been an athlete at professional levels with football and hockey, he transformed those energies into his own and the world's "Spiritual Olympics."

When John moved to Victoria in 2002, I knew I would follow him and continue our earthly journey. One could call these matters soul contracts from Source and from before a particular incarnation; however, I prefer to give ourselves more free will and choice and be able to change and switch up earlier agreements when necessary in order to follow a "Higher Love." On Vancouver Island, we spent many days hiking, sharing, and giving workshops on Heartways of Knowing and Being.

As with many middle-aged members of our society, aging is unfortunately replete with age-prejudice. Though he was a Senior Vice-President at Lenscrafters, had a Masters Degree in Environmental Studies at York University, and was a consummate businessman, the only work he could acquire in Victoria was working in the lumber and framing section of Home Depot. Our society wastes so many of our highly qualified and remarkable citizens. This too must and will change, and soon I trust.

I made him lunch every day and we ate outdoors at Thetis Lake and talked about Jesus, the changing of our age, and the beauty of Nature and the overarching Spirit world.

During our workshops in the various venues John always started with the spiritual aspects of Source, the Christ I AM Presence, and Jesus. Then, he wandered off or listened absent-mindedly to Miriam and I taking individuals and the group through their emotional-karmic-psychological-spiritual healing process. John had many personal psychological issues, co-dependencies, and addictions, just as every one of we seven billion on Earth have. One of the reasons people have no soul, no individuation, no pure love, no spiritual liberation is because we have split off from our unconscious psyches in our physical bodies, and we prefer for now to let the dark evil side of our present conditions take over, keep us wounded, and eventually kill us. This is what happened with John.

It was John's choice not to deal with any personal emotional-psychological challenges that came to him through his family of origin, his three failed marriages, and his dysfunctional relationships with his children. It is most distressing and sad as an outside observer to see someone love others so much and not really love themselves enough to do their inner shit work, to sincerely process to turn all the darkness into light, and the pain and hurt into love. Each of us needs to transmute the shit and lead into gold. Every time I suggested to John that his life would be better served through emotional healing than the bottle, he simply and directly commanded, "Don't go there!"

Every day, for every one of us, there are countless "Open Doors" and synchronous opportunities for us to learn, to love our Self more truly, and garner greater Self-worth and Self-esteem. John chose not to go there. For me, a day is worth more when I surrender and grow more.

In the end, John hooked up with a dark female projection of his un-lived inner feminine side and withdrew from his friendships with Miriam, Mary, and me. One day when going to see him at Home Depot, I heard he had a heart attack, was unconscious, and was taken to the local hospital. After several days, he finally came out of a coma and was receiving visitors.

When I went to visit, the abusive language I heard revealed that whoever was present and operating this mind and body was not John. John had "walked out" and gone home permanently to Spirit. The new entity in John threw me out of his hospital room and told me to never contact him again.

Now and again I see "John" riding his bicycle along the streets of town.

I roll down my window, and call out, "Hi John!" just to see a response. "I'm not John, who are you?"

I still communicate with John who is in a high Spirit place. We share and connect around Jesus in the most profound and elucidative ways. We will always love each other as powerful Brothers in Christ. One day, however, John will be required by the cosmic and earthly Divine-human laws of karma to come back and clear his emotional and psychological baggage. I will support him from wherever I AM when he comes back to an earthly incarnation for this liberating, lifestyle-changing journey.

CHAPTER 16
WHY AND HOW I BECAME
A REAL ESTATE AGENT

During the first three months in Victoria while I lived on Emerald Road, I had three very perplexing unusual dream-vision visitations. I have continuously had experiences almost every day and night of my life with Jesus, my closest friend. During the first month in Victoria, Jesus came to me in a dream and clearly stated, "Joseph, I want you to become a real estate agent!"

I immediately woke up, laughed, and said, "Thanks for the joke, Jesus! I needed a little pick-me-up." I went back to sleep and never thought about it again.

Then a few weeks later, Jesus appeared even more sharply and abruptly in the Dreamtime and pronounced, "Joseph, I told you I need you to become a real estate agent."

"I have never thought of becoming a real estate agent; that's a great joke, and I appreciate your sense of humour, Jesus!" I responded and I went back to sleep and again forgot all about it. Even though workshops were not bringing in enough money to really cover my bills and I did not really know what my dharmic source of income might be, I let the thought of real estate go.

Then, after another few weeks, Jesus came a third time in my Dreamtime, and exclaimed clearly, "Joseph! I thought I told you I need you to become a real estate agent... When you awake in the morning, the first thing you will do is call the UBC Sauder School of Real Estate business, give them your credit card number, enroll, start studying, do the 20 mini-exams online, and the final 3-hour written one. Please do as I ask. I need you to do this for me, Joseph."

So, dutiful as always to Jesus, I did as he asked. Now, eight years later I am still a Realtor®. First I was with RE/MAX for one year to learn the ropes, and now with Pemberton Holmes Ltd for seven years. Though I was asked by Jesus to give up counseling several years before I listened to him, I realized that holding space for so many people was very deleterious to my physical, emotional, and mental health. And I knew I would never do counseling for the rest of this life. However, real estate has allowed me to be kind, respectful, and compassionate with individuals, couples, and families during stressful, life-changing moments in their lives when they need to sell or buy a home. I thoroughly enjoy giving my friends 100% service and support in finding and purchasing their dream home. My expertise in Feng Shui, Prepping, Staging, colour, art, and energy flow in homes is a direct outer extension of my previous facilitation of peoples' inner energy bodies and fields.

Now my friends' homes, offices, and yards have harmony, balance, flow, peace, and joy. I am truly blessed to offer this life-enhancing science for them. Real estate has turned out to be a great service and learning for me. I never thought I would be a real estate agent. However, the door opened and I walked through it, trusting Jesus all the way as I always have. This is my experience throughout all my lives on Earth, especially in this one! Real estate has given me the needed income to enable me to write and publish the books I will leave to humanity as my humble legacy.

CHAPTER 17
ART, INSPIRATIONAL MEDITATION, MUSIC CDS, AND BOOKS

During my sojourn on the Canadian west coast, I have been able to be creative in the ways that fulfill my heart. Although I am certainly no computer techie, I have been able to create over 500 computerized artistic healing coloured mandalas from powerful images and photos of great Spiritual Masters and natural beauty. I call these "personalized healing mandalas." You may view some of these at www.sourceco-creations.com/mandala.php.

I have co-created several inspirational Meditation and Music CDs. The two most valuable may be "The 61-Point, 5-Pointed Star, Blue Light Ancient Vedic Meditation," and "Making Money Through Soul Gold Alchemy: Spiritual Prosperity and Abundance Through Jungian Psychology." You can view these at www.sourceco-creations.com/musicmeditationcds.php.

Other than loving everyone I meet and creating many great friendships, the main reason I am here as I told my mother Alieda at my 18th birthday party, is to leave over 50 books that will be the knowledge of essential personal Divine-human processes, and give heart-warming inspiration for individuals and humanity on Earth over the next 500 years.

Here are some of the books I have been called to offer for people's benefit.

18 MIRACLES FOR YOUR HEALING JOURNEY INTO THE LIGHT

This book is to help you celebrate the fact that you are a miracle yourself. The book shows you how to Surrender, Open, Allow, Release, and Receive (SOARR) and apply these miracles daily to your every breath, thought, feeling, and sensation. Love is All. The Light is Everything.

BABAJI MANTRAS, CHANTS, MEDITATIONS, MESSAGES WITH CD

Babaji Nagaraj is the infinite Universal Creator and well known as an incarnation of Shiva worldwide. This original document is Babaji's gift to all people of this world at a time of great transformational crisis. The sweet, powerful, illuminating, incisive emanations of His Great Love will provide light, love, healing, courage, strength, decision, and action for any who listen and receive.

BUDDHA'S HEART SUTRA

The pure light of Shakyamuni Gautama Buddha's teachings has spread to all corners and cultures of the world. In this clear, brief, relevant discussion of the approximately 250 words of the focal point of all Buddha shared—the Prajna Paramita or Heart Sutra—you can find practical and truthful answers to your loneliness, depression, and personal suffering, along with the violent malaise and chaotic social changes of our time— the ghettoization of the planet. The time-tested steps to end all pain, fear, sorrow, and suffering are found in the psychological commentary that is woven into this book.

PEACEFUL WAR: ASSERTING VICTORY

This compilation of original poetry was written at the turn of the millennium as we moved into the next aeon of the 21st century. The battle between the spiritual and animal sides of our human nature has always been at the centre of our psychology and our civilizations. As we move into what our Indigenous sisters and brothers call The Fifth World after 2012, we must find revolutionary new methods of interpersonal relations and resolutions in order to evolve, thrive, and leave a healthy planet and increasing world unity for our coming descendants and All Our Relations.

SKENNEN KOWEN, THE PEACE IS GREAT

Through the centuries the ravages of war, disease, murder, cultural geno-cide, and incarceration in residential schools and other forms of prison have killed millions of First Nations individuals and cultures in Canada, on Turtle Island, and all over Mother Earth. However, the Spirits of the Ancestors, great Peace Chiefs, Warriors, Visionaries, and Leaders are stronger now than ever. At this time of the Seventh Generation Fire, the spirits of the Great Ones have indeed returned to bring us back to The Way of Peace, the Kayenerehkowen. Tashunke Witko Crazy Horse proclaimed, "We shall return, we shall return again, all over the Earth; my people, we shall return again and bring harmony and peace to All Our Relations." These poems honour the native soul of each and every one of us, along with All Our Relations and the welcome heart gifts of the great Native Spirit Masters.

TRAVELLING LIGHT: A CALL TO GREAT POWER THROUGH THE NINE INNER PLACES OF TRUTH, FREEDOM AND LOVE CONSCIOUSNESS

As mentioned, Travelling Light, co-written with Miriam Sanua, is the first published compilation of four volumes from the four training years of The Soul Initiative Coaching-Training Program in Toronto in the 1990s.

The introduction of Travelling Light shares qualities of the spiritual peacemaker-warrior through ancient Toltec knowledge. This life-chal-lenging, adventurous story follows the hero and his teacher don Miguel through Latin America. The main text then becomes a self-help book for you the hero-heroine to open gateways to the Nine Inner Great Power Places of Truth, Freedom, and Love, which is your true identity as con-scious Source Light and greater Pure Love. Based on 37 years of intensive experience with individuals and groups, Travelling Light embodies all the Eastern, Western, and First Nations modalities of the world, including particularly Ayurveda and Kriya Kundalini Yoga. Inspirational and prac-tical, you will transform your life through ancient and modern physical, emotional, mental, and spiritual techniques. The book is based on and therefore useful as a text for individual and group classes and study.

SEVEN SACRED TEACHINGS

The Seven Sacred Teachings is a book co-written with my fine Brother and great friend, David Bouchard. It is a timeless message of traditional values and hope for the future. The Teachings are universal to most First Nation peoples. These teachings are close to the heart of Aboriginal communities from coast to coast, and they link these communities together as a unified sisterhood-brotherhood.

The Seven Sacred Teachings embody the exemplary values of what it means to be a "true-hearted, good human being." They include respect, humility, courage, unity, and most of all, love. It is our hope that this telling will unite and thus heal divisions among all peoples. Prophecies tell that this is the time for "One Heart, One Mind, and One Drum." We are the ones we have been waiting for; the time of the "lone wolf" is over. We must come together, accept, and live these values, revitalize our culture, and co-create a harmonious, Nature-respectful life for ourselves and for 77 generations of our descendants to come.

For more background and information on these books, please view the following link: hwww.sourceco-creations.com/books-and-cds.php.

CHAPTER 18
COMING FULL CIRCLE, 2011–2013

My life seems to be in synch with the changing tides of the World Soul. I have always known that these two souls are inextricably linked. I feel the history of the Earth periods in the depths of my being. I resonate with all the ups and downs of the conscious cycles of evolution and devolution of our humanity. Luckily for those alive now, we are coming out of the end of the Kali Yuga as of 1873 AD. In this new era ruled by Archangel Mikael, Sananda, Melchizedek, Metatron, and the Violet Ray of Mahachohan Saint Germain, we have the possibility of gaining ground in this Dwaparu Yuga cycle, which after thousands of years will consciously lead us back to yet another Golden Age on Mother Earth.

Our two steps forward and one step back will not occur without a horrendous conscious struggle to accept our hidden darkness, evil, and treacherous posturing with ourselves and one another. It will likely be more dramatic than traumatic. While individual minds and the collective will glides superficially on the outermost layer of the unconscious, wild eruptions of darkness, chaos, and madness will come to light—all to bring us home to our soul and pure love nature.

While the world has been going crazy the last few years, my health also greatly deteriorated. Even though I have always been an athlete, worked out almost daily for decades for at least an hour, have had a great diet since I was a teenager, and do not drink or smoke, my heart and lungs were giving out on me.

I love swimming outdoors in the natural lakes around Victoria. Up until late November, I swam without a wetsuit in Durrance Lake and Matheson Lakes. Swimming is my greatest joy as recreation. In January of 2011 I came down with pneumonia. My lungs filled up with water; I could scarcely breathe. My legs and ankles also filled with fluid. I realize now that I was going through serious cardiac failure. On another level, although my spirit and soul always bound in the endless love, peace, and friendship I feel with my Spiritual Master friends in Source, my earthly emotional and astral heart were sad beyond reckoning. Sad for All Our Relations, Mother Earth, and all the people I met and experienced near me and around the planet.

Humanity is severely depressed more than we know; we are all sad and unknowingly grieving for all kinds of unresolved losses. As a result of our unconsciousness we are bipolar. We survive and suffer through our catatonic sadnesses, hurts, and thus rarely become manic. Each of us is triggered to soon blast open our hidden rage, anguish, torment, dejection, gloom, felt inferiority, poor-me, sense of injustice, misery, and our numbing fears.

From January to April I could not sleep. I could not lie down, knowing that I would drown and asphyxiate with the water in my lungs. I did not sleep for four months. I read books. I watched the BBC Merlin series over and over on the computer. I called Miriam in Toronto every night and into the early hours of the morning where we would talk about matters of interest and great import; and she also condoled me and sang me the Medicine Buddha Mantra, which is one of the loveliest healing sayings and melodies ever. When you listen, you will feel immediate sustenance and healing, www.youtube.com/watch?v=yUJucA-mrgE.

I was overly fatigued, adrenally worn out, and my body was stressed to the max. I took a five-day holiday up-island at an oceanfront resort in mid-April. On the drive up, I kept falling asleep through anoxia so I had all the windows down to stay awake during the three-hour drive. I was unwise to have gone, let alone go alone. The stay there was miserable. I could only walk a few steps before tiring. I could not sleep because of the fluid topping my lungs. In retrospect, I should have driven to the Hospital.

Miriam came out from Toronto in the end of April. My heart and lungs were so not functioning that my usually lean tall body frame that weighs about 195 pounds was weighing 280 pounds—with over 80 extra pounds of water. I felt like my legs were waterlogged pants and I was slogging through a swamp. So I decided to go to the nearby Hospital. The emergency doctor said I was about a week away from packing it in. He prescribed me massive doses of water-reducing pills and I went home. Within a week I lost most of the extra water. He sent me to a cardiologist. She prescribed the typical heart failure medications of beta-blockers, angiotensin-converting enzyme (ACE) inhibitors, and more of the same diuretic.

Miriam went back to Toronto, packed up her house, and moved to

Victoria to live here permanently on July 4th. She supported me in my ongoing struggle to get well. The cardiologist said that I was in dire need of surgery for two heart valves and my aorta, and I was not well enough yet for surgery. At home I rented an oxygen machine to get enough oxygen to my brain, heart, and muscles. A number of times I scared myself passing out while driving my truck.

I kept up my daily regimen of great diet, exercise, and walking. On my birthday June 21st 2011, I could hardly move. Making it up a small hill of 100 feet took 20 minutes. This is not how I saw my life moving forward.

More than a full year later in July 2012, the cardiologist sent me to the local cardiac surgeon Dr. Jovan (John) Bozinovski. You might recall him from the beginning of this story. He did more cat-scans, angiography or heart catheterization, X-rays, and other tests. He felt I was in good-enough shape, and he scheduled me for a repeat heart surgery on October 4th. You know the rest of the story from there. I didn't have the operation on that day; it was rescheduled for October 10th.

SPIRITUAL CONNECTIONS

So much is made of Near-Death Experiences (NDEs) these days. Although I had a major NDE during this last heart operation and recall being in the Great Clear Light, these one-off connections with the Other Side are really not the key for me. Not at all. Instead, through the strict mental-emotional discipline of Kundalini Kriya yoga meditation and by following the eight-runged yogic ladder to final liberation, I am in constant communication and contact with Source, all the Spiritual Masters of all times and cultures, and the realms of the highest heavenly beings. Most of these loving, refined Light Beings are unknown to humanity so far.

Listening to The Creator in all Her-His glory is the key to living. Doing the will of the Creator and "Being the Great Love You Are" is the simplest yet most meaningful way of being, knowing, and living. Everyday I listen to Babaji, Jesus, Dendreah, Mother Mary, Mikael, Yogananda, Crazy Horse, Geronimo and all my other loving friends in Spirit. They are all and everything for me. They are my greatest lovers and friends. Through them, I bring the sweetness of unconditional love to everyone

I meet. I do not need to like everyone, nor do I judge him or her. Yet I want to have each person as my friend. I understand where they are at, and that they are doing the best they can for what they know about themselves so far, and what their karmas have delivered to them.

HONOURING THE DARK SIDE

Throughout all this, from my awareness of Spirit, Heavens, Hells, and our "Middle Earth," I know that I can only flourish in paradox when I hold the tension between all the pairs of opposites in life—Spirit and matter, soul and body, Self and ego, mind and body instincts, good and evil, light and dark, inside and outside, life and death, and mostly love and fear.

All my life, since I was a baby, I realized I had hundreds of discrete nameable fears to deal with again in this lifetime. It is part of everyone's Earth walk, karma or no karma. One after another I tackled each fear, held it, demanded it teach me, and transmuted its force into pure love. And then each time I was set free. When I completed transforming the energies of well over 500 fears in my early 40s I knew I was once again eternally and infinitely free and liberated. You can take as long as you want to work with your own fears, and by doing so you claim your birthright as "The Love You Are." It can take 500 years, 500 days, or 500 minutes. It is your choice. These days, there are more of us doing this Essential Inner Work, so it's easier, more natural, and quicker. Just get it done! That is my hope and suggestion for you. I have the faith and trust that you will accomplish these goals.

We are engaging upon and co-creating a new superconscious Sisterhood-Brotherhood of love that will eventually unite all humanity on Earth, regardless of gender, race, class, status, ethnicity, skin colour, and sexual orientation. When you work diligently towards your own liberation, you ease the collective path towards our "One World, One Peace, and One Love."

By honouring and surrendering to Spirit and Source, to the love your friends have for you, and your complete surrender to the Dark Earth Feminine and Masculine, you thereby bring all your inner opposites to the higher vibrations of the Eternal Soul-Self. Then you are in bliss!

You premanently live in the flow honouring each now moment. You stay centred inside your pure heart love in order to open the love in the hearts of everyone and everything else.

STARTING A NEW LIFE HERE AND NOW

My heart is happy I have shared this with you. I trust the truth of my stories have inspired and brightened your path. Remember love and forgiveness make life perfect, just the way it is. May you feel blessed and blissed forevermore.

As the aeons shift into a new way of being for this emerging Meruvian Age of Aquarius over the next 2,000 years, we are setting the stage for our untold millions of descendants who depend upon you and me, and who are watching us from the astral planes.

We can live in harmony with our Self, each other, Nature and All Our Relations. Babies and dogs can do this; so can each of us—individually and together.

These days, I compose new songs on the piano every day. I love to write down my thoughts about co-creating the best visionary and down-to-Earth world we can all imagine. Challenge your consciousness; get out of the box. Fly free with me and bring the dawn of another new way of healing and loving.

Bless each and every one of you.
I will see you in the Dreamtime and perhaps in the flesh.

All my love, Joseph

And now as we say in India, and wearing a great big smile,
I say, "Namasgo!"

AUTHOR BIOGRAPHY

Founder and Director of The Academy of World Psychology and Creative Arts, Psychotherapist and Medical-Psychological Anthropologist Joseph Martin has taught and trained thousands of students and clients for 42 years. He incorporates a vast network of complementary ancient and modern quantum healing modalities for the unity of the spiritual, intellectual, emotional and physical. Joseph is a composer, artist and writer currently living in Victoria BC.

Dr. Joseph Martin can be contacted at:
www.josephmartin-living-in-two-worlds.com

Contact directly for public speaking and healing musical events at:
josephmartin@shaw.ca

Other Published Books by Joseph Martin

Available at www.SourceCo-Creations.com

Peaceful War: Asserting Victory—Peace and War Poems for the
Healing of the Earth Soul and All Our Relations

18 Miracles For Your Healing Journey Into the Light
(Keys to Spiritual Living)

Babaji's Mantras, Chants, Meditations, Messages

Babaji's Messages of Infinite Love, Hope and Peace
Regarding the Earth Changes

Skennen Kowen—The Peace is Great: Indigenous Poems for the
Renewal of the Earth

Celebrating the Flow of Life:
27 Ancient and Modern Psychotherapies (2nd Edition, 1998)

Pure Mind Training Life Manual (NLP Plus)

Buddha's Heart Sutra: Why the World is Now a Ghetto
(with a psychological-spiritual commentary)

Travelling Light: A Call to Great Power Through the Nine Inner
Places of Truth, Freedom and Love Consciousness
(Volume 1; 537 pages)

If you want to get on the path to be a published author by
Influence Publishing please go to
www.InspireABook.com

Inspiring books that influence change

More information on our other titles and how to submit
your own proposal can be found at
www.InfluencePublishing.com

CPSIA information can be obtained at www.ICGtesting.com
Printed in the USA
LVOW01s1710041013

355490LV00026B/1752/P